# ·ans Hals
# ·fe Work Restoration

# Frans Hals

## Life Work Restoration

Norbert Middelkoop
Anne van Grevenstein

Uniepers, Amsterdam
Frans Halsmuseum, Haarlem
Alan Sutton Publishing, Gloucester

Published in co-production with the
Dutch-language edition *Frans Hals - Leven Werk Restauratie*



Consultant editors: Neeltje Köhler and Derk Snoep
Advisers: Pieter Biesboer, Alexander de Bruin, Koos Levy, Irene van Thiel and Jan Baptist Bedaux.
Translation: Rollin Cochrane
Design and production: Uniepers b.v., Amsterdam

Printed in The Netherlands



ISBN 0-86299-699-6

# Foreword



According to a certain tradition, the directors of the Frans Halsmuseum have published monographs on Frans Hals. Gratama and Baard both set their stamp on the reputation of Frans Hals as promoted by their museum of the same name. Until now their successors have not devoted themselves to such a project.

In 1970-74 an imposing standard work in three volumes came from the hand of Professor Seymour Slive - unfortunately this is now out of print. At the present time a work of such dimensions is not likely to be realized. In the museum, however, a need was felt for a convenient book for the general reader which, taking into account the most current discoveries and views, would tell more about Hals than the richly illustrated but modestly annotated monographs that are still to be had.

The book also acquired a side-function. It is intended as a kind of guide to the works of Frans Hals in museums in Belgium and the Netherlands. The geographical limitation is perhaps somewhat arbitrary, but on the other hand much attention has been given to the historical and cultural framework of Hals's life and work in Haarlem. From this angle, the art historian Norbert Middelkoop has treated the discipline's rich historical information in such a way that aesthetic considerations are more implicitly woven into the text than is the case in most other publications about Hals. It is an approach to this genius of painting which the museum also favours. An introduction to the history-making recent restoration of works by Frans Hals in the museum's collection was considered appropriate to this 'objective' vision. The five militia portraits, three regents portraits, three individual portraits, as well as the interdisciplinary research into and execution of methods of treatment, have attracted widespread attention. Certainly in large measure thanks to the museum's promotion of open discussion and publicity. The conscious emphasis on the scientific, rather than traditional, analysis of Hals's works has greatly clarified the techniques he used and to a perhaps even greater extent shed light on later 'well-meant' restorations. The most recent restoration methods, formulated and developed by Anne van Grevenstein, former restorer of the Frans Halsmuseum, have proved eminently successful, judging from the abundance of positive reactions. For the sake of openness and public awareness, I have therefore asked the restorer to contribute to this book about Frans Hals so that the ideas which were practically applied might be made clear and accessible to one and all. Given Anne van Grevenstein's wide experience in openly promoting her new views on conservation, restoration and the reversibility of treatments once they have been carried out, her share in this book will be of interest to layman and specialist alike.

*Dr. Derk P. Snoep,*
*director Frans Halsmuseum*

a. *Drinking boy (taste)*, ca. 1628. Schwerin, Staatliches Museum.
b. *Boy holding a flute (hearing)*, ca. 1628. Schwerin, Staatliches Museum.
c. *Portrait of Catharina Hooft with her nurse*, ca. 1620. Berlin-Dahlem, Gemäldegalerie.
d. *The Haarlem brewer Claes Duyst van Voorhout*, ca. 1635. New York, The Metropolitan Museum of Art.

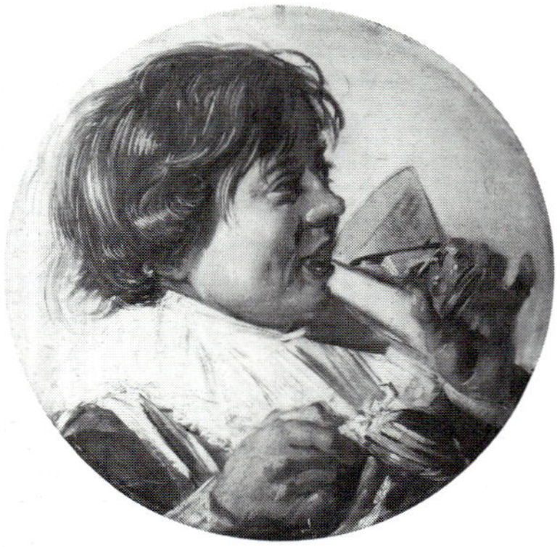
a

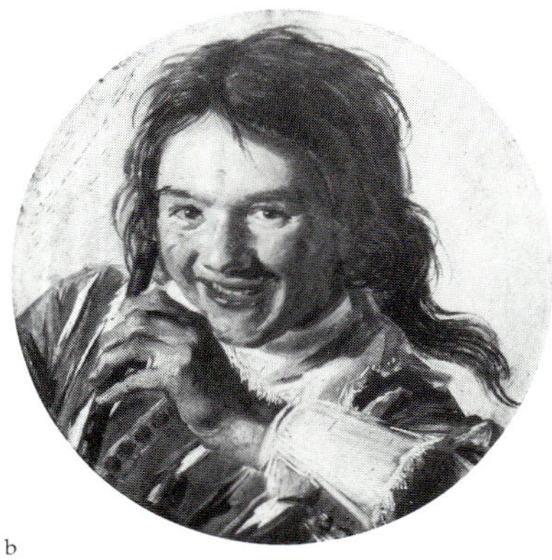
b

# Introduction

Frans Hals (1581/85-1666) is one of the Low Countries' most celebrated painters, his name invariably mentioned in a single breath with such colleagues as Rubens, Van Dyck, Rembrandt and Vermeer. But fame came to him differently. Rubens, Van Dyck and Rembrandt were well known while they were alive; compared to theirs, Hals's reputation was limited. Like Vermeer, Frans Hals was rediscovered in the latter half of the nineteenth century, thanks to a renewal of interest in Dutch painting which sprang up in France. His style accorded perfectly with developments taking place in painting at that time and inspired such artists as Courbet, Manet and Van Gogh. Although his work has been esteemed ever since, views about Frans Hals and his time have changed considerably. Many studies

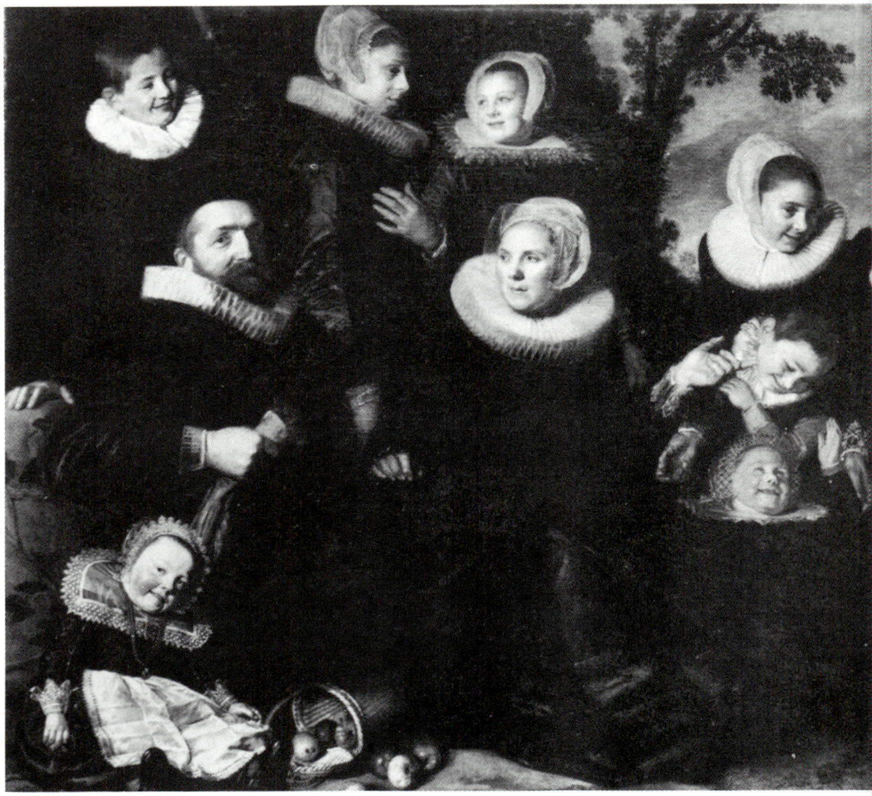
e

about him have been written since his rediscovery.

The restoration of the five militia portraits by Frans Hals in the Frans Halsmuseum has prompted a review of the painter's life and work. Photographs taken at the time show the treatment which the militia portraits underwent. A separate chapter deals with the problem of restoration in general.

The illustrations in this book centre on works by Frans Hals in Dutch and Belgian collections. These forty paintings, providing a representative survey of Hals's *oeuvre* , are reproduced in full colour, accompanied by explanatory texts. Also included are many other works by Hals and his contemporaries. This book could not have been written without the dedicated contribution of Neeltje Köhler and Derk P. Snoep.

*The authors*

e. *Family portrait,* ca. 1620 Reconstruction from two fragments, one in Cardiff, National Museum (on loan from Viscount Boyne, Bridgnorth), one in Brussels (plate 5). Possibly the right side of the painting was originally even larger. In 1628 the painter Salomon de Bray (1597-1664) added to the composition the portrait of a child (lower left), probably born after the family portrait was completed.

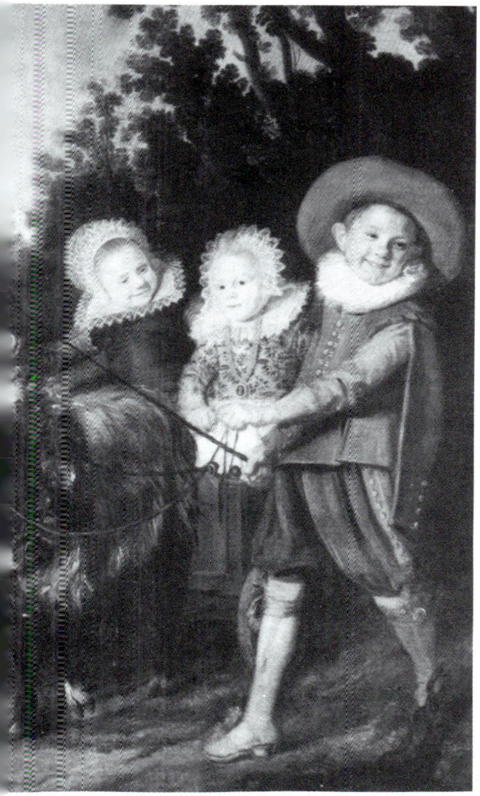

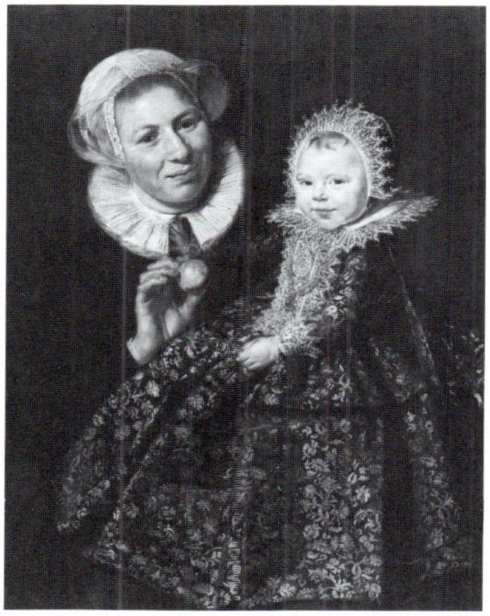

c

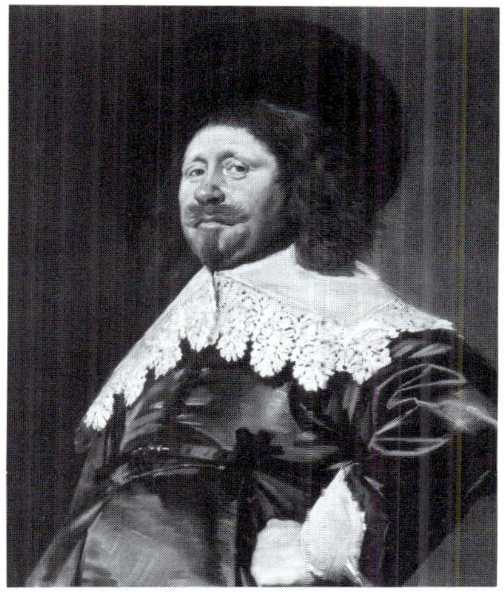

d

# Frans Hals

f. *'The merry lute player' (intemperance),* ca. 1626. London, Mansion House. This painting was bequeathed to the city of London in 1987.
g. *St. Mark,* ca. 1626. Private collection. This portrait was discovered underneath an old overpainting in 1974.
h. *St. Mark,* before its restoration.

Not much is known about the life of Frans Hals. What little was written about him was always at second hand and his youth is a complete mystery. Even his work gives rise to some important questions: no preliminary studies or drawings have come to light - is this evidence of the ease and quickness with which he painted? But who taught Hals his fluent brushwork? This style of painting, boldly conspicuous in the seventeenth century, allowed Hals to immortalize in a direct and spontaneous way the people around him: children, folk figures and notably the prominent citizens of Haarlem.

The two hundred and some known paintings by Frans Hals - his original *oeuvre* was doubtless much larger - constitute a perpetual testimony to the individuality of his talent. Their profound eloquence justifies a place for Frans Hals among the very greatest artists of all time.

**The Low Countries**

On 17 August 1585 Antwerp was taken by Spanish troups. The conquerors reinstated the Catholic religion and Protestants were given two years to leave the city. In the same year Holland closed off the mouth of the Schelde, thereby bringing

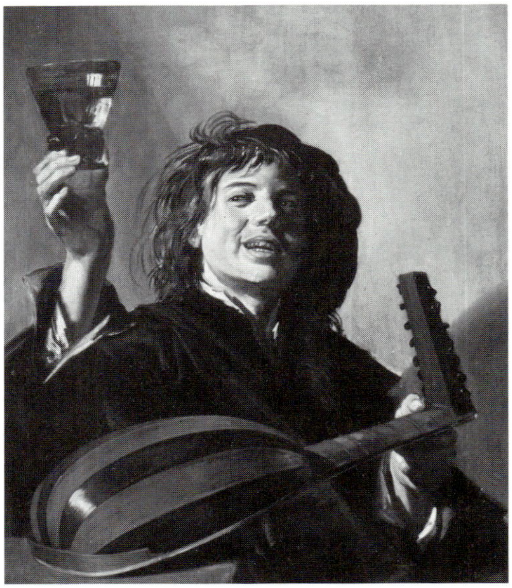

f

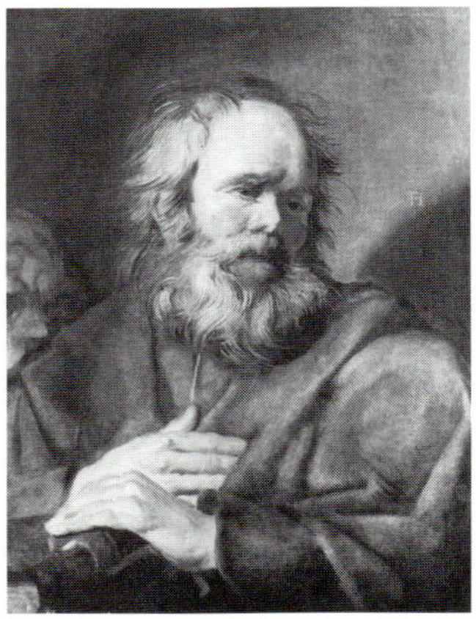

g

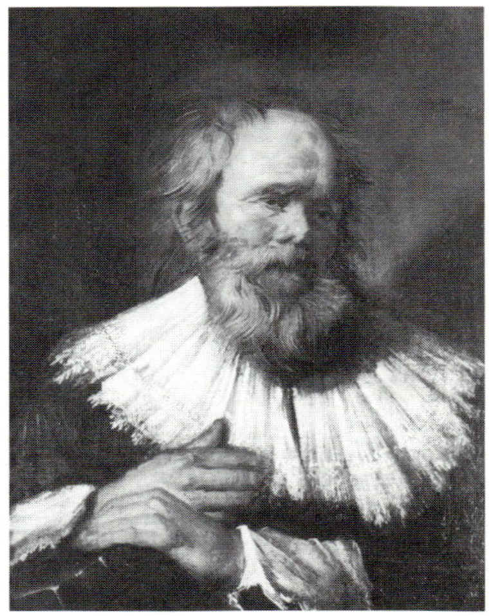

h

economic ruin to what had been the most powerful city in the Low Countries; this also compelled many to leave Antwerp in order to seek a new life elswhere. One of the emigrants was the weaver Franchoys Hals who, together with his wife Adriana van Geestenryck and his sons Joost and Frans, sought refuge in Haarlem.

In the northern Netherlands economic prospects were more favourable. Revolt against Spanish domination had led to the withdrawal of the armies of King Philip II in 1576. The towns worked energetically at building up the economy.

The northern provinces felt that the growing economy would be better served by an independent government without a sovereign. In about 1588 this gave birth - out of practical necessity, but not for economic reasons alone - to the Republic of the Seven United Netherlands. Foreign recognition of the Republic, and the territory's relative peacefulness, led to an unprecedented upsurge in the economy. For the cities of Holland and Zeeland, the principal backers of the revolt, the closing of the Schelde was of crucial importance. Ships bearing precious cargo were forced to detour to ports in Holland and Zeeland; trade flourished. An era of unknown prosperity dawned in the young Republic.

a. Pieter Wils, *Map of Haarlem*. 1646. Haarlem, Municipal archives.
1. Great or St. Bavo Church; 2. Town hall and Prinsenhof; 3. Meat hall; 4. Weigh-house; 5. New or St. George Doelen (doelen = a hall for military meetings and exercise), also called Doelen of St. George; 6. Old Doelen or Cluveniers Doelen; 7. Work-house; 8. Leper Hospital; 9. St. Elisabeth's Hospital; 10. Old Men's Alms House (now the Frans Halsmuseum); 11. Orphanage; 12. Site of the 'Hofje van Heythuysen'.

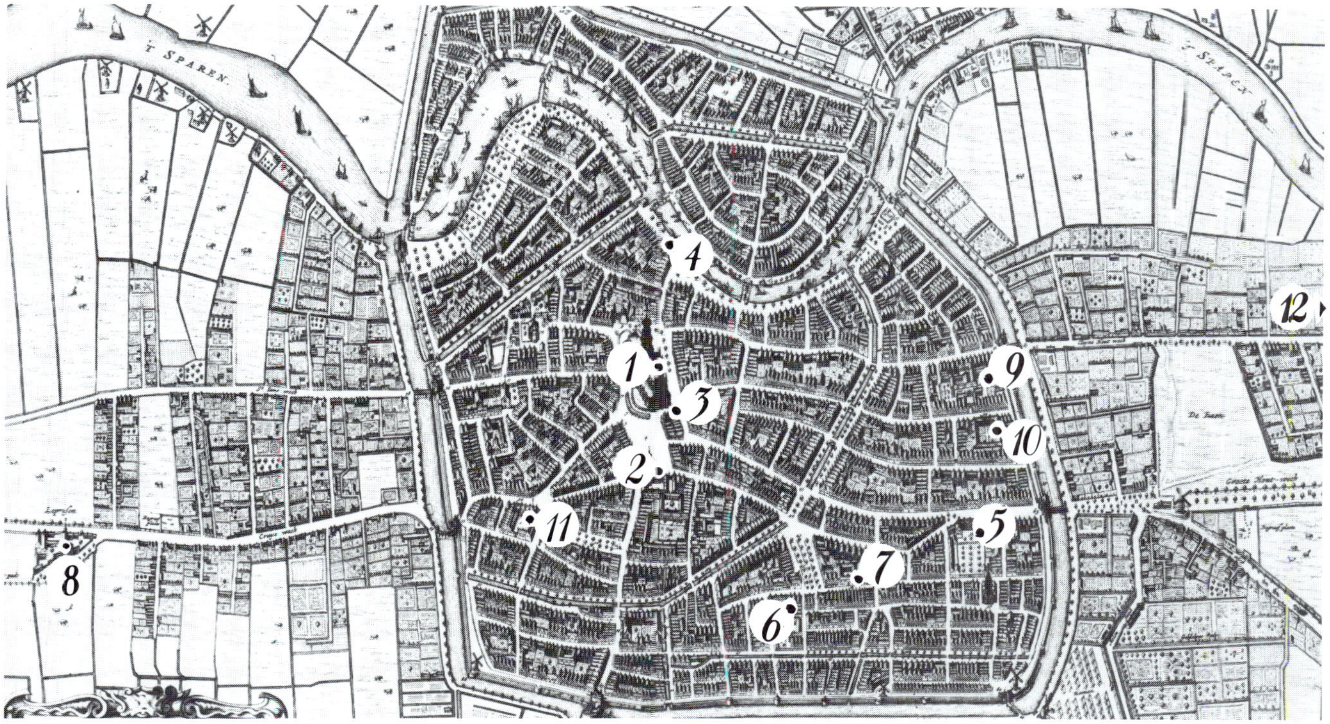


a

b. Gerrit Berckheyde (1638-1698), *The Grote Markt (Market-place) at Haarlem*, 1696. Haarlem, Frans Halsmuseum (on loan from the Rijksdienst Beeldende Kunst). Next to St. Bavo at the right, Lieven de Key's Meat Hall.
c. Cornelis Cornelisz. van Haarlem (1562-1638), *Portrait of Dirck Volckertsz. Coornhert* (1522-1590), ca. 1600. Haarlem, Frans Halsmuseum.
d. Hendrick Goltzius (1558-1617), *Massacre of the Innocents*, ca. 1584. Engraving. Haarlem, Teylers Museum.
e. Carel van Mander (1548-1606), *The worshipping of the golden calf*, 1602. Haarlem, Frans Halsmuseum.

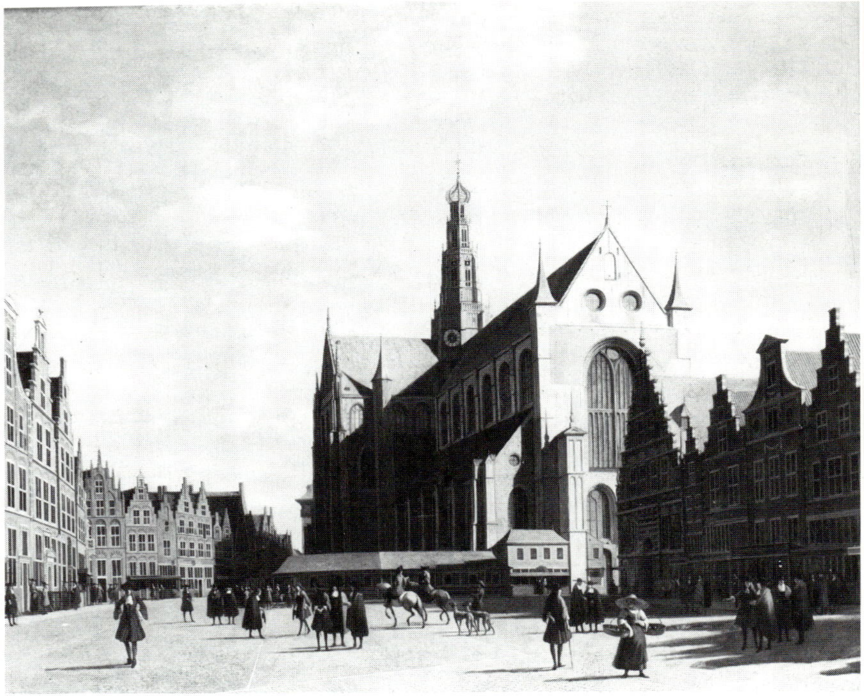

b

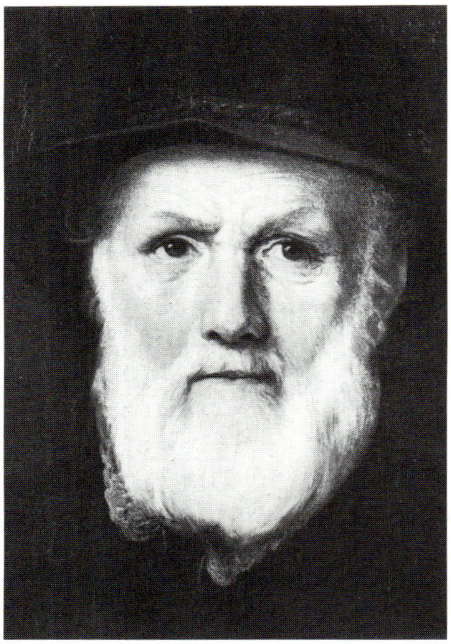

c

### Haarlem

When the Spanish forces withdrew in 1576, Haarlem was at an economic low point. Now the policies of the city authorities were aimed primarily at restoring the economy. For this purpose religious tolerance was given high priority. Soon after the departure of the occupying armies, immigrants began pouring into the town, attracted by the favourable economic prospects and a reasonable degree of religious freedom. Particularly after the fall of Antwerp in 1585 many people from the southern Netherlands found their way to the north. Each year thousands of Flemings and Walloons arrived at Haarlem's gates, drawn by advantageous living conditions and tax benefits. The population of the town swelled enormously: from eighteen thousand in 1572 to nearly forty thousand fifty years later (ill. a).

The population explosion had a positive effect on the economy. Not only did the immigrants bring their industrial skills with them, they also brought capital which was used to start new business ventures. Haarlem's traditional industry, beer brewing, which had declined during the crisis years, awakened to fresh activity. But it was above all the textile industry that blossomed because of the flood of immigrants; within only a few years their skills and experience won Haarlem a strong position in the foreign and domestic textile trade.

But the new prosperity had its dark side. Work conditions were far from ideal and at the slightest slow-down of the economy, poverty spread like wildfire through the overpopulated town. In many cases the guilds into which the different professions were organized bore the financial burdens of their members; but their principal efforts were devoted to keeping an eye on the quality of their products and the varying needs of the market.



## Haarlem and the arts

The flourishing economy formed a rich soil for cultural expansion. Haarlem's two societies of drama and rhetoric again began presenting theatrical productions, and the Flemish immigrants set up a society of their own. Thanks to the skills of Flemish printers, book publishing developed into an important branch of culture. In 1593 Lieven de Key, an architect from Ghent, was appointed 'head mason and stone-worker' for the town of Haarlem. In his exercise of this function he added a new wing to the town hall and built a weigh-house and meat hall, three concrete symbols of Haarlem's new-found prosperity (ill. b).

Productivity in the plastic arts increased in the various towns, and Haarlem was prominent among them. Earlier in the sixteenth century, Haarlem had been the home of the painters Jan van Scorel and Maerten van Heemskerck, who had introduced the style of the Italian Renaissance to the northern Netherlands. The humanist writers Adrianus Junius and Dirck Volckertsz. Coornhert had also been among the town's residents, but had fled from 'the Spanish tyranny' (ill. c). However, in 1577 Coornhert returned to Haarlem. His presence in the town greatly influenced the cultural climate. In writings and prints he pled the cause of religious tolerance. Also coming with him to Haarlem was Hendrick Goltzius, a prominent

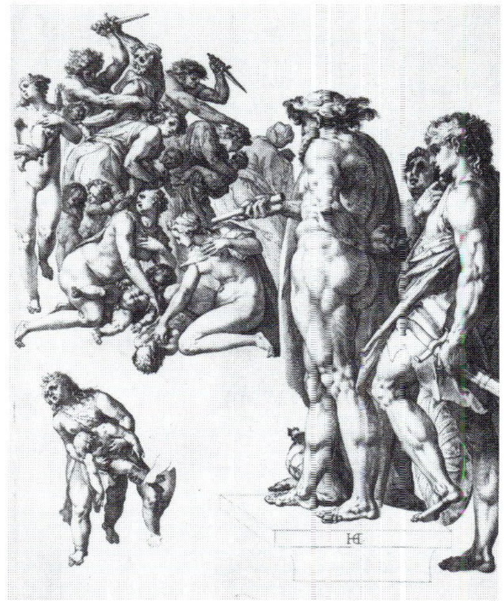

d

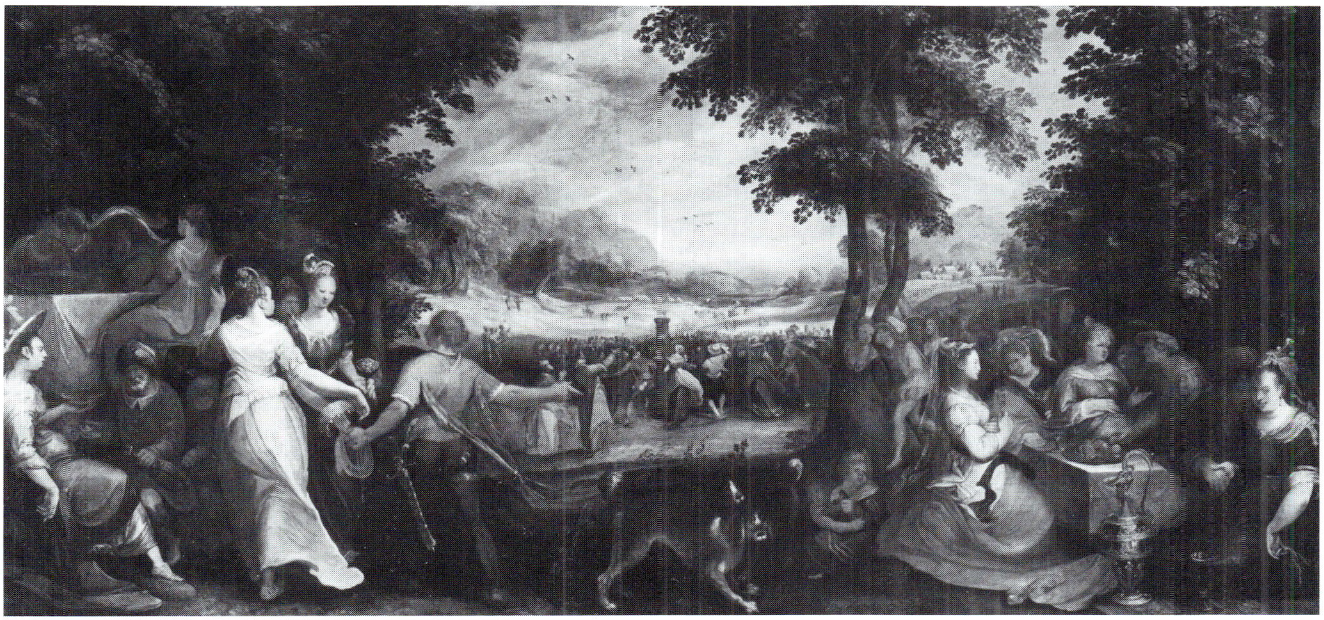

e

engraver and draughtsman (ill. d). He set up a print-shop for graphic arts which formed the basis for Haarlem's important print trade in the seventeenth century.

Of great significance to the development of the art of painting in Haarlem was the arrival in 1583 of the Flemish poet and painter Carel van Mander. He had studied the art of the Renaissance in Italy and announced to Haarlem the criteria which the ideal artist should fulfil. Van Mander was firmly convinced that painting 'histories', depiction of subjects borrowed from mythology, the Bible and the historical past, was the highest pinnacle towards which a painter could strive (ill. e). Depicting human beings demanded a great deal of inventiveness on the part of the artist and was therefore a loftier exercise than the strict imitation of nature, as in the case of still life or landscape painting. Together with Hendrick Goltzius and the young painter Cornelis Cornelisz. van Haarlem, Van Mander founded an academy in order to put his theories into practice. Years later, in 1604, he published them in the *Schilder-boeck*, where he also chronicled the lives of many Dutch and Italian artists. For him, Cornelis was the ideal artist. He worked on large canvases, showing himself to be in possession of a thorough knowledge of anatomy and capable of rendering his subjects' state of mind. From the town council Cornelis received the estimable assignment of decorating the Stadholder's residence in Haarlem, the Prinsenhof (ill.

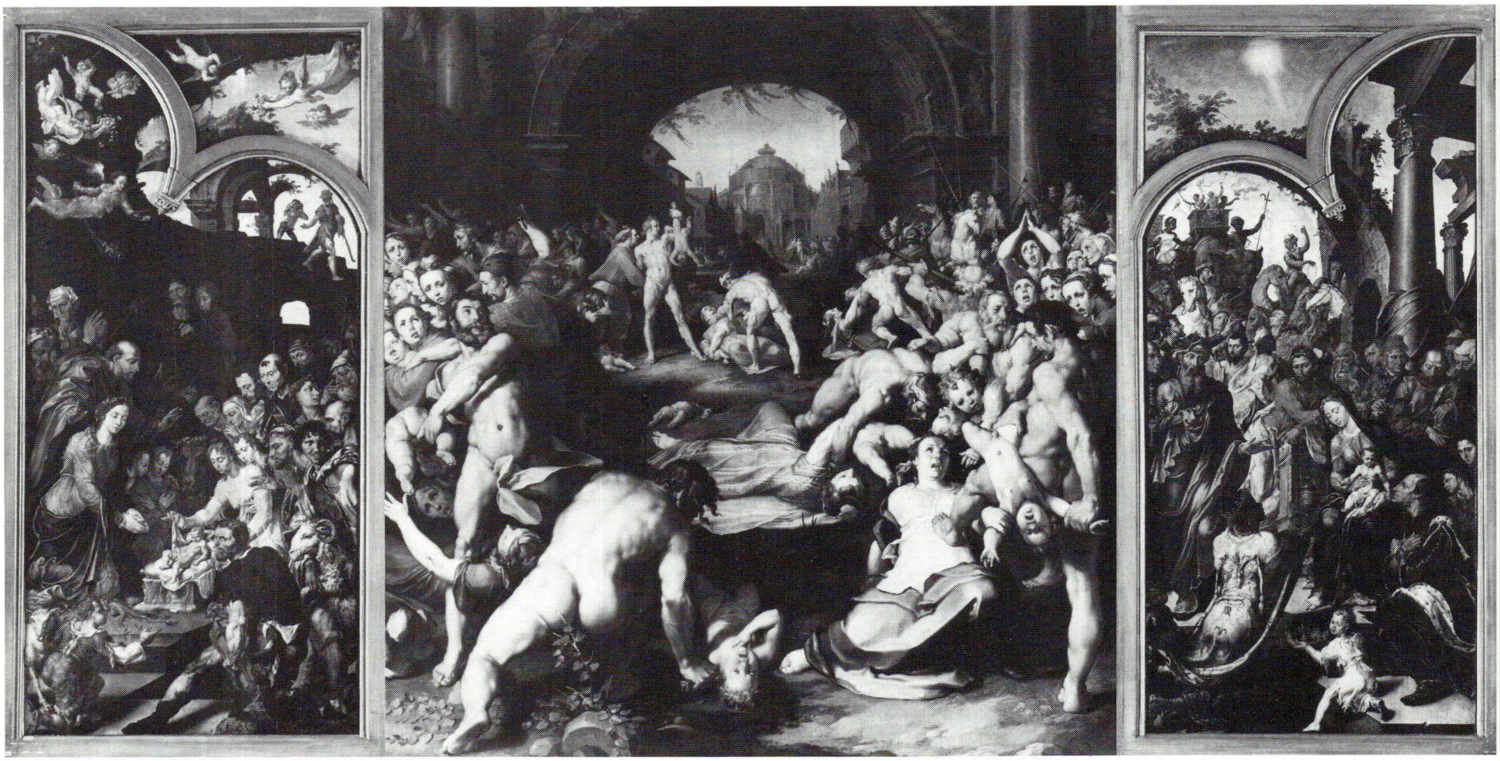

f

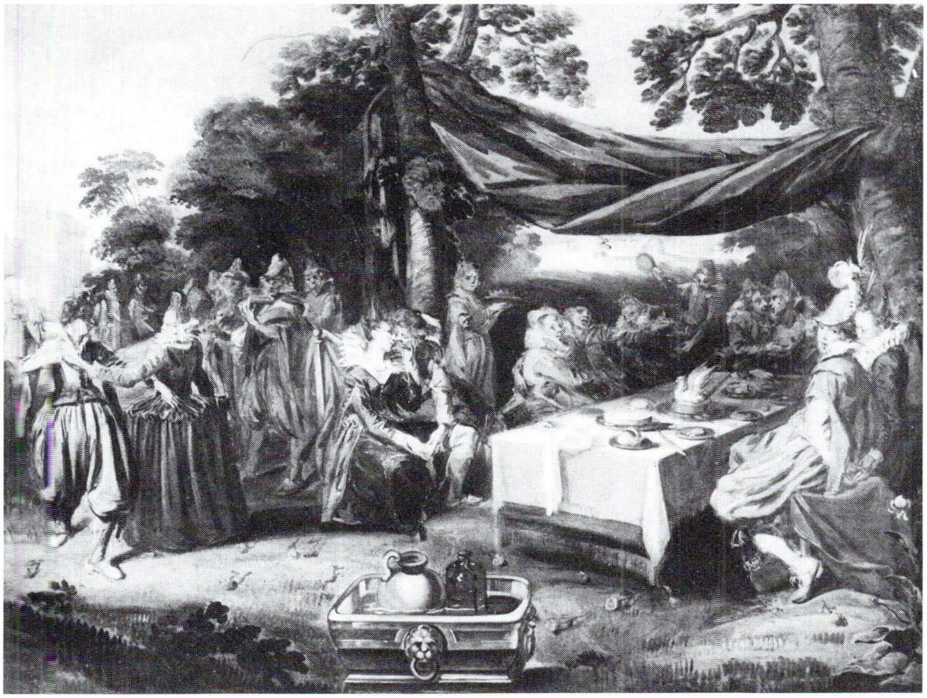

h

f). He was considered the natural successor to Maerten van Heemskerck.

Despite the efforts of Van Mander, Cornelis van Haarlem and Goltzius, increasing specialization earmarked the next generation of artists. After the revolt, the Catholic church was no longer the primary source of commissions for works of art; and the new-found prosperity now alllowed citizens and local governments to take over this role. Painters devoted themselves to genres popular with their new 'commissioners': landscapes, still lifes and portraits (ill. g). One of these specialists was Frans Hals. In the second edition of the *Schilder-boeck,* from 1618, he is named as a pupil of Carel van Mander. A certain influence deriving from Van Mander's principles of composition can be seen in Hals's *Banquet in a park,* unfortunately lost in the Second World War (ill. h). However, within his total output this small painting is an exception. For the remainder of his long life, Hals devoted himself exclusively to portraiture.

f. Maerten van Heemskerck (1498-1574) and Cornelis Cornelisz. van Haarlem, *Drapenier's altar,* 1546 (side panels) and 1591 (centre panel). Haarlem, Frans Halsmuseum (on loan from the Rijksdienst Beeldende Kunst). The original central section of this altarpiece from St. Bavo, which probably consisted of a wood-carving, was lost during or shortly after the siege of Haarlem by the Spanish armies (1572-73). Once the side panels were in the town's possession, Cornelis van Haarlem was commissioned to make a new centrepiece. The triptych was then placed in the Prinsenhof.

g. Cornelis Cornelisz. van Haarlem, *Banquet of the militia companies of St. George and St. Adrian,* 1599. Haarlem, Frans Halsmuseum. Cornelis van Haarlem too was a painter of portraits, of which this is an example.

h. *Banquet in a park,* ca. 1610. Formerly Berlin, Kaiser Friedrich Museum (destroyed in the Second World War).

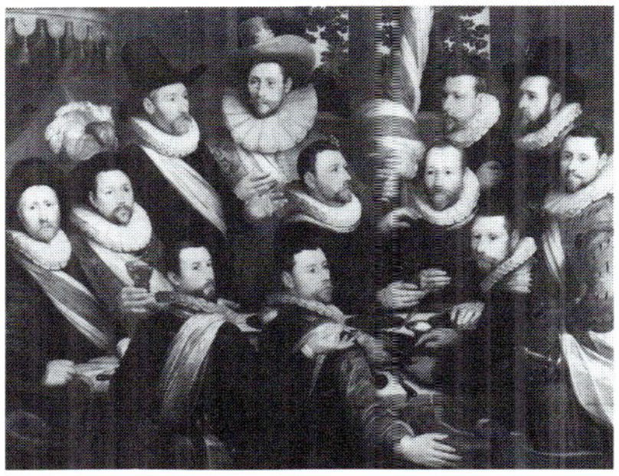

g

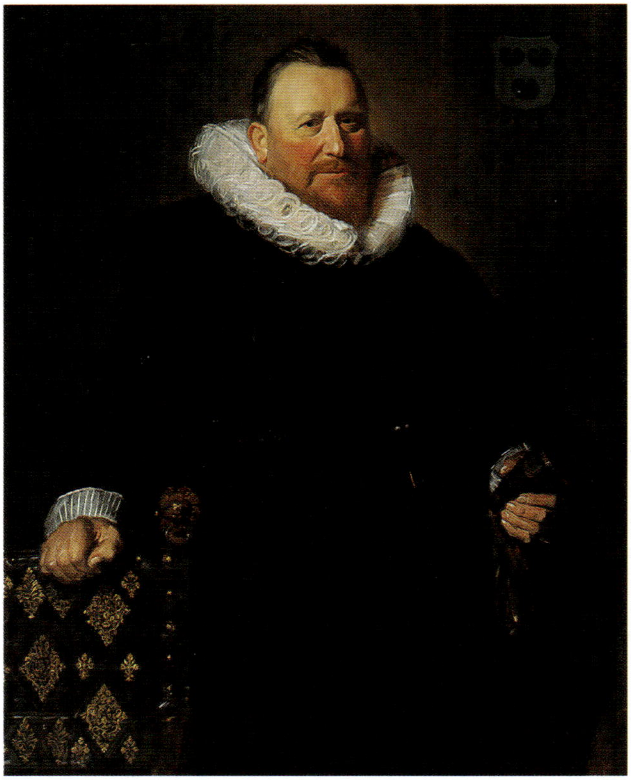

1

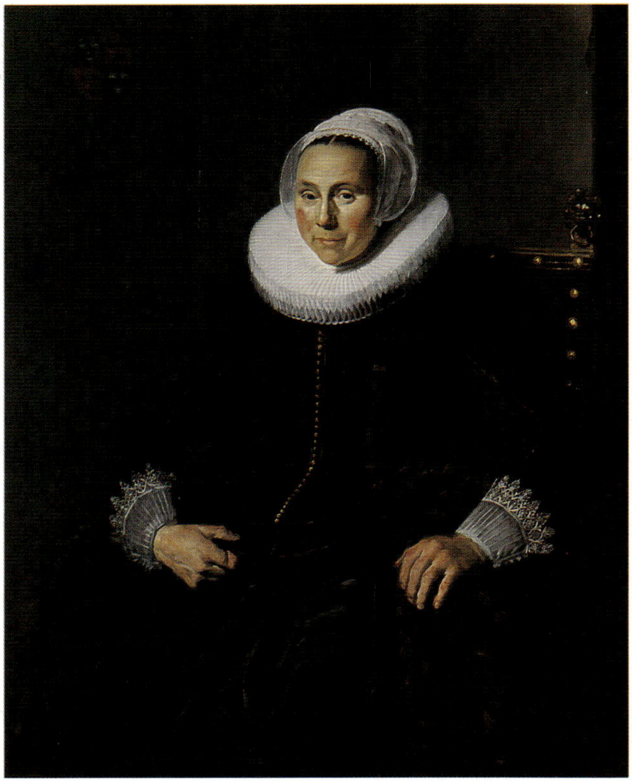

2

Plate 1. *Nicolaes van der Meer.* Panel, 128 x 110.5 cm. Inscribed 'AETAT SVAE 56/AN° 1631'. Haarlem, Frans Halsmuseum.

Plate 2. *Cornelia Vooght Claesdr.* Panel, 126.5 x 101 cm. Inscribed 'AETAT SVAE 53/AN° 1631'. Haarlem, Frans Halsmuseum.

Much of Frans Hals's work consists of portraits of this type, so-called pendants, showing a man and a woman. Traditionally the man is pictured at the right side, the woman at the left. In many cases the identity of the subject can be determined from the family coat of arms in the painting, together with the inscription which gives the subject's age and the year in which the portrait was done. The Haarlem brewer, magistrate and burgomaster Nicolaes van der Meer (1575-1638) was also recognized from a similarity to his portrait in Hals's *Banquet of the officers of the St. George militia company,* painted fifteen years earlier (plate 4). Conclusive evidence, one would think. However, a recent restoration showed that other portraits lie beneath the two by now familiar faces. In addition, the family arms and inscription in Cornelia's portrait were added at a later date. These discoveries raise questions about the two paintings, previously thought to be eminently 'identifiable'. Were Van der Meer and his wife dissatisfied with their likenesses and did they have Hals make new ones? Or did the two portraits perhaps come into other hands and were the new owners responsible for the overpainting? The museum has decided, at least for the time being, to leave the two portraits as they are. Co-operation between art history and the science of restoration will determine what is to be done about them in the future.

Plate 3. *Jacobus Zaffius*. Panel, 54.6 x 41.2 cm. Inscribed and dated 'AETATIS SVAE/77 AN° 1611'. Haarlem, Frans Halsmuseum.
An engraving by Jan van de Velde shows Zaffius seated in a chair with his hand resting on a skull. Jacobus Zaffius (1534-1618) was provost and archdeacon of the episcopal chapter of Haarlem.
Ill. 3a. Jan van de Velde (ca. 1593-1641), *Jacobus Zaffius*, engraving after Frans Hals, 1630.

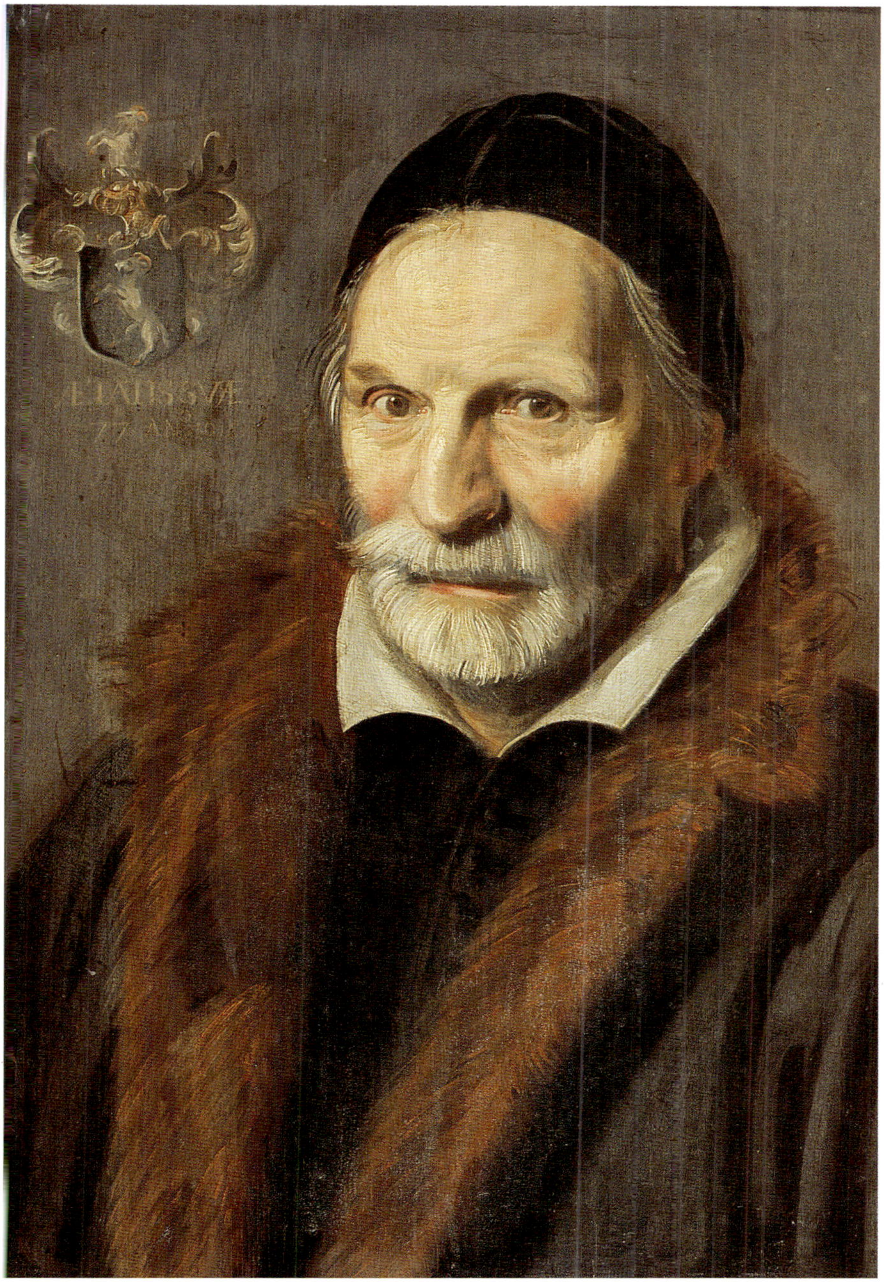

3

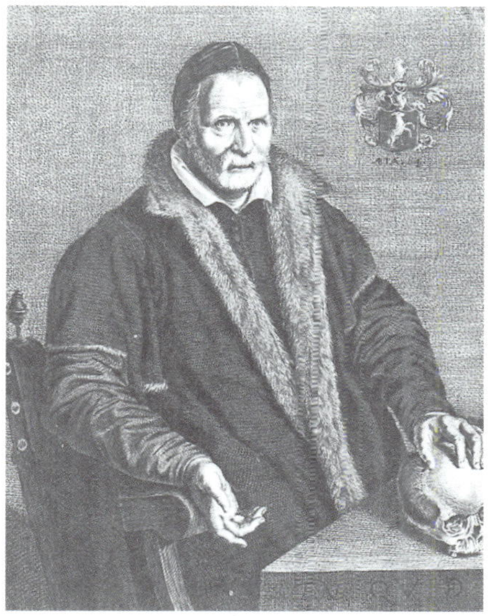

3a

# 1581-1620

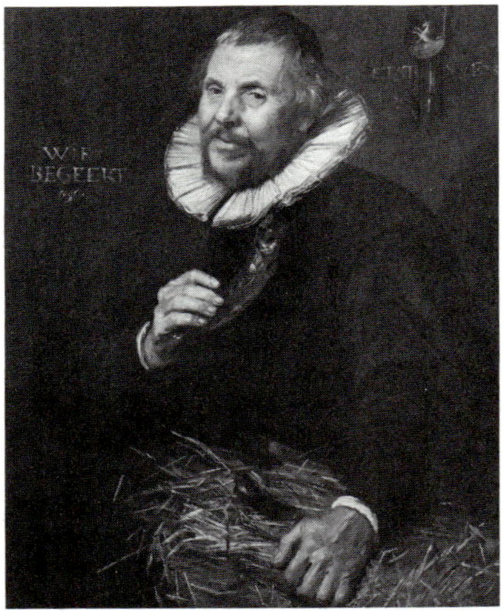

a

Exactly when Frans Hals was born is not known. The marriage of his parents, Franchoys Hals and Adriana van Geestenryck, must have taken place in the last half of 1581 or at the beginning of 1582. The weaver Franchoys Hals and his family belonged to those that fled from Antwerp after the town was captured in 1585. Frans Hals's birth must therefore have occurred between 1581 and 1585, since in official documents he repeatedly listed Antwerp as his place of birth. Before the family's departure for Haarlem, another son was born, Joost Hals. By the time the third son, Dirck, was baptized on 19 March 1591 the family was living in Haarlem.

If Frans Hals indeed studied with Carel van Mander, his study could not have extended beyond 1603, the year in which Van Mander withdrew to his country home near Alkmaar in order to devote himself to finishing the *Schilder-boeck*. Frans Hals's activities in the following years are uncertain. Not until 1610 did he register as a member of the St. Lucas Guild in Haarlem and paintings from his hand are known as of that year. Frans Hals's early work follows the manner of traditional portraiture, but his distinctive, fluent brushwork is already unmistakably present (ill. a, b, c).

In about 1610 Frans Hals married Anneke Harmansdr. from Haarlem. Their son Harmen was baptized on 2 September 1611. A second child died - probably shortly after birth - in the spring of 1613. Possibly the birth of a third child, whose name is also unknown, was the cause of Anneke's death in May or June 1615. From 1616 onwards Frans Hals was a member of the St. George militia company. The officers of this citizen soldiery had themselves painted in 1616 at the traditional farewell banquet (plate 4). This militia portrait is Hals's first large commission. In the same

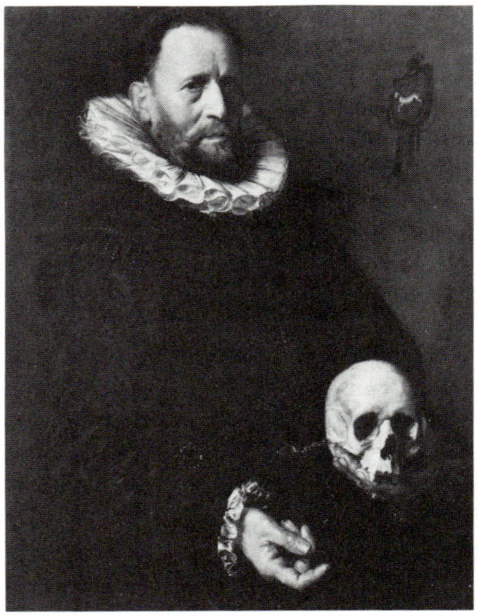

b

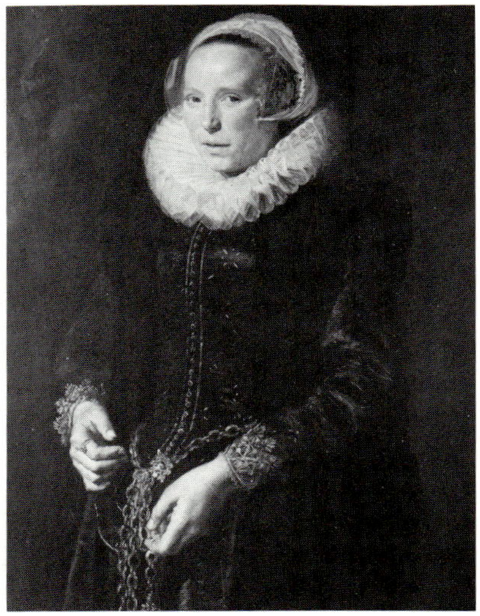

c

year Frans Hals travelled to the city of his birth, Antwerp, possibly to take care of family business. There, Pieter Paul Rubens, Anthonie van Dyck and Jacob Jordaens were the leading masters of the moment. Hals's absence from Haarlem prevented him, on 6 August, from appearing in court; a charge had been brought against him because he had purchased several paintings and not yet paid for them. Apparently, like many painters, Frans Hals dealt in the art trade. In September 1616 he still had not returned. Now a charge was brought against him by the nurse of his two children to whom he owed money. The magistrates reached an agreement with Hals's mother on 11 November to the effect that the amount owing would be paid from part of the money he still had coming to him from the St. George militia company. By then one of the children had already died. Four days later Frans Hals reappeared in Haarlem and agreed to the ruling.

In 1616 Frans Hals joined the 'rederijkerskamer' *De Wijngaertrancken,* one of Haarlem's three drama and poetry societies. Many artists were members. Probably the atmosphere of their performances is reflected in the scene portrayed by Frans Hals in *'Shrovetide revellers'* (ill. e). On the crowded canvas can be seen the traditional stage figures of Peeckelhaering and Hansworst. Both of these also appear regularly in paintings by Dirck Hals and Willem Buytewech (ill.e). Frans Hals remained a member of *De Wijngaertrancken* until 1625.

On 12 February 1617, in Spaarndam, a village near Haarlem, Frans Hals married Lysbeth Reyniers, nine days before the birth of their daughter Sara. In 1618 Frans Jr. was born, and a third child, Jan Hals, followed in about 1620.

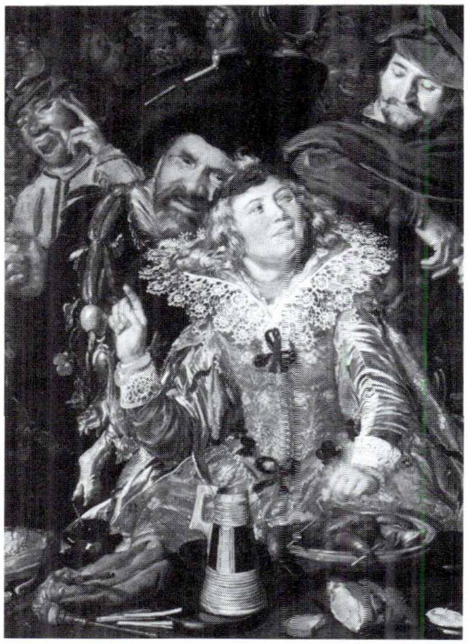

d

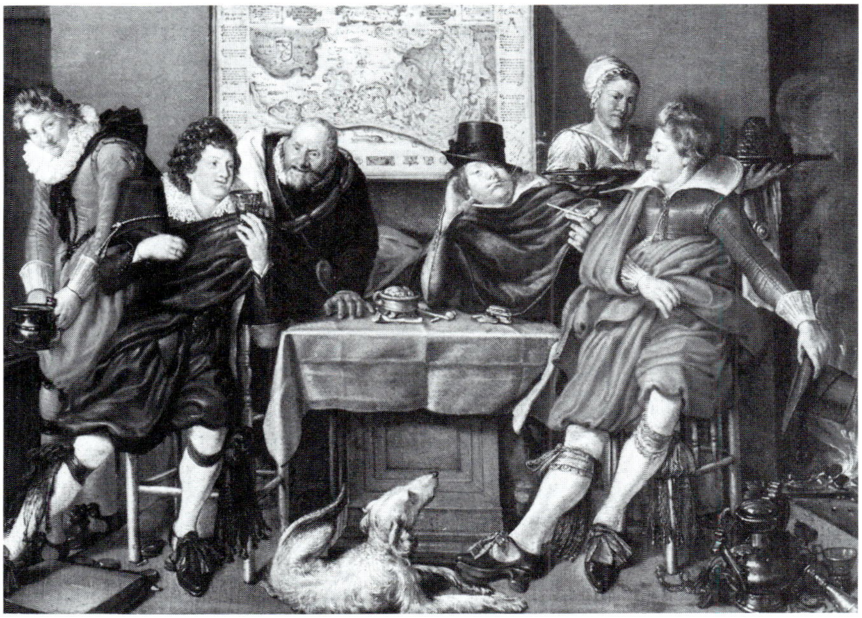

e

a. *The 'rederijker' (dramatist) Pieter Cornelisz. van der Morsch of Leiden*, 1616. Pittsburgh, Carnegie Museum of Art.
b. *Portrait of a man*, ca. 1610. Birmingham, The Barber Institute of Fine Arts.
c. *Portrait of a woman*, ca. 1610. Chatsworth, Devonshire Collection, The Trustees of the Chatsworth Settlement.
d. *'Shrovetide revellers '*, ca. 1617. New York, The Metropolitan Museum of Art.
e. Willem Buytewech (1591/92-1624), *Merry company*, ca. 1620. Rotterdam, Museum Boymans-van Beuningen.

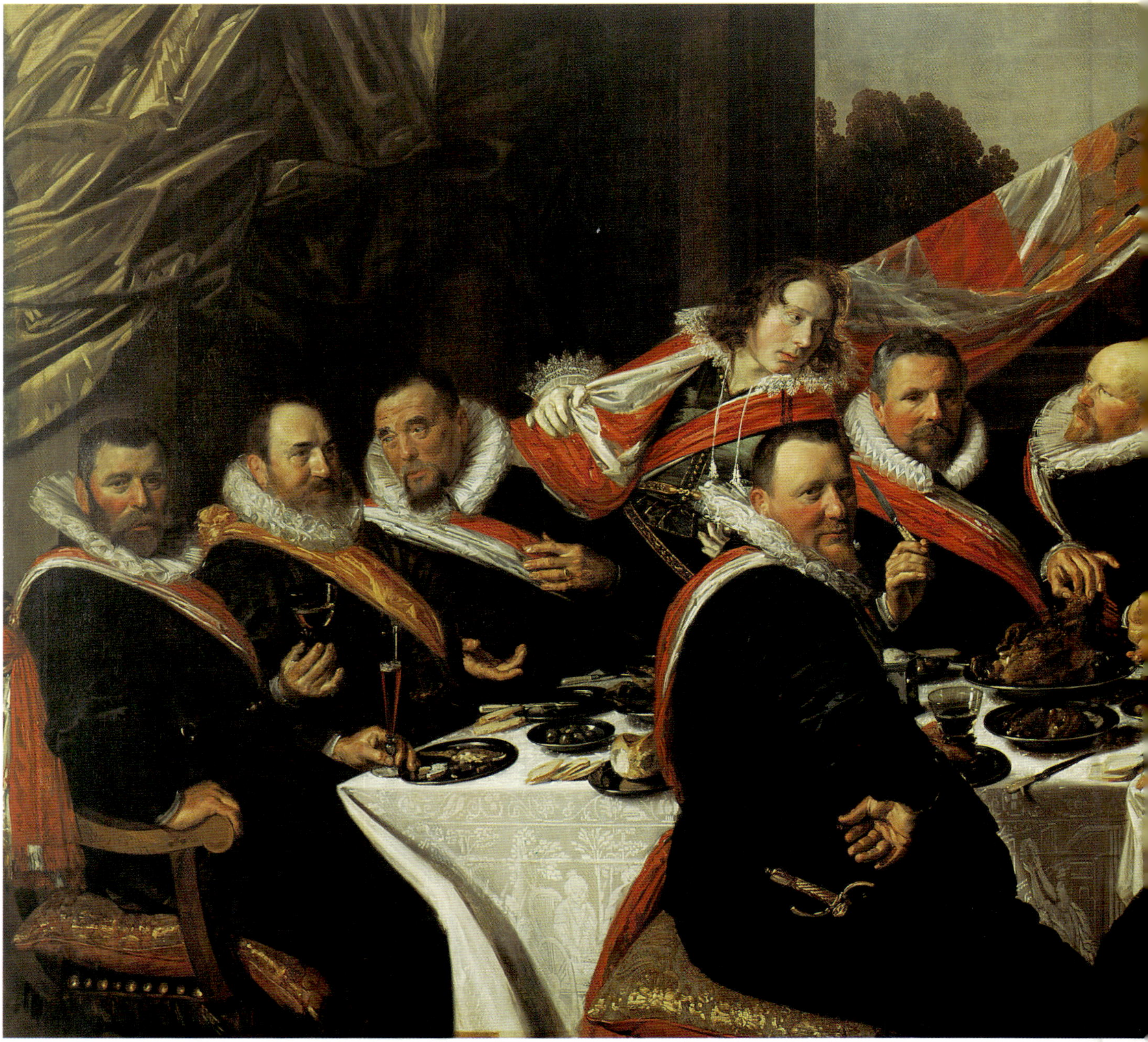

4

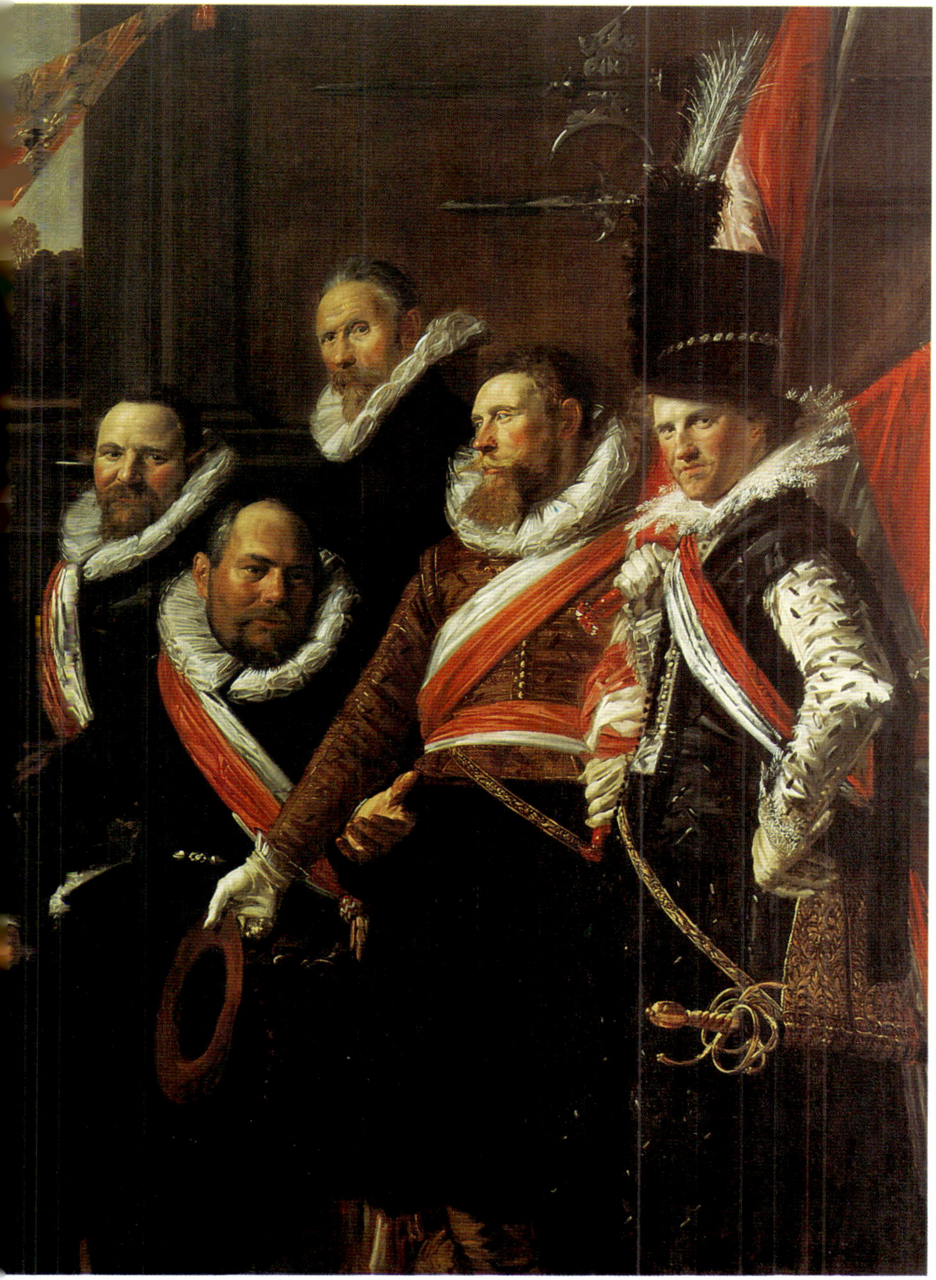

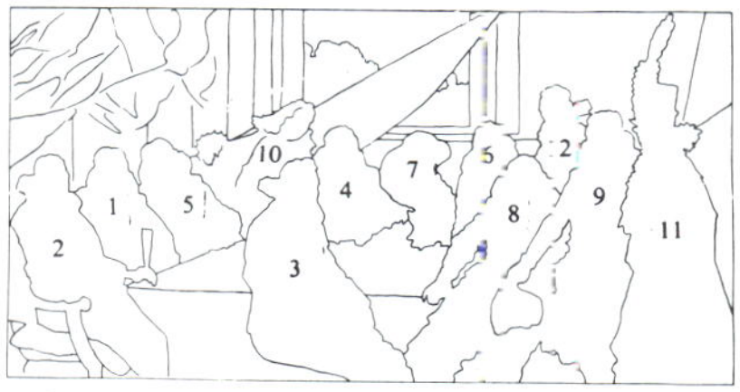


1. Hendrick van Berckenrode, colonel; 2. Johan van Napels, provost; 3. Nicolaes Woutersz. (van der Meer), captain (see also plate 1); 4. Vechter Jansz. (van Teffelen), captain; 5. Jacob Laurensz., captain; 6. Hugo Steyn, lieutenant; 7. Cornelis Schout, lieutenant; 8. Pieter Verbeek, lieutenant; 9. Gerrit Vlasman, standard-bearer; 10. Jacob Schout, standard-bearer (see also plate 14); 11. Boudewijn van Offenberg, standard-bearer (see also plate 14); 12. attendant.

Plate 4. *Banquet of the officers of the St. George militia company.* Canvas, 175 x 324 cm. Dated on the chair, left, '1616'. Haarlem, Frans Halsmuseum.
Frans Hals depicted the officers of the militia at the banquet traditionally offered them by the town council at the end of their three years of service.
The militiamen sit casually at the festively decked table with the standard-bearers entering the room. It is as if the observer has been given the opportunity to gaze freely at the spectacle for a time. A few militiamen are aware of him, others are busy conversing and the attendant hurries in with another platter of food. It is this momentary character which gives the painting its great distinction: the militiamen do not seem to have posed but to have been 'caught in the act' and set down on canvas in the twinkling of an eye.

## HISTORY OF THE BANQUET OF THE OFFICERS OF THE ST. GEORGE MILITIA COMPANY, 1616

*1616* The painting is made, dated at bottom left, on the chair.
*1692* The painting is taken to the Prinsenhof in Haarlem before 1692.
*1862* The painting is already lined when taken to the Stedelijk Museum in Haarlem, opened this year.
*1885* Lining comes loose, is removed and a new lining is provided by Hopman, Amsterdam.
*1889* The varnish layer is regenerated and partially removed by F. Vos, the museum's restorer.
*1894* Varnish layer regenerated by F. Vos.
*1906* Idem. As a result of being photographed in the open air, the canvas sags and a new lining is required. During its application, part of the facing paper on the front with its attached varnish comes undone. The paper is again made fast with alcohol and work continues.
*1913* Transfer to the newly opened Frans Halsmuseum.
*1919* Restoration under the supervision of D. de Wild.
*1986* Restoration by Anne van Grevenstein, Michaela Burek and Carol Pottasch.

## THE RESTORATION IN 1986

June-December

This is the only militia portrait to be taken to the Prinsenhof before 1692. It was still in good condition, with only a small number of losses or damaged spots, and does not appear to have shrunk. The paint surface remained smooth, adhering securely to the canvas. The original cusping was still visible; there had been virtually no cutting down. The tension was reasonably good.

The mastic varnish applied by De Wild, strongly yellowed, was removed with acetone and cotton swabs. The black areas, given a generous black glaze by De Wild, were judiciously cleaned. Due to the thin, almost sketchy application of paint in the clothing, as well as to abrasion in the past, these areas were extremely delicate. The brown curtain (formerly copper-green), the grey sky (formerly smalt blue) and the brown trees (formerly copper-green) represent changes that can not be restored to their initial state. Since the relation of colours was clearly not the original one and in order not to emphasize the light-dark contrast unnecessarily, a thin layer of old varnish was retained over the entire surface.

An intermediate layer of dammar varnish was applied, then the losses were filled with a mixture of wax, chalk and pigment in the light rose tint of the ground layer, fixed with paraloid B72 in acetone.

The surface of the fillings was treated with a silicone mould made from the original paint in an effort to recreate the surface structure.

Retouching was done with dry pigment bound with dammar varnish. The top coat of varnish was sprayed on sparingly; a thin layer of varnish is naturally less subject to yellowing and accentuates to a lesser extent irregularities in the painting's surface.

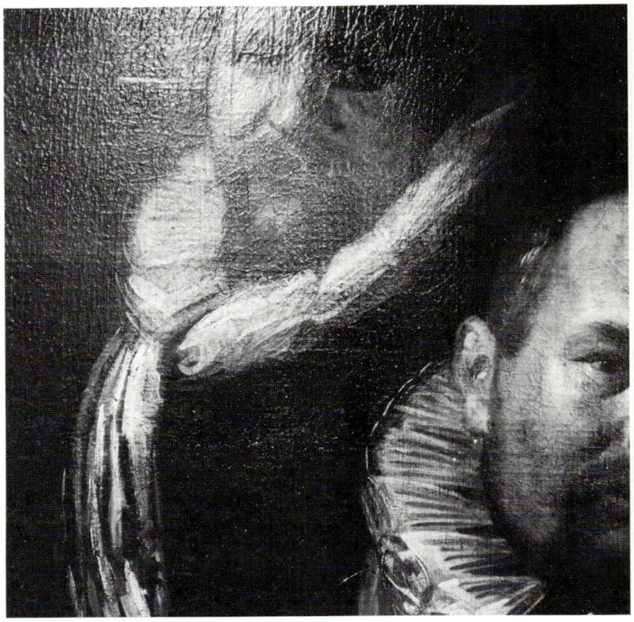

4a

Ill. 4a.
The head of figure 6 in reflected light. The old filling is smooth and reflects light differently than the surrounding paint. This adds to the effect of disharmony produced by discoloration and too much overpainting.

Ill. 4b.
The head of figure 6 after the losses have been filled.
The loss is filled with a mixture of chalk and wax in the colour of the ground layer (a very light warm beige). The filling is treated with a silicone impression of the surrounding paint (see also ill. 8e, p. 34) in order to reproduce the original surface structure.

Ill. 4c.
The head of figure 6 after retouching. Current requirements for the highest quality in retouching were met as fully as possible: the filling gives a good reproduction of the craquelure. The paint work was respected, retouching limited to filling. Nostril, cheek and shadow now show to better advantage.

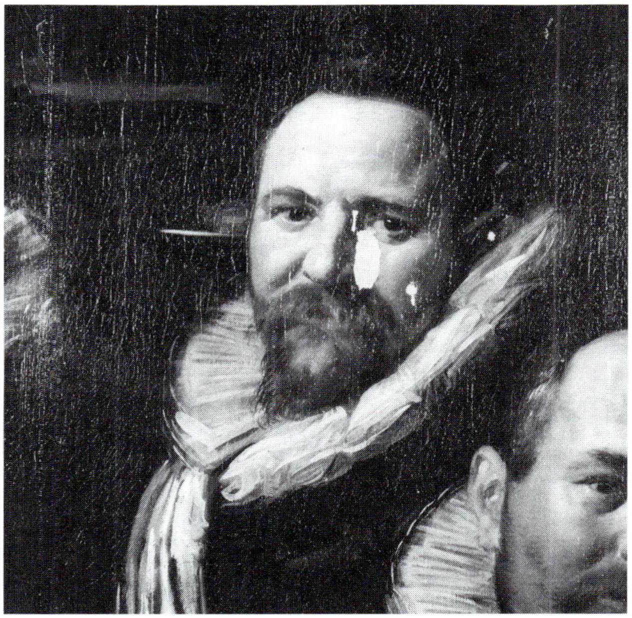

4b

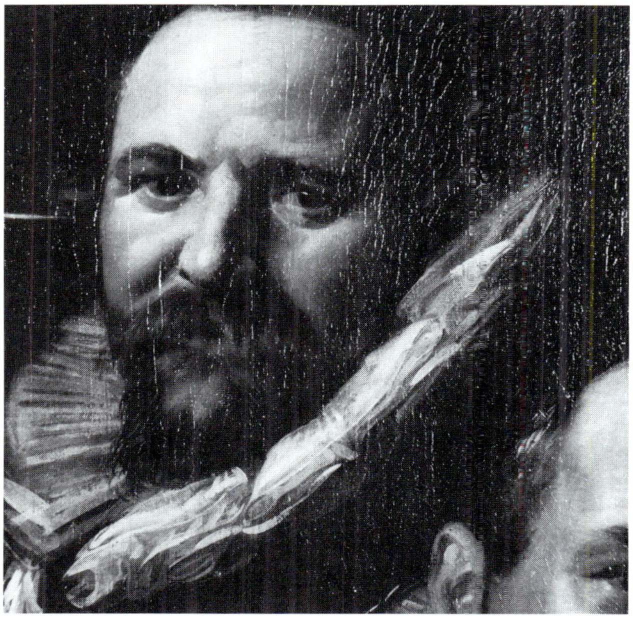

4c

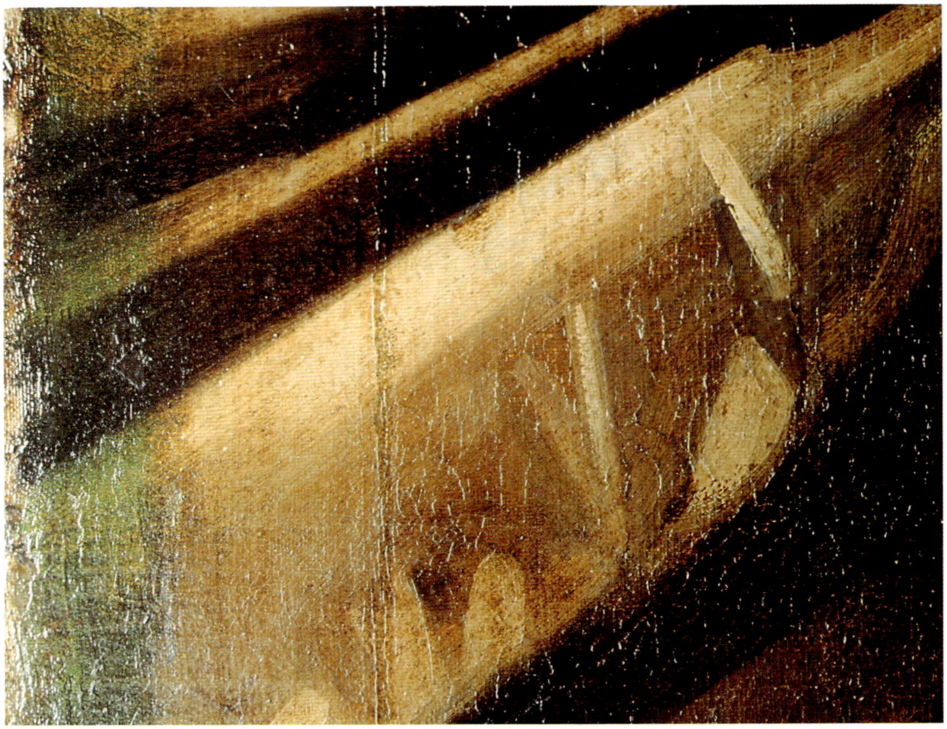

Ill. 4d. Detail of the curtain in the background: discoloration of copper-green. Removal of the old varnish and overpainting revealed a strip of copper-green on the left which had been covered by a frame. This is a thin layer of paint, rich in binding medium, providing little cover and sensitive to solvents. Where not protected by the frame, this copper-green layer had turned brown, probably from exposure to light, and during an earlier restoration it had been abraded along with the varnish. A layer is thus missing on the curtain as it looks today. An irreversible deterioration due to the kind of paint Hals used and improper restoration in the past. Green overpainting of the curtain is theoretically possible. But exactly what shade of green? What sort of brushwork? Such questions can not be answered. Hence the unacceptability of taking such a step.

4d

Plate 5. *Three children with a goat-cart,* ca. 1620. Canvas, 150.8 x 107.5 cm. Brussels, Koninklijke Musea voor Schone Kunsten. This children's group was originally part of a family portrait. The left half, showing the father and mother, is in the museum at Cardiff (see p. 6, ill. e). The paint surface is quite thin, probably as a result of an overly intensive restoration in the past.
Seventeenth-century family portraits were frequently situated in the open air, nature providing the painter with a variety of reference points where flora and fauna could be used to symbolize the harmony of family life. The most striking symbol in this fragment is the goat-cart, indicative of proper child-raising. The goat is associated with lust. The boy shows his good upbringing by keeping a tight rein on the animal. He has learned to keep his sensual appetites under control.

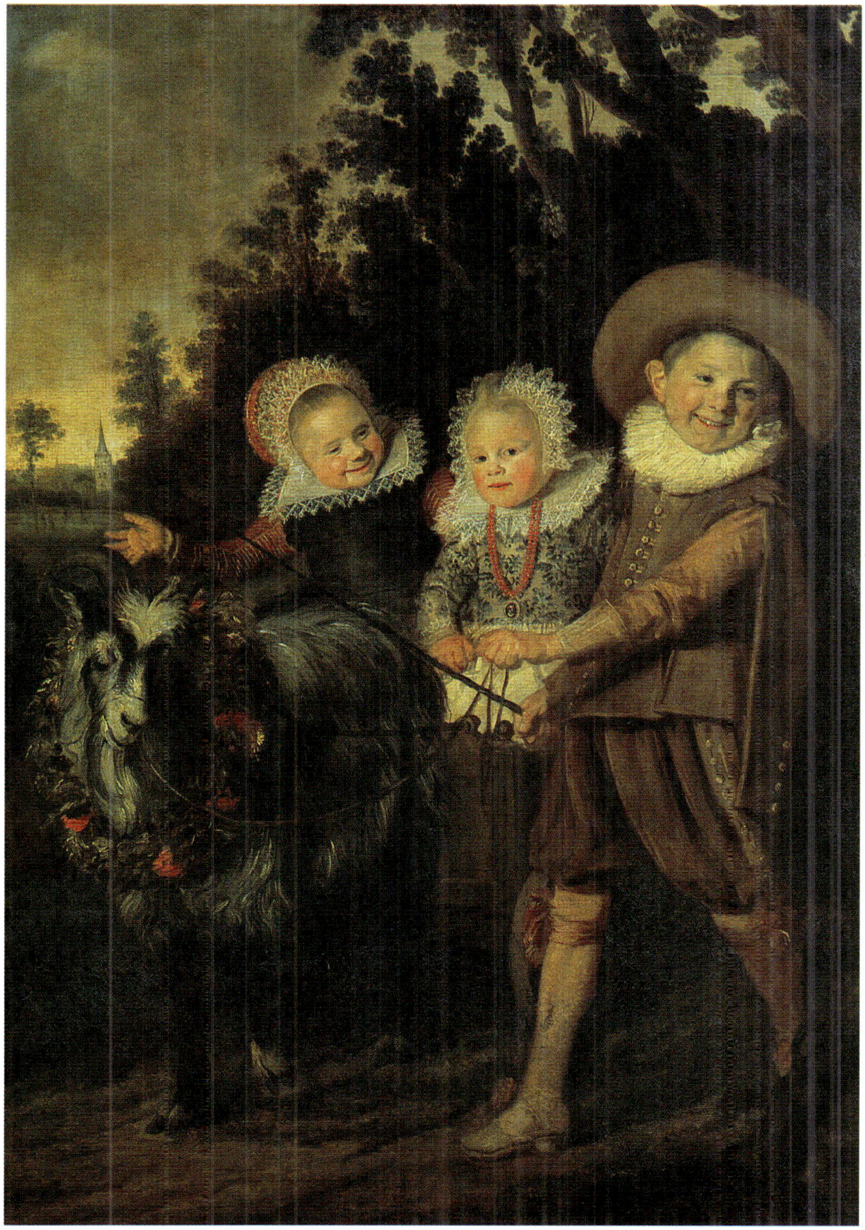

5

# 1620-1630

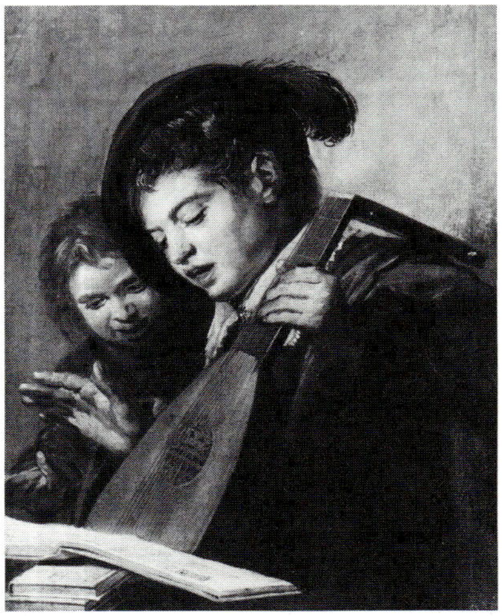

a

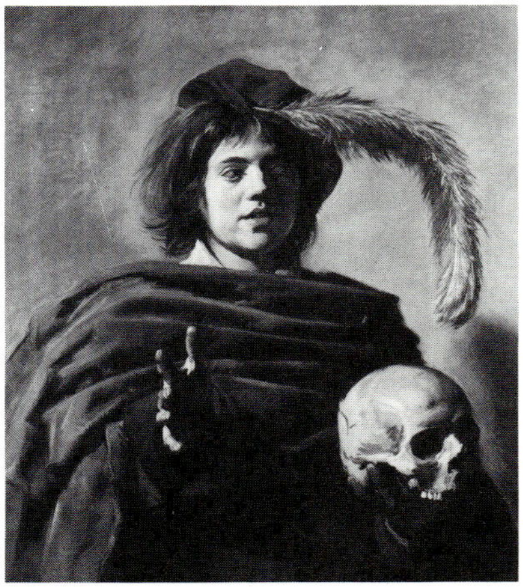

b

In the years after 1620 the Frans Hals family expanded with the births of at least eight children: Adriaentgen (1623), Jacobus (1624), Reynier (1627), Nicolaes (1628), Maria (1631) and Susanna (1634); the birth dates of Pieter and Anthonie Hals are not known. Like Harmen, Frans Jr. and Jan, Reynier and Nicolaes were to follow in the footsteps of their father.

During this period the paintings came into being which have made Frans Hals so popular with the public: the folk types (see pp. 36-38) and the figures of children (ill. a and b). For the latter, Frans Hals perhaps used his own brood as inexpensive models; the faces of some of the children clearly resemble one another. Or it is possible that Frans Hals had an ideal type of child in mind? The children's figures were not commissioned as portraits; with their attributes, they depicted the five senses or the seven deadly sins. Instructive series of this kind had been popular since the sixteenth century, and Hals's pupils painted them as well. With his emblematic child figures, Frans Hals made a significant contribution to the blossoming in the 1620s of 'genre piece': a narrative scene, apparently taken from everyday life, carrying with it an edifying message.

In the work of Frans Hals from the 1620s the influence can be seen of the Utrecht painters, the so-called Caravaggists. Hendrick ter Brugghen and Gerrit van Honthorst had studied the work of Michelangelo Merisi da Caravaggio (1571-1610) in Italy and introduced his style in the north. From their paintings Hals took over not only the direct fall of light but also the composition: he depicts only the upper body of his models, as seen from below. The choice of subjects also seems to have come from Utrecht. In imitation of the Caravaggists, Hals painted both children and a series of four evangelists, possibly destined for a clandestine Catholic church (ill. d, e, f).

Given the widely fluctuating income from his work, Frans Hals was repeatedly in debt. Precisely during these years, he received several valuable commissions. In about 1627 he painted two militia portraits, one for the St. George militia company and one for the other citizen soldiery, the St. Adrian militia company (plate 9 and 14). In 1629 Hals received from the city treasury the sum of 24 pounds 'for the lightening and changing of a few pieces of Painting from the Convent of St. Johans'. Exactly what was meant by this is not clear, but probably Hals gave several paintings a 'touch-up' after they had come into the possession of the town of Haarlem from the Convent of St. John.

a. *Two boys singing (hearing),* ca. 1625. Cassel, Hessisches Landesmuseum.
b. *Boy with skull (transience, vanity),* ca. 1626. London, National Gallery.

c. *The lute player,* ca. 1625. Paris, Musée du Louvre.
d. Hendrick ter Brugghen (1588-1629), *St. John,* 1621. Deventer, Town Hall.

e. *St. Luke,* ca. 1626. Odessa, State Museum.
f. *St. Matthew,* ca. 1626. Odessa, State Museum.
g. *Samuel Ampzing,* 163(0?). England, private collection.

In his *Beschrijvinge ende lof der Stad Haerlem in Holland (Description and praise of the city of Haarlem in Holland)* the city historian Samuel Ampzing (ill g) devoted a few lines of praise to the brothers Frans and Dirck Hals:

*Come Halses, come forth*
*Take your place here, as is your right.*
*How strongly Frans paints men to the life,*
*How fine the images Dirck gives us!*
*Brothers in art, brothers in blood*
*Raised by a mother who nurtured art.*

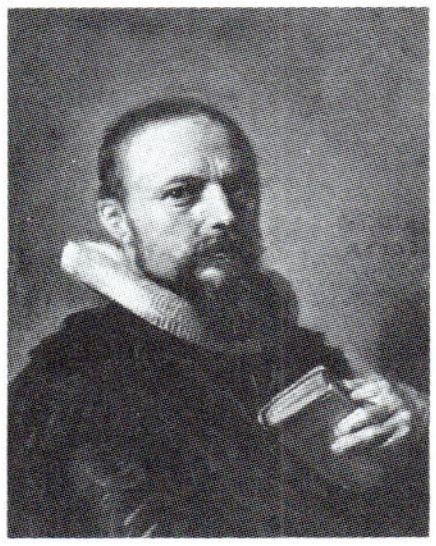

g

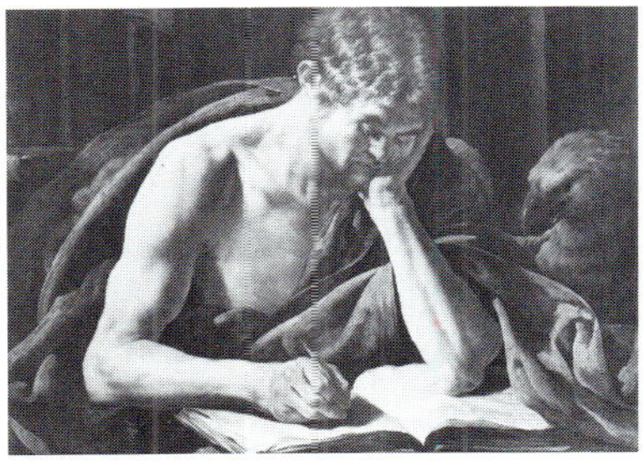

d

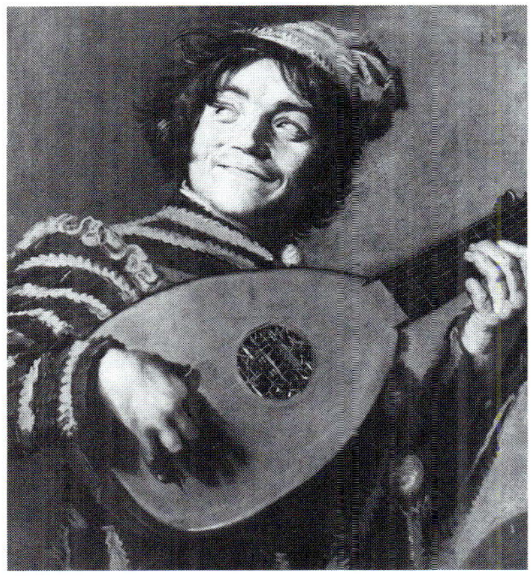

c

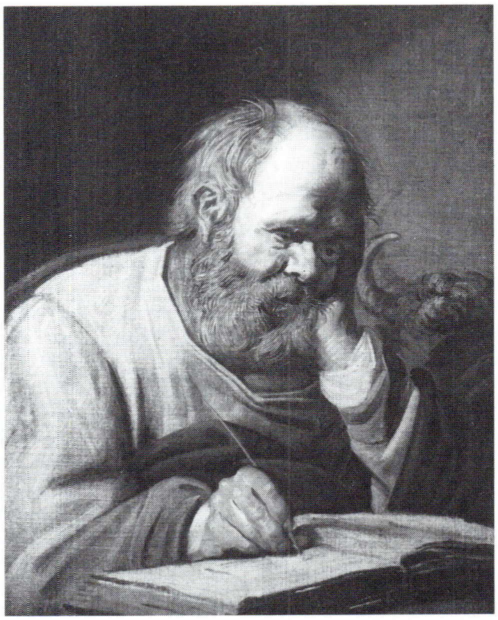

e

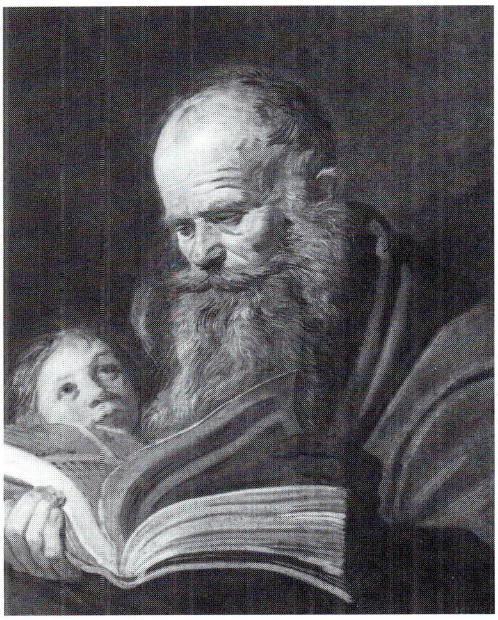

f

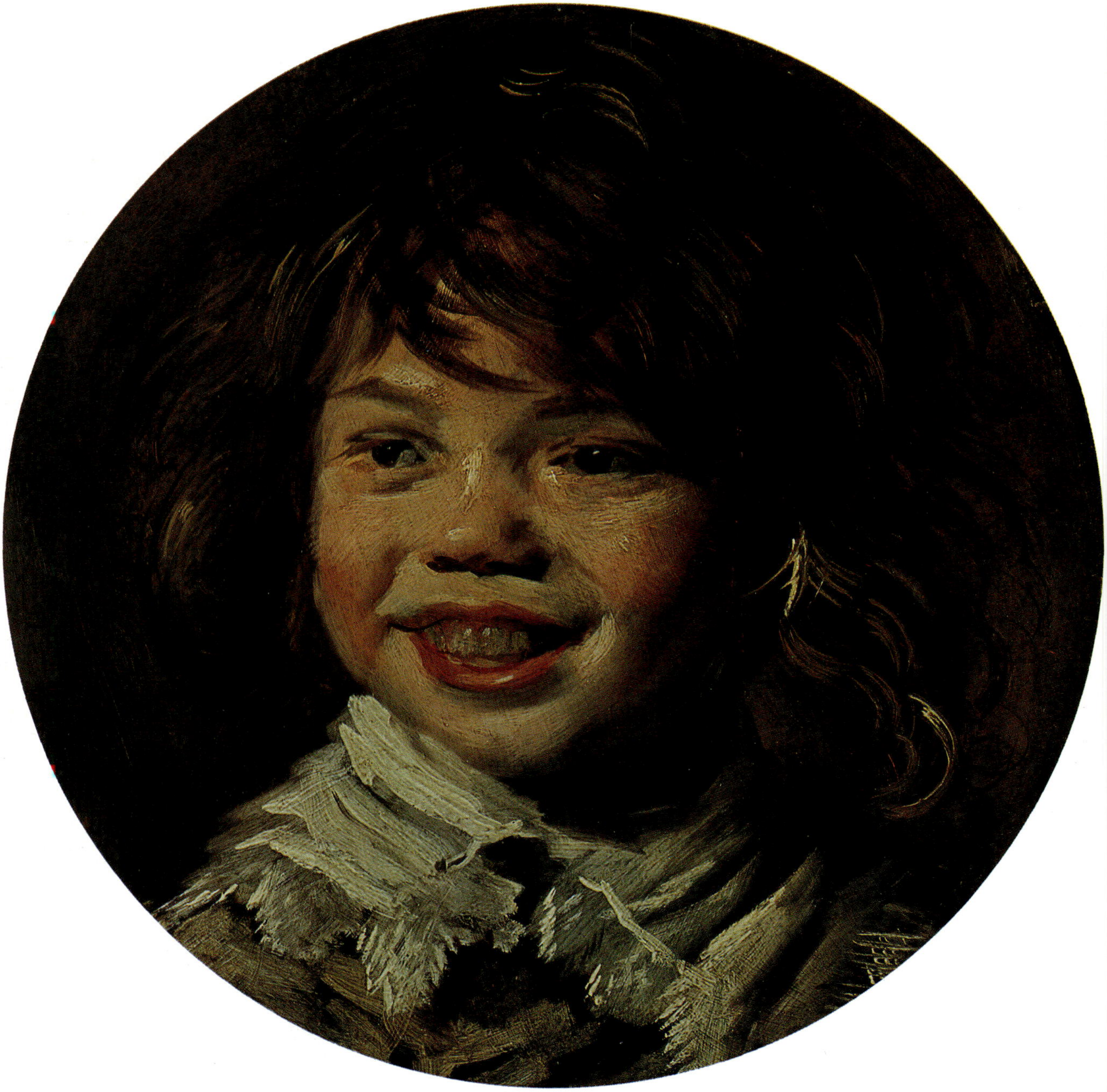

6

Plate 6. *Laughing boy,* ca. 1625. Round panel, 29.5 cm. Signed left with the monogram 'FH' and above left (vague) 'FHF'. The Hague, Mauritshuis.
Plate 7. *Laughing boys with a jug,* ca. 1627, 69.5 x 58 cm. Signed right with the monogram 'FH'. Leerdam, Hofje van Aerden.
This representation may be interpreted as 'sight', one of the five senses. It also can be seen as depicting one of the seven deadly sins, the merry boys with their empty jug symbolizing 'intemperance'.

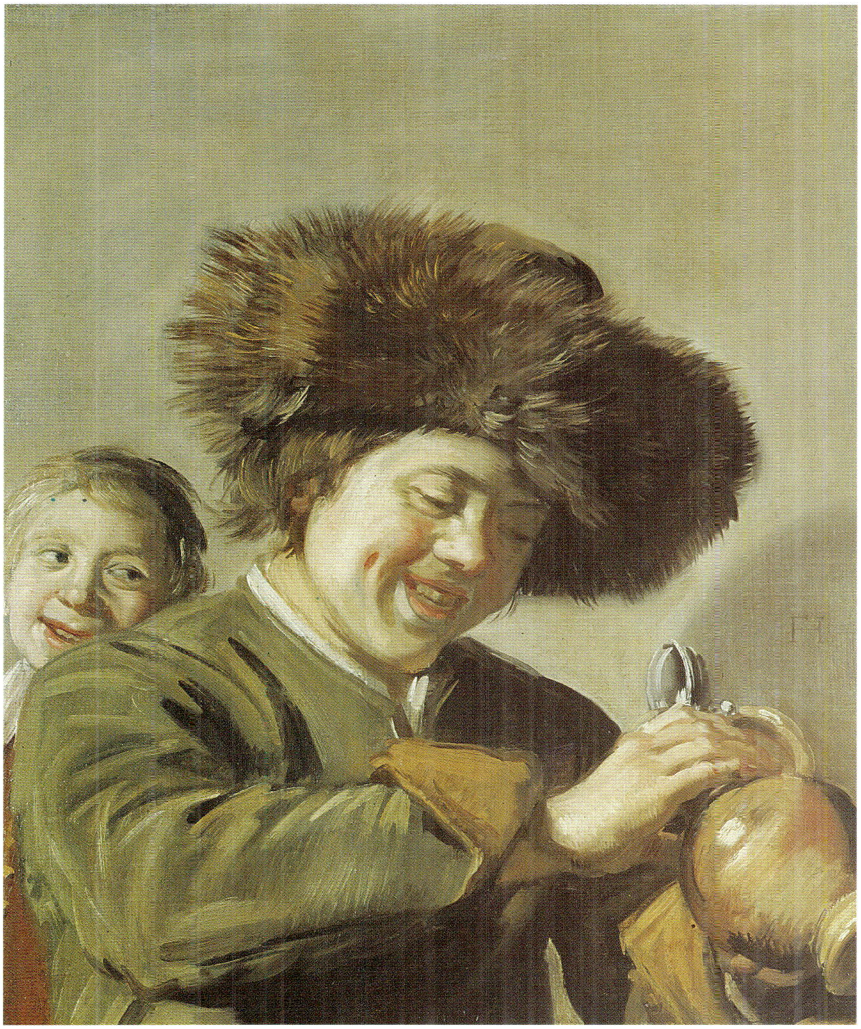

7

## The Haarlem militia companies

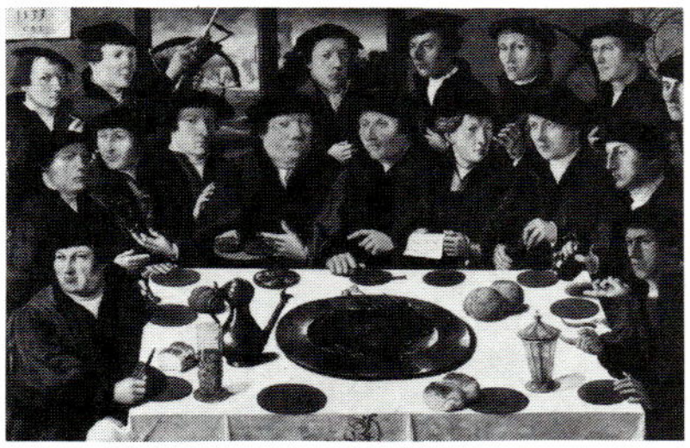

a

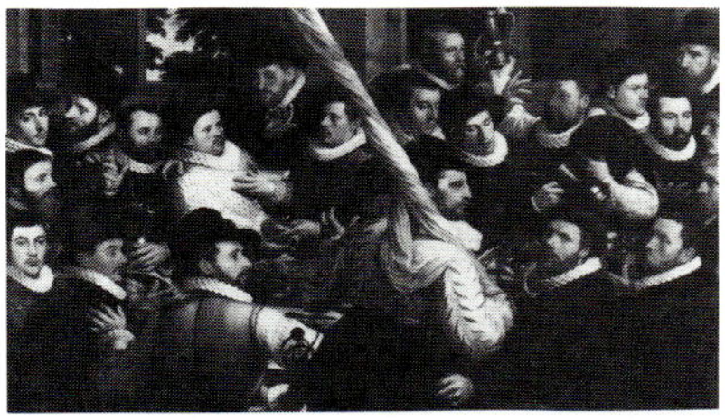

b

During the period in which Frans Hals painted his militia portraits - between 1615 and 1640 - there were two corps of militia companies in Haarlem. The older militia stood under the protection of St. George and gathered in the New Doelen or St. George Doelen. The association's old headquarters had been destroyed by fire in 1576 which reduced a large portion of the town to ashes. The other militia had St. Adrian as its patron saint and met in the Old or Cluveniers Doelen.
After the retreat of the Spanish armies in 1576, the Haarlem militias were reorganized. They were integrated into the military structure of the northern Netherlands and also charged with guarding the city gates. Both militia companies were responsible to the city council, which every three years chose a new officers' corps from among the well-to-do citizens of Haarlem. The colonel was the leader. He was assisted by the provost, later called the fiscal, who managed the finances. From 1612 onwards both militias consisted of three companies, each headed by a captain, a lieutenant and two sergeants. Each had its own standard-bearer, a position which traditionally could be held only by a bachelor. Belonging to a militia was by no means available to everyone. Each member was expected to pay for his own weapons and uniform, and to possess at least one hundred Flemish pounds. This gave the militias a somewhat elitist character.

Every year the traditional militiamen's banquet was held, partially financed by the town council. Such a festive occasion was apt to go on a bit - a banquet lasting a week was no exception - and led to 'great and immoderate gorging with Food and Drink'. In 1617 the town council determined that the event was not to exceed four days. In addition, the militia officers were treated to a banquet by the town council at the close of their three years' tour of duty. These banquets were taken by Frans Hals as the basis for three of his militia portraits.

Initially the militia portrait as a genre existed only in Amsterdam. In 1533 Cornelis Anthonisz. portrayed seventeen militiamen on a single panel, using the soberly laid table as the mid-point of his composition (ill. a). Fifty years later Cornelis van Haarlem made the first known militia portrait in Haarlem (ill. b). He also grouped the militiamen round a table and managed to achieve a fuller use of space, partly by choosing a lower vantage point. Carel van Mander praised his colleague's work for its liveliness and faithful likenesses.

The composition of Frans Hals's first militia portrait, the *Banquet of the officers of the St. George militia company*, from 1616, clearly shows the influence of Cornelis van Haarlem. But under Hals's direction the militiamen are allowed to carry on their revels in a realistic space, without crowding. Twice again, in about 1627, he was to portray Haarlem citizen-soldiers in this way: the officers, some with swords, relaxedly seated at table, surrounded by colourful standard-bearers.

In Hals's militia portraits of 1633 and 1639 the men are no longer pictured sitting at a banquet but in the open air. Now, in addition to the officers - colonel, fiscal, captains and lieutenants - and the standard-bearers (plate 9 and 14), Frans Hals included the militia's sergeants (plate 21 and 40). In a corner of *The officers and subalterns of the civic guard of St. George* of 1939 he very probably added his own image (see p. 54, ill. 21 and p. 93, ill. b). Since the identity of most of the militiamen is known, as are the years in which they served, Hals's militia portraits can be dated with reasonable accuracy. A number of the subjects appear in more than one portrait.

For two centuries the militia portraits by Frans Hals hung in the associations' meeting halls. An engraving from 1787 shows *The officers and subalterns of the St. Adrian militia company* from 1633 high on the wall of the Cluveniers Doelen (ill. c). Theodorus Schrevelius, in his *Harlemias* of 1648, describes Hals's militia portraits in the St. George Doelen:

> *'there are still many paintings in the old Militia Doelen in which he portrayed to the life Colonels, Captains, Fiscals, Standard-bearers, Sergeants fully weaponed. And in another Scene brothers in the Militia sitting at table drinking one another's health.'*

In 1819 the militia portraits by Frans Hals were taken to the town hall. From 1862 onwards they would form the heart of the municipal collection, examples of civic virtue and proud symbols of Haarlem's Golden Age.

a. Cornelis Anthonisz. (ca. 1499-ca.1557), *Banquet of 17 members of the crossbowmen's militia company (the St. George Guards), known as the 'Banquet of the Copper Coin'*, 1533. Amsterdam, Amsterdams Historisch Museum.
b. Cornelis Cornelisz. van Haarlem (1562-1638), *The Banquet of the militia companies of St. George and St. Adrian*, 1583. Haarlem, Frans Halsmuseum. (See also p. 13, ill. g).
c. Engraving after Wybrand Hendriks (1744-1831), *Interior of the Old or Cluveniers Doelen in 1787*. Haarlem, Municipal Archives.

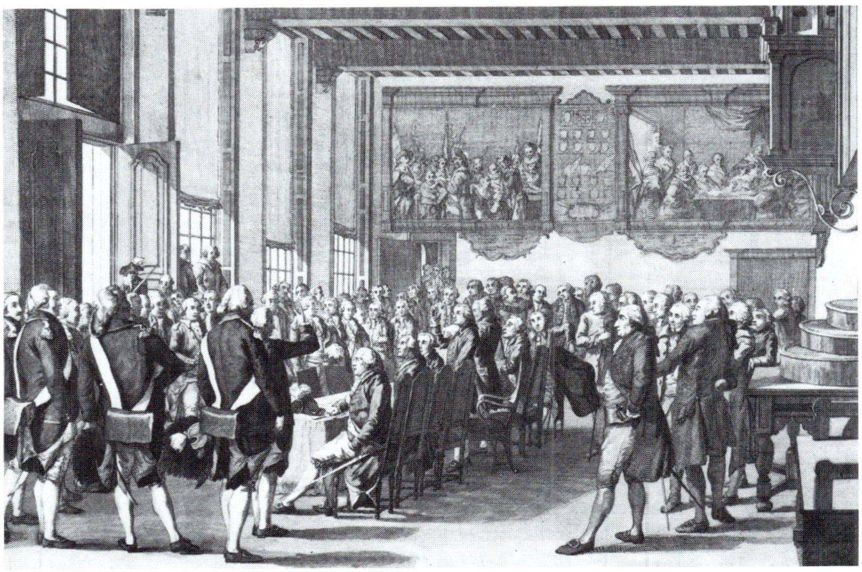

c

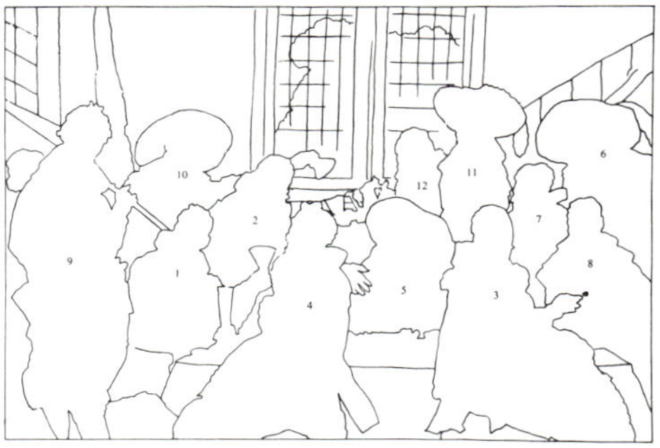

1. Willem Vooght, colonel; 2. Johan Damius, fiscal; 3. Willem Warmont, captain; 4. Johan Schatter, captain (see also plate 40); 5. Gilles de Wildt, captain; 6. Nicolaes van Napels, lieutenant; 7. Outgert Akersloot, lieutenant; 8. Matthijs Haeswindius, lieutenant; 9. Adriaen Matham, standard-bearer; 10. Lot Schout, standard-bearer; 11. Pieter Ramp, standard-bearer; 12. Willem Ruychaver, attendant.

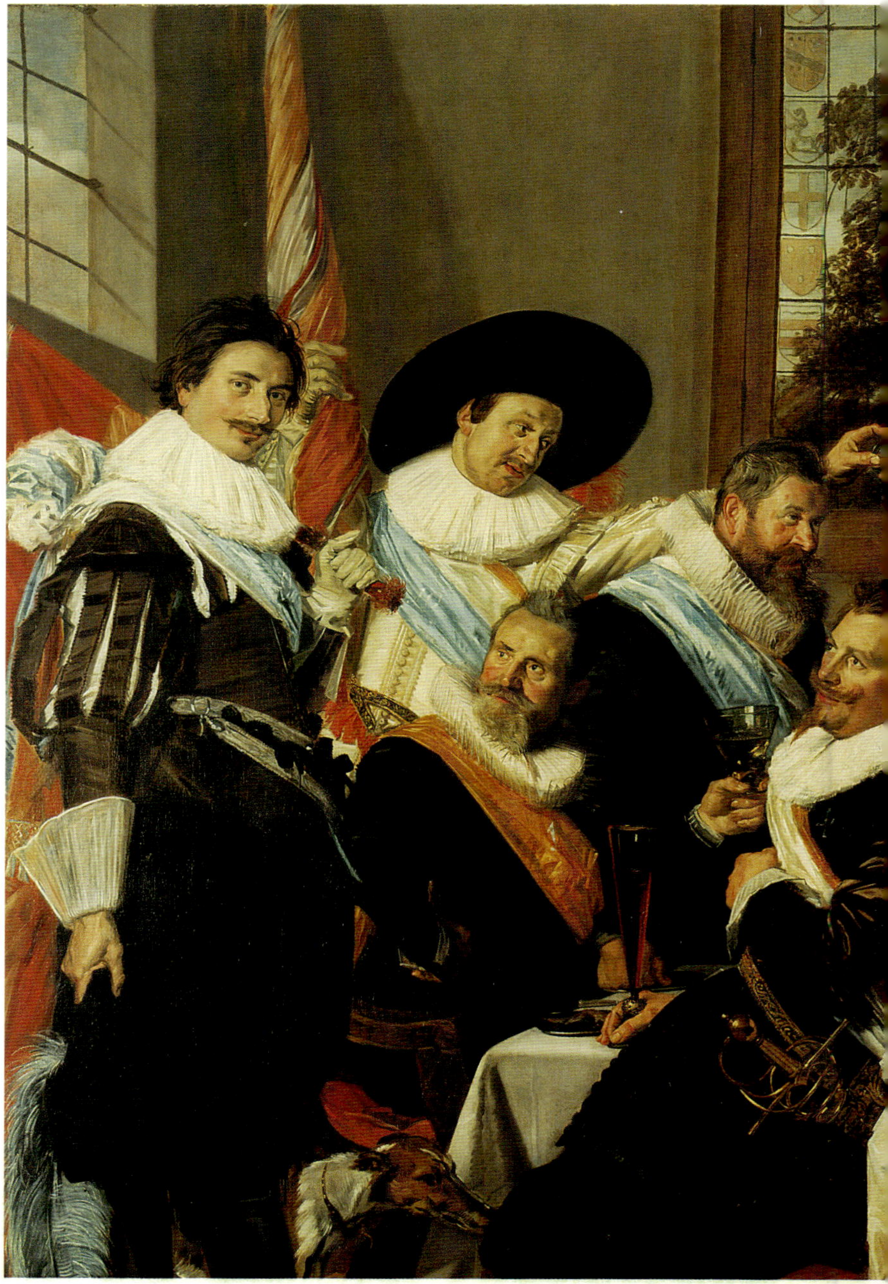

8

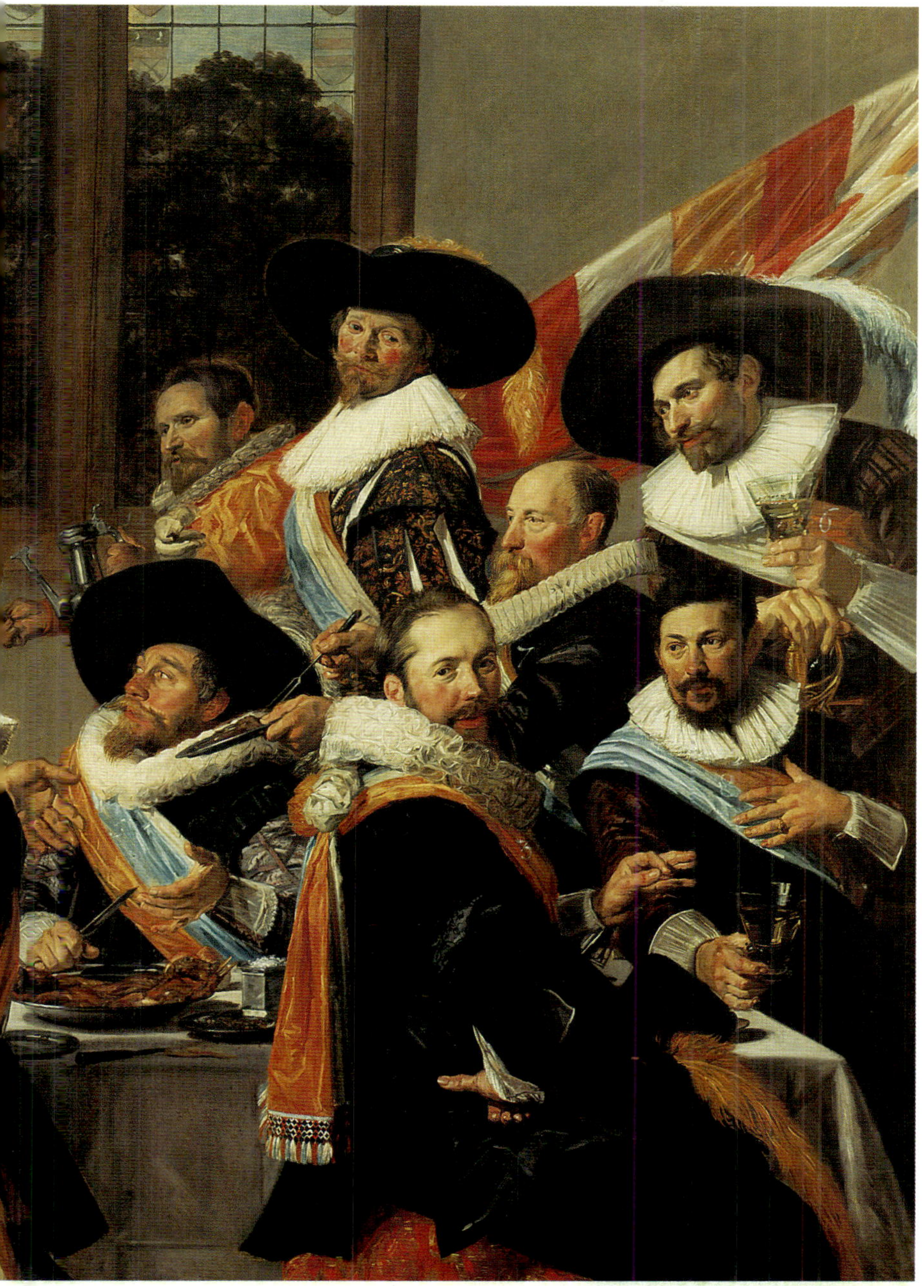

Plate 8. *Banquet of the officers of the St. Adrian militia company,* 1627. Canvas, 183 x 266.5 cm. Signed on the chair at the left with the monogram 'FHF'. Haarlem, Frans Halsmuseum. In the eighteenth century the militiamen were given identification numbers.

In his *Beschrijving ende lof der Stad Haerlem in Holland (Description and praise of the City of Haarlem in Holland* ) of 1628, Samuel Ampzing wrote about this militia portrait: 'There is a large painting by Frans Hals of some Officers of the militia in the Old Doelen or Cluyveniers, very close to life.' Following Haarlem tradition, Hals grouped the officers according to the hierarchy within the officers' corps: at the head of the table, the colonel with the fiscal next to him. The three captains form the middle group and the three lieutenants are at the far right. Compared with the militia portrait of 1616 (plate 4) Frans Hals gave this hierarchical ranking greater variety; the officers are no long pictured exclusively in a sitting position, making for a more compact grouping.

## HISTORY OF THE BANQUET OF THE OFFICERS OF THE CLUVENIERS MILITIA COMPANY, 1627

*1627* Dated, based on information about the subjects portrayed.
*1695* Item of expenditure for cleaning paintings in the Cluveniers Doelen.
*1721* Idem.
*1740* A 'Painting Commission' occupies itself with identification of the militiamen. Their names are given on a plaque below the portrait. The men are numbered.
Item of expenditure for cutting frames, 50 guilders.
*1810* Mention of damage to paintings caused by soldiers at exercise.
*1819* New mention of damage, after restoration of painting two years earlier.
*1821* The paintings are brought to the town hall.
*1862* The painting is transferred to the Stedelijk Museum in Haarlem.
*1872* Lined and restored by Mr. Scholten.
*1895* Restored by F. Vos, the museum's restorer.
*1913* Taken to the Frans Halsmuseum, opened this year.
*1925* Restoration under the supervision of D. de Wild.
*1985* January-December: restoration by Anne van Grevenstein, Amelia Jackson and Karin Tams.

## THE RESTORATION IN 1985-86

January-December

This militia portrait suffered a great deal. The canvas had shrunk considerably, causing the edges of the cupped paint to stand up. Past attempts to make the paint lie smooth again were unsuccessful and high temperatures and pressure have left their mark on the paint layer. Since there is little likelihood of improvement, structural conservation has been limited to localized fixing of the paint where necessary (particularly in the right quarter). This was done with wax resin applied with a heated spatula.

Holes in the canvas were filled with old pieces of treated canvas; several layers of old filler covered the areas around the losses. In the past these were sanded smooth (often all the way down to the canvas) and the new fillings were treated with a scraper in an attempt to imitate the surface structure. De Wild's intervention apparently involved removing the old varnish, reducing the overpainting and improving old fillings here and there, with extensive 'touch-ups' throughout.

Not only losses but also large areas of the original were covered or 'brought into line', as this is sometimes euphemistically described. All black surfaces were covered with a thick glaze which blurred details and subtle differences in the way forms were reproduced.

When the overpainting and old filler were removed, small traces of the original paint were found, permitting reconstruction, as of the hat in fig. 5. This and the reconstruction of the shoulder of fig. 8 were derived from the copy made by Wybrand Hendriks before the damages in 1810.

An intermediate layer of dammar varnish was applied, then the losses were filled with a mixture of wax, chalk and pigment in the tone of the ground layer (very light pink). The losses in the black clothes were filled with black. In order to keep the new fillings from standing out like smooth scars in the craquelure, a silicone mould was made of the original paint.

The mould was pressed into the surface with a heated spatula. Thanks to extensive photographic documentation, it was not necessary to leave the restored losses visible in the painting (by, for example, filling them smoothly or marking them with a line or small groove or - as is customary in Italy - retouching with vertical hatched lines).

The final layer of varnish was sparingly applied by spraying in order to avoid a shiny surface, thereby accenting the uneven structure of the paint as little as possible.

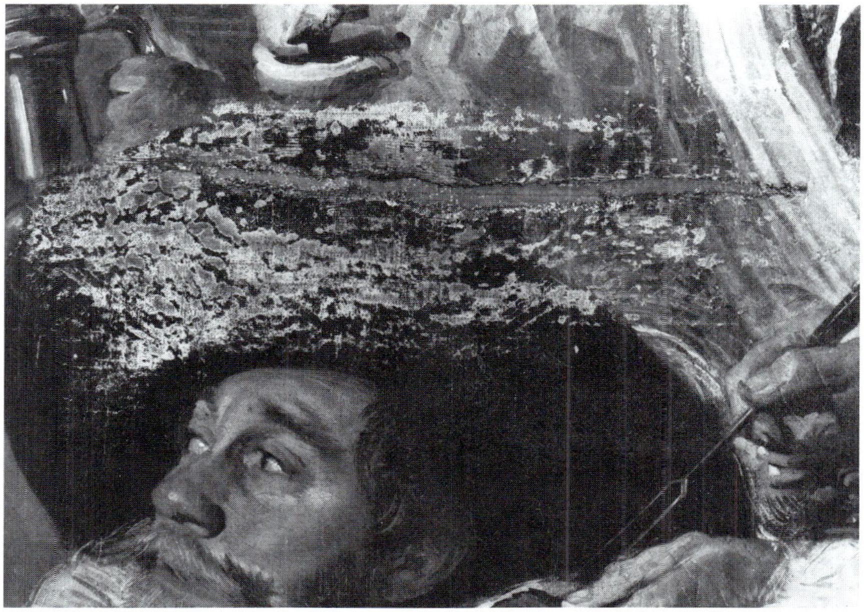

8a

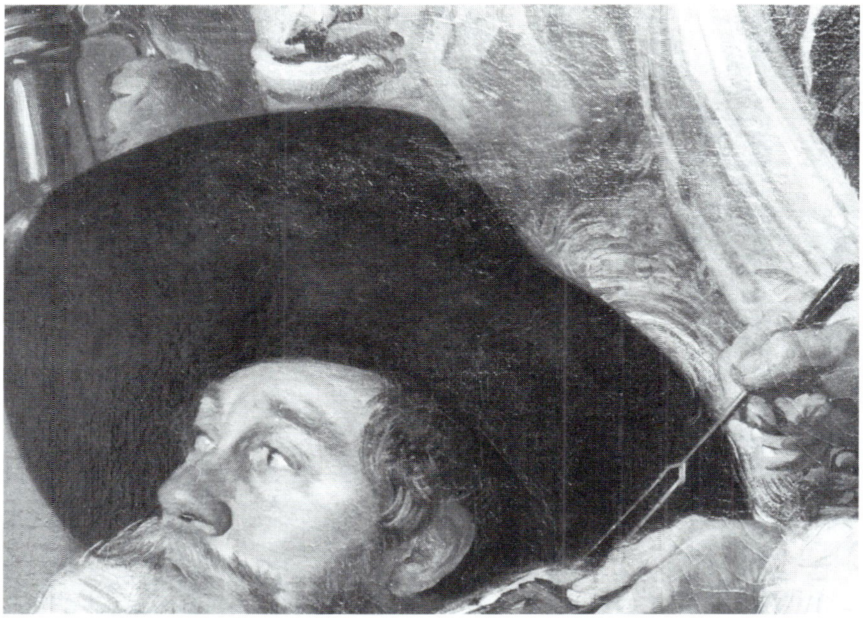

8b

Ill. 8a. Irregularities in the paint surface of the hat of figure 5 and the area above it indicated damage. The extent of the damage came to light in the X-ray. This photo was taken after cleaning. Varnish, overpainting and old filling have been removed. Remnants of the original paint permitted the form of the hat to be reconstructed. The water-colour by Wybrand Hendricks was also taken as a model.
Ill. 8b. Detail of the hat of figure 5, after treatment. The hat was not overpainted in full, but only where necessary; the original paint remaining was left intact. A solution more ethical than aesthetic, resulting in an uneven surface.

Ill. 8c. Detail of the area above the arm of the chair, before treatment. Variations in surface structure indicate places of damage.
Ill. 8d. Detail of the area above the arm of the chair. After removal of the old filling, the damaged section is filled again with a wax mixture containing pigment. The surrounding area is carefully protected with Japanese paper.
Ill. 8e. Detail of the area above the arm of the chair. Using a silicone mould with a light relief of the surrounding surface structure and a heated spatula, an imprint is made in the wax.

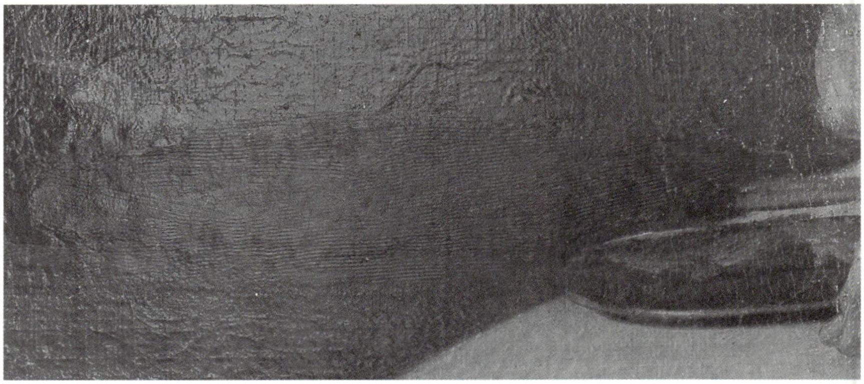

8c

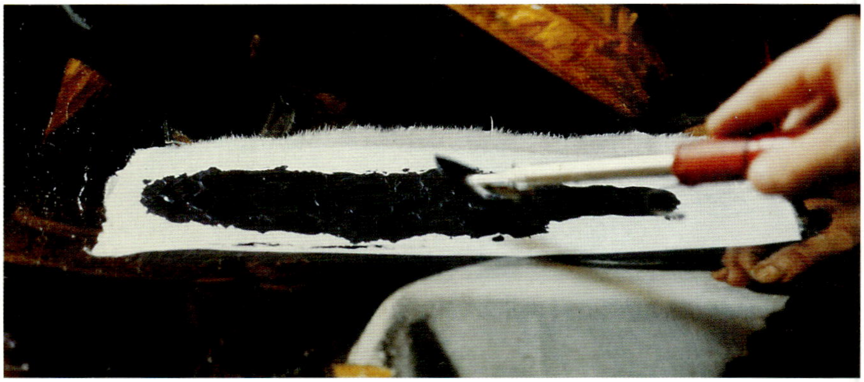

8d

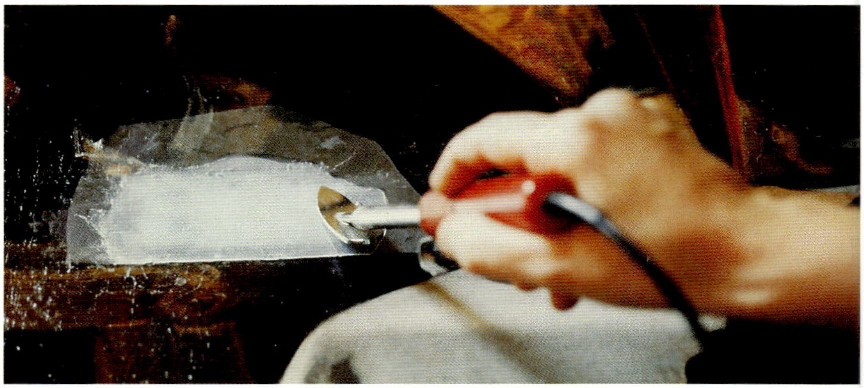

8e

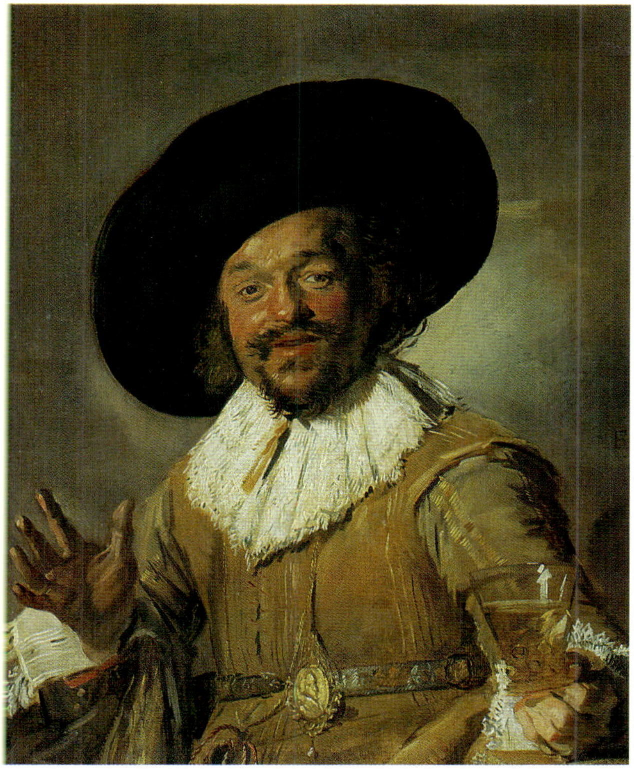

9

Plate 9. *'The merry drinker'*, ca. 1628. Canvas, 81 x 66.5 cm. Signed at right with the monogram 'FH'. Amsterdam, Rijksmuseum.
*'The merry drinker'*, is one of Frans Hals's most popular works, and rightly so; the painting combines Hals's virtuoso technique with an exceptionally appealing representation. But the work raises an important question: how should it be interpreted? The cheerful drinker could represent 'taste', one of the five senses. However, in this case Hals would have been more likely to show the man in the act of drinking, as with the child figures (see p. 6, ill. a). Another possibility is that the painting was intended as a portrait. The medallion the man is wearing suggests this and can be taken as a personal attribute. The same is true of the glass; this merry - but not drinking - drinker is perhaps an innkeeper or one of the many Haarlem brewers. The answer may well lie somewhere in between. The gesture with the right hand and the friendly facial expression are undoubtedly meant for the observer, whom the subject seems to be inviting to share a glass with him.

Plate 10. *Fisherboy*, ca. 1630. 74 x 61 cm. Signed bottom right with the monogram 'FH'. Antwerp, Koninklijk Museum voor Schone Kunsten.
The 'fisherchildren' by Frans Hals were widely imitated by other painters of the past, so much so that some are tempted to eliminate all such paintings from his work for the sake of a more reliable overview of his *oeuvre*. As regards the Antwerp fisherboy, this seems rash. The piece is a fine example of Hals's style in about 1630 when he began handling the brush more freely than ever before. Hal's's fisherchildren can be considered as successors to his child portraits, representing the senses or deadly sins. With his arms resting on each other, this youngster could symbolize 'indolence'.

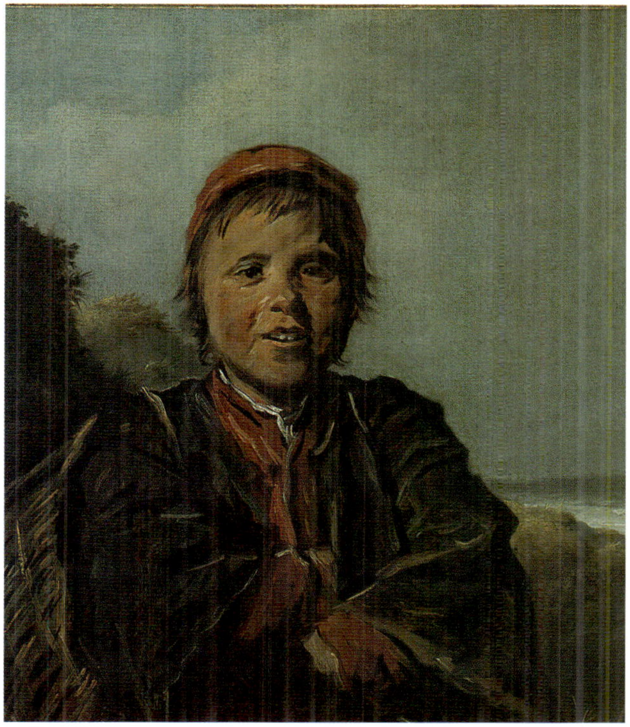

10

## Portraits of irony

In the folk portraits from the late 1620s, Frans Hals used his brush more freely than in official portraits from this period. Details in clothing and faces are only suggested with an occasional dab of paint, giving the figures an unprecedented spontaneity. The merriment of the subjects should be taken ironically; they seem to be lightly mocking their own appearance in a portrait.

a. *Verdonck,* ca. 1627. Edinburgh, National Gallery of Scotland.

*'This is Verdonck, bold fellow,*
*Whose jaw-bone strikes at everyone,*
*Sparing no one, small or great,*
*He fetched up at the workhouse gate.'*

This old man is probably Pieter Verdonck. He was a Baptist belonging to the 'Old Flemings', a group of strict fundamentalists who spurned any departure from religious tradition. The jaw-bone Verdonck is waving is a symbol of oratorical power. At the same time it evokes the Biblical character Samson, who slew the Philistines with the jawbone of an ass. Verdonck always got the better of his opponents, so much so that he drew the wrath of the authorities in Haarlem. According to the poem, his sharp criticism spared no one 'small or great' and he ended up in the workhouse. The smile on Verdonck's face suggests self-mockery; his attribute is not the jaw-bone of an ass but of a cow.

b. *'The gipsy girl',* ca. 1628. Paris, Musée du Louvre.

When in the last century this painting was given the romantic title *'La Bohémienne',* no one yet suspected that it had probably hung in a brothel. Visiting gentlemen made their choice with the aid of portraits. The girl's 'spontaneous' smile therefore had a specific significance. Floodlighting her bosom brings out an interesting detail: the painting of her *décolletage* was originally far less provocative.

c. *Peeckelhaering,* ca. 1629. Cassel, Hessisches Landesmuseum.

*'See Monsieur Peeckelhaering,*
*He loves a cool, full mug*
*And keeps up with the drinking cup*
*Because his throat is always brackish'*

In seventeenth-century comedies Peeckelhaering is the fool who, as the poem says, usually carries a 'cool, full mug'. The painting should not be regarded so much as the portrait of a drunken man but rather as the typification of a stage character. A 'Peeckelhaering' by Frans Hals was auctioned in 1631 from the possessions of innkeeper Hendrick den Abt. This may indicate that portraits such as this one hung in various public houses in Haarlem. In a painting by Jan Steen, the *Peeckelhaering* by Frans Hals can be seen hanging on the wall of an inn. Only recently 'The gipsy girl' was identified as Judith Leyster (see p. 61, ill. 9).

d. *'The mulatto'* , ca. 1629. Leipzig, Museum der bildenden Künste.

This painting, given the title *'The mulatto'* in the last century, also depicts Peeckelhaering. With his pointing finger, a gesture of mockery, the stock comedy figure seems to be ridiculing someone. The canvas, recently restored, was originally larger on the left side.

e. *Malle Babbe,* ca. 1630. Berlin-Dahlem, Gemäldegalerie.

*'Babel of Haarlem, to you*
*your owl for a falcon, O Babel,*
*I am glad of it.*
*Play with an illusion*
*You are not alone.'*

Almost nothing is known of Malle Babbe, identifiable thanks to an inscription on the back of the painting. She was referred to as 'the Witch of Haarlem'. This canvas, painted with exceptional virtuosity, shows an owl sitting on Malle Babbe's shoulder. Although the owl often symbolizes wisdom, it can also suggest foolishness and drunkenness. According to the poem - written at a later date - Malle Babbe thinks her owls is a falcon, meaning: she pretends to be more important than she is. But the poet is not critical and cheerfully notes that Malle Babbe is not alone in her illusions.

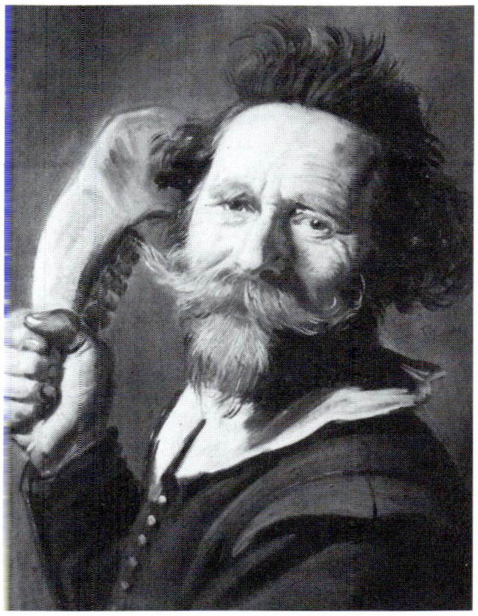

a

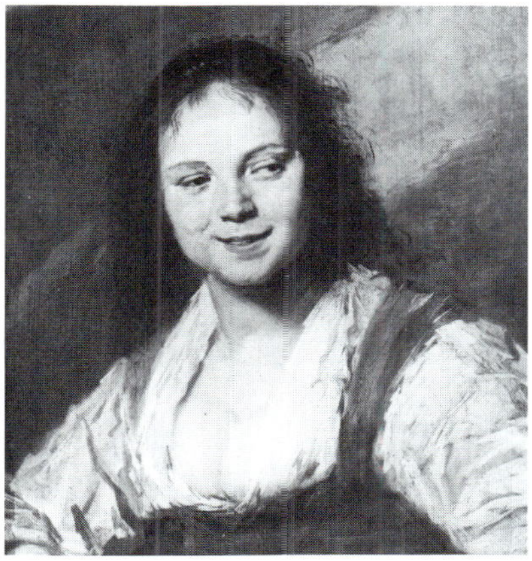

b

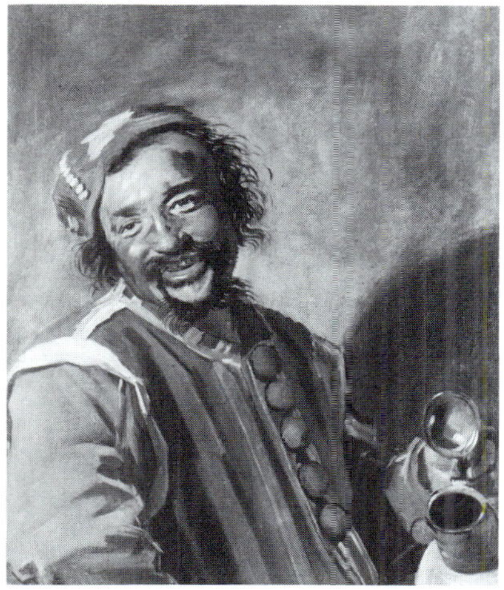

c

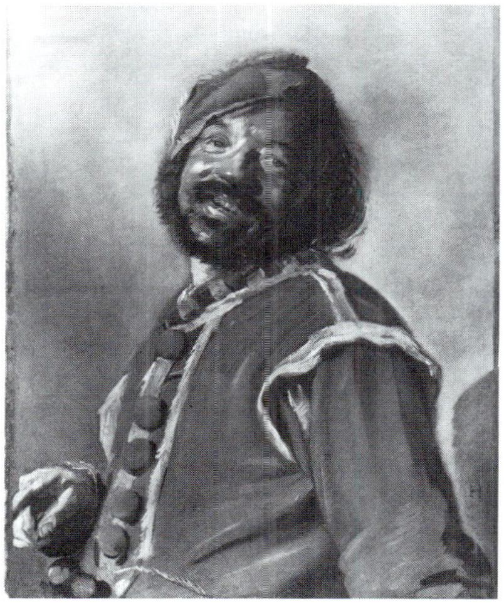

d

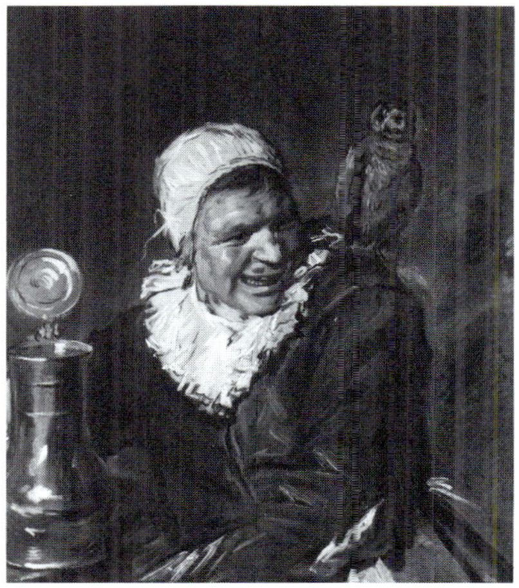

e

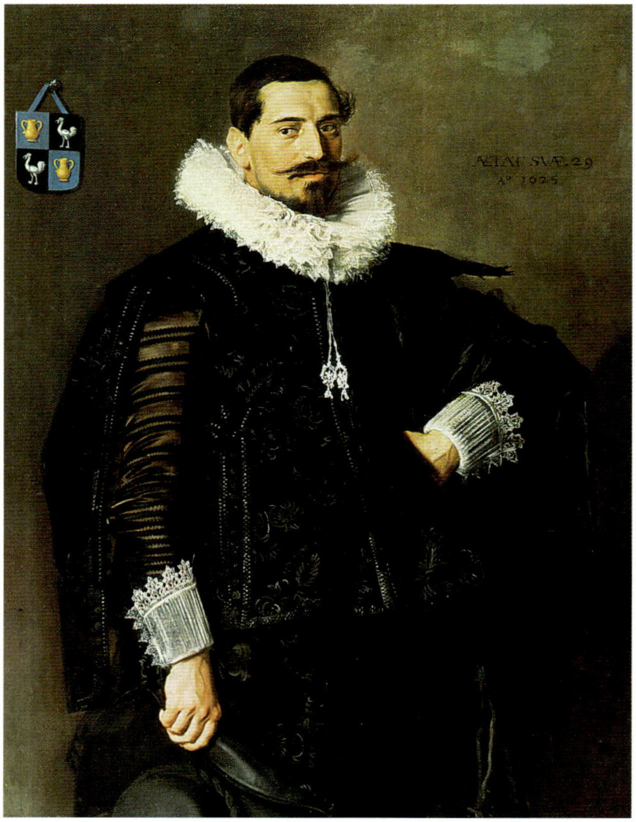

11

Plate 11. *Jacob Pietersz. Olycan.* Canvas, 124.6 x 97.3 cm. Inscribed above right 'AETAT SVAE 29/A° 1625'. The Hague, Mauritshuis.

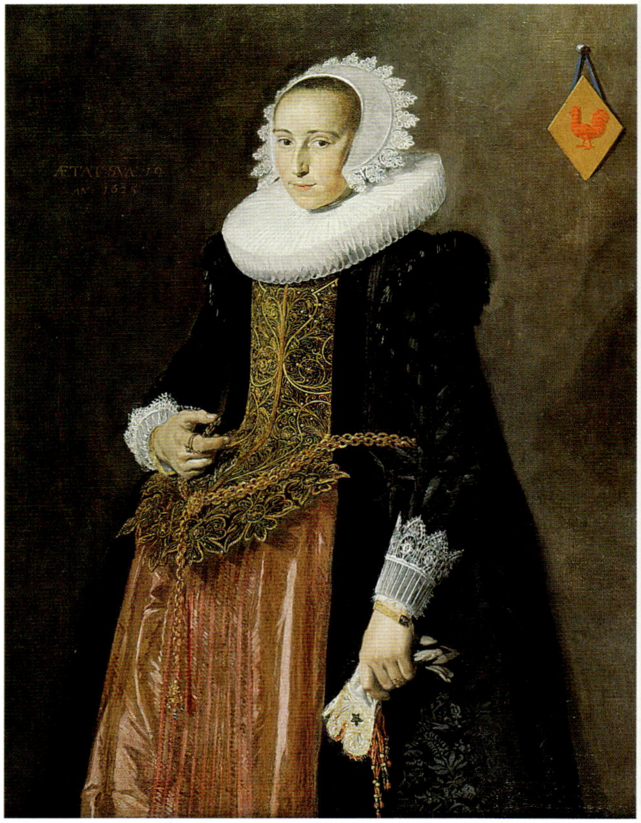

12

Plate 12. *Aletta Hanemans.* Canvas, 124.2 x 98.2 cm. Inscribed above left 'AETAT SVAE 19/AN° 1625'. The Hague, Mauritshuis.

Jacob Olycan (1596-1638) was the son of Pieter Olycan, whose portrait was painted by Hals in 1631 (plate 25). In 1624 he married Aletta Hanemans (1606-1653). Jacob Olycan can also be seen in the *Banquet of the officers of the civic guard of St. George* of 1627 (plate 14). After his death, Aletta Hanemans remarried in 1641. She also survived her second husband Nicolaes van Loo (see plate 21), who died six months after their marriage.

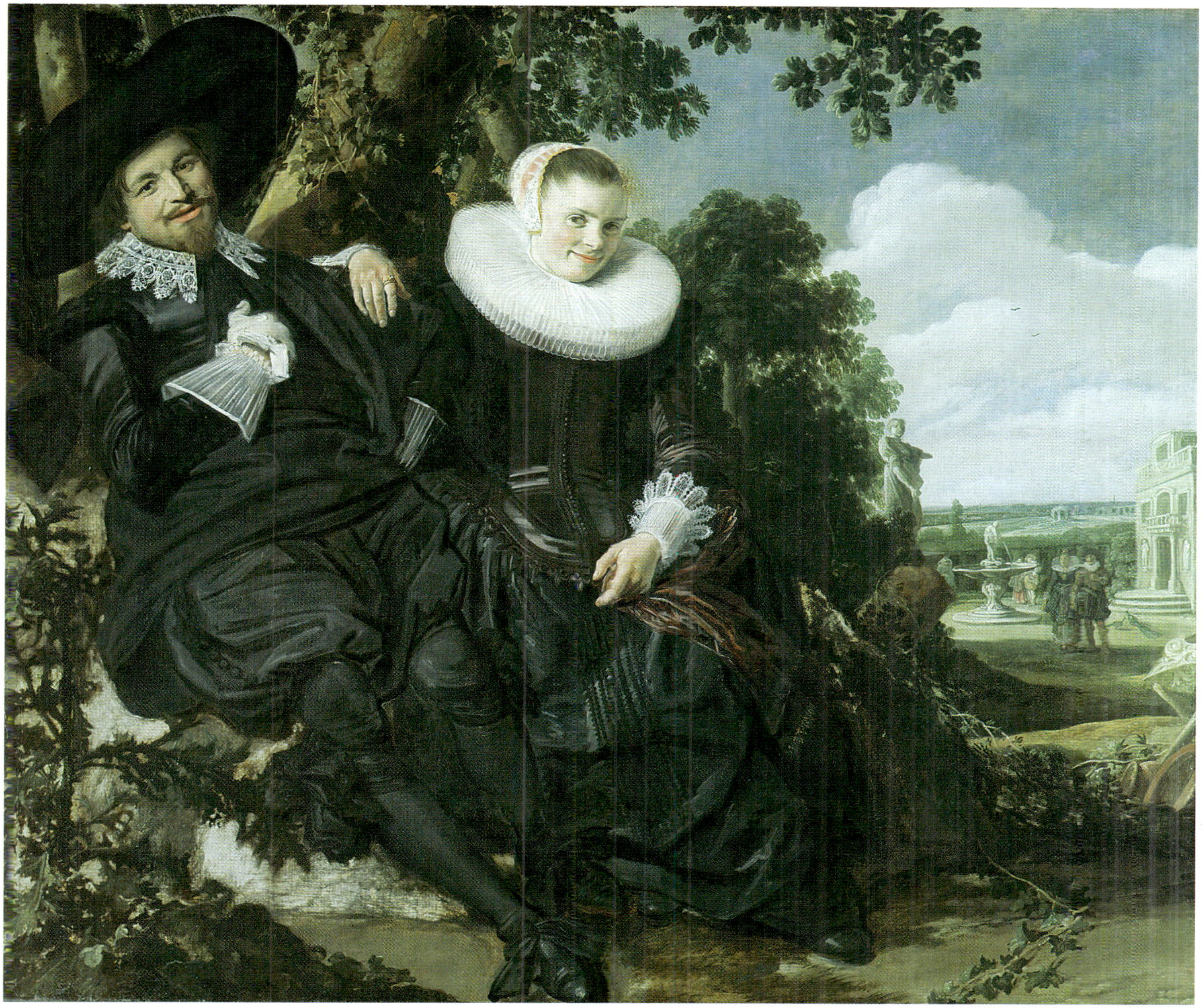

3

Plate 13. *Wedding portrait of Isaac Massa and Beatrix van der Laen*, ca. 1622. Canvas, 140 x 166.5 cm. Amsterdam, Rijksmuseum

## The symbolism of a wedding portrait

Many have identified the happy pair in Hals's double portrait in the Rijksmuseum as Isaac Massa and Beatrix van der Laen (plate 13), because Frans Hals painted other portraits of Massa which bear a resemblance to the man in this painting (ill. a, b, c, d). This double portrait, which can be dated from the early 1620s for stylistic reasons, was probably made in honour of Massa's marriage to the daughter of the burgomaster, Beatrix van der Laen, on 25 April 1622. The vegetation in the foreground and the garden in the distance play a symbolic role in this wedding portrait.

The garden was traditionally regarded as the province of the goddess Venus and was therefore a most suitable setting for portraying a pair of lovers. A good example of this is the portrait of Rubens and his wife Isabella, made in 1609, the year of their marriage (ill. e). And so Frans Hals deliberately placed the bridal pair in the open air. Probably following Isaac Massa's instructions, he included a number of symbols relating to the nobler aspects of love.

Between the heads of the couple a vine-tendril curls around the trunk of a tree. The meaning of this symbol can be found in one of the many 'emblem books', collections with instructive plates and accompanying texts. The vine twined round a tree trunk indicates love that survives after death (ill. f). Even if the tree dies, the vine lives on. The vine-tendril can also be seen as a symbol of fertility. Just as the vine-tendril needs the support of the tree to bear fruit, so is the woman dependent on the man in order to produce children. This wedding portrait not only expresses the dependence of the wife but also the faithfulness of the husband. This is symbolized at the bottom left by the thistle, also called 'man's faith'. Frans Hals repeated the two

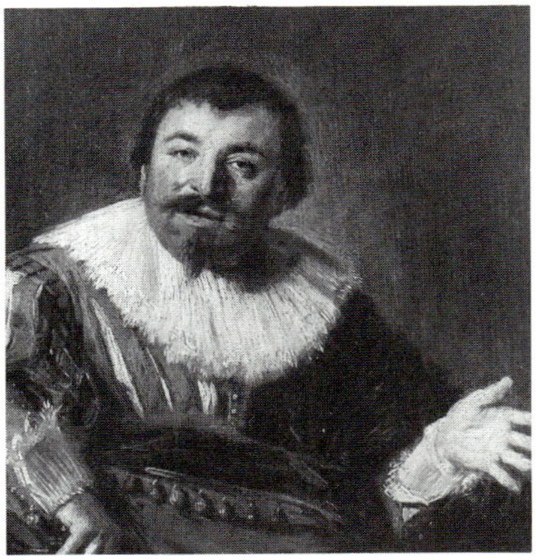

a

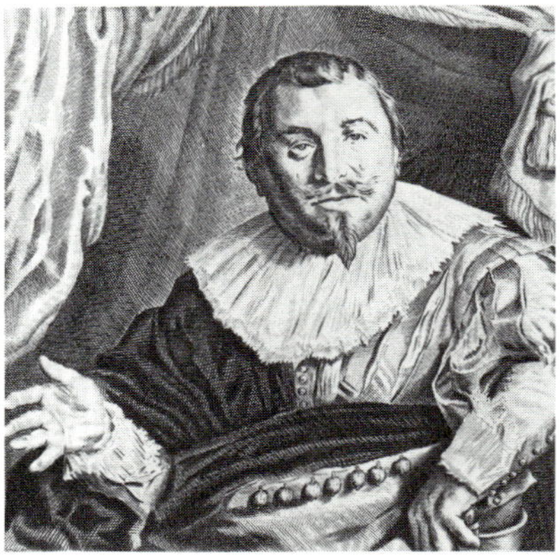

b

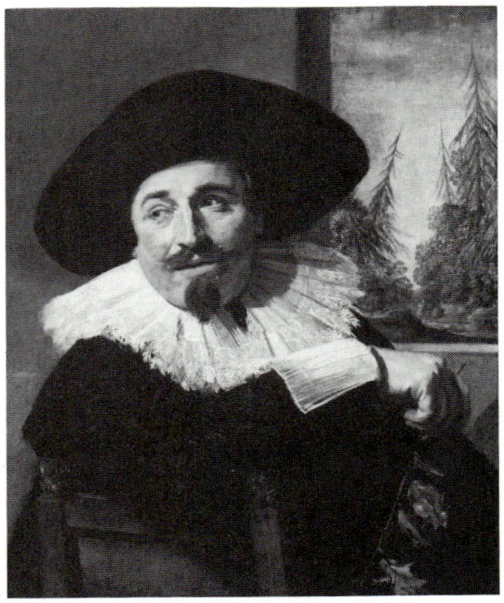

c

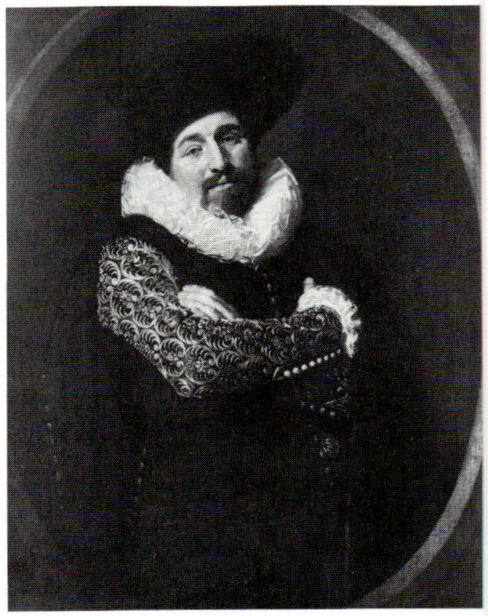

d

symbols in an original way in the pair's pose. Beatrix's arm rests on Isaac Massa's shoulder and he holds his hand over his heart, a sign of faithfulness.

Surrounded by symbols of noble love, the bridal pair seem to want to separate themselves from or even oppose what is going on in the background of the painting where couples stroll in an idyllic garden with statues, fountains and pavilions. But their superficial amorousness differs totally from true love. Two strutting peacocks show that this dalliance is based on external display. The negative aspect is reinforced with emblems. The ivy on the right side is a symbol of lust. In contrast to the vine, this plant will never bear fruit and will even kill the tree it embraces. The urns on the ground also point to the fleetingness of this type of love. The couples themselves, in their pride, will not enter into such serious affairs as marriage. The customary head-dresses are missing from the women and the men are wearing showy sabres. The colourfully got up couples stand in obvious contrast to the newlyweds in the foreground. Despite their costly clothing, Isaac Massa and Beatrix van der Laen give no sign of excess. The happy pair testifies in a becoming way to the proprieties of marriage.

Isaac Abrahamsz. Massa (1586-1643) belonged to Haarlem's rich middle class. He had made a name for himself as a diplomat in Russia. Massa was an erudite man; he spoke Russian fluently and acquired a reputation as a cartographer. He must have been well acquainted with Frans Hals. Not only was he a witness at the baptism of Hals's daughter Adriaentgen in 1623, he also posed for Hals a number of times. The various portraits of Massa offer a unique opportunity for comparison.
a. *Isaac Massa,* ca. 1634. San Diego, Museum of Arts.
This small panel - 21 x 20 cm. - probably served as a model for the engraving of Isaac Massa by Adriaen Matham.
b. Adriaen Matham (ca. 1599-1660), *Isaac Massa,* 1635. Engraving.

c. *Isaac Massa,* 1626. Toronto, Art Gallery of Ontario.
This canvas was recognized as a portrait of Massa from its likeness to the subject in the panel in San Diego. The inscription on the chair, 'AETA/41/1626', also fits Massa.
d. *Isaac Massa,* 1622. Chatsworth, Devonshire Collection, The Trustees of the Chatsworth Settlement.
The inscriptions in this portrait, 'AETAT SVAE 36' and 'AN 1622' also correspond with Massa's age in 1622, the year of his marriage.
e. Pieter Paul Rubens (1577-1640), *Self-portrait with Isabella Brant,* 1609. Munich, Alte Pinakothek.
f. Andrea Alciato, *Amicitia etiam post mortem durans.* Woodcut from *Emblematum Libellus,* Paris, 1534.

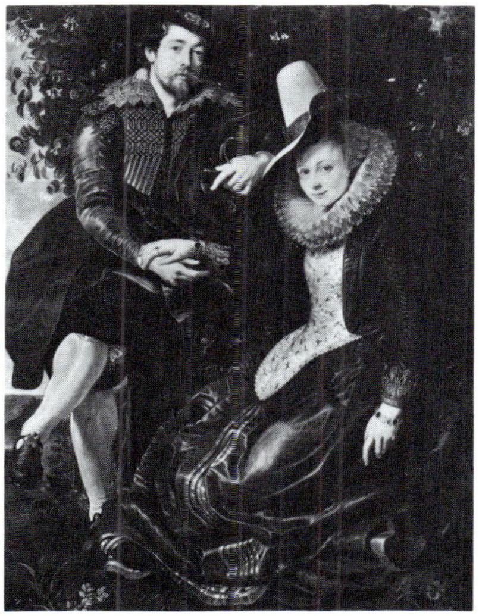

e

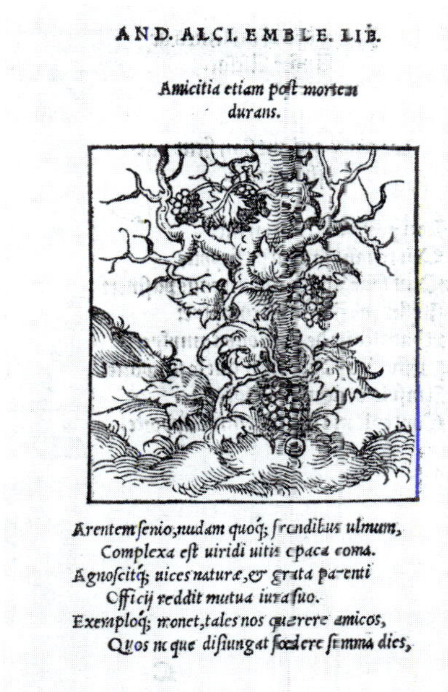


f

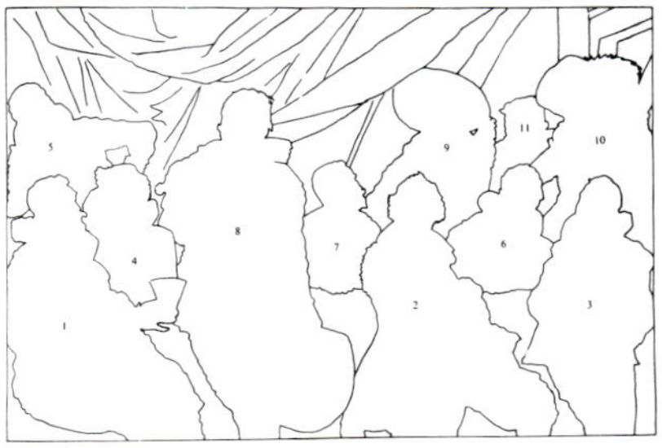

1. Aernout Druyvesteyn, colonel; 2. Michiel de Wael, captain (see also plate 21); 3. Nicolaes le Febure, captain; 4. Nicolaes Verbeek, captain; 5. Cornelis Boudewijnsz., lieutenant; 6. Frederik Coning, lieutenant; 7. Jacob Olycan, lieutenant (see also plate 11); 8. Boudewijn van Offenberg, standard-bearer (see also plate 21); 9. Dirck Dicx, standard-bearer (see also plate 21); 10. Jacob Schout, standard-bearer (see also plate 4); 11. Arent Koets, attendant.

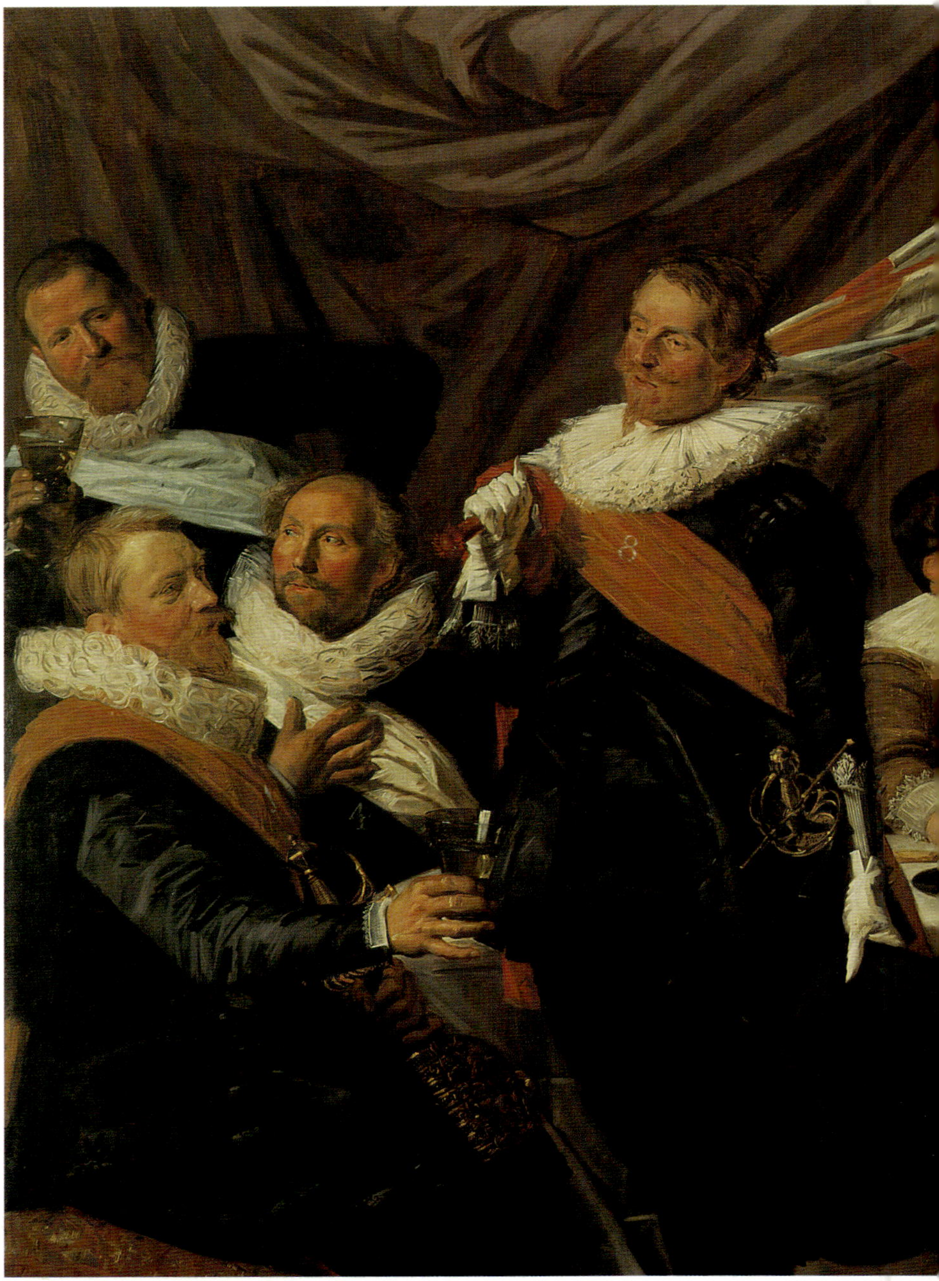

14

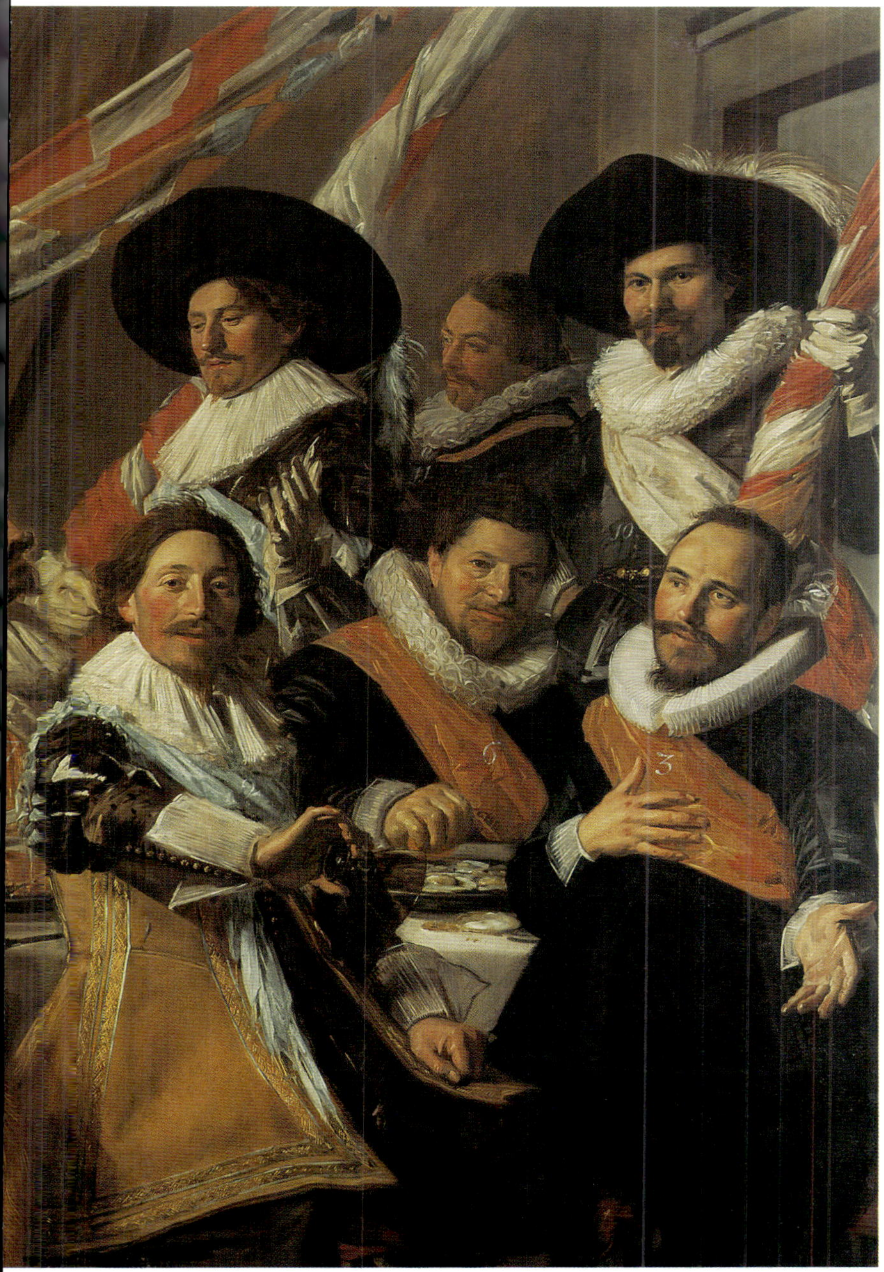

Plate 14. *Banquet of the officers of the St. George militia company,* ca. 1627. Canvas, 179 x 257.5 cm. Haarlem, Frans Halsmuseum.
In the eighteenth century the militiamen portrayed were given identification numbers.
The two militia portraits Frans Hals painted in about 1627 exhibit considerable differences. Compared with the group portrait of the officers of the St. Adrian militia company (plate 8), the composition of this painting is strikingly natural, the brushwork looser and freer. Possibly these differences can be explained by the fact that Hals himself was a member of the St. George militia company. Not only is the work's composition highly original, Hals also broke with the Haarlem tradition of portraying the hierarchy of the militiamen within the officers' corps from left to right. Captain Nicolaes le Febure is pictured standing at the extreme right, disguising the fact that he was a very short man.

**HISTORY OF THE BANQUET OF THE OFFICERS OF THE ST. GEORGE MILITIA, 1627**

*1627* Dated, based on information about the identity of the subjects.
*1701* Item of expenditure for the cleaning and 'repainting' of the paintings in the Doelen of St. George.
*1721* Before this year the painting was taken to the Doelen of St. Adrian.
Item of expenditure for cleaning the paintings in the Doelen of St. Adrian.
*1740* A 'Painting Commission' occupies itself with identification of the militiamen. Their names are given on a plaque below the portrait. The men are given identification numbers.
*1810* Mention of damage to paintings caused by soldiers at exercise.
*1819* New mention of damage, after restoration of painting two years earlier.
*1821* The paintings are brought to the town hall.
*1862* The painting is transferred to the Stedelijk Museum in Haarlem.
*1880* Lined by Hopman in Amsterdam.
*1906* Lined by F. Vos, restorer of the Stedelijk Museum in Haarlem.
*1913* Taken to the Frans Halsmuseum, opened this year.
*1925* Restoration under the supervision of D. de Wild.
*1985* January-December: restoration by Anne van Grevenstein, Amelia Jackson, Claudia Breuer-Castelli and Beate Federspiel.

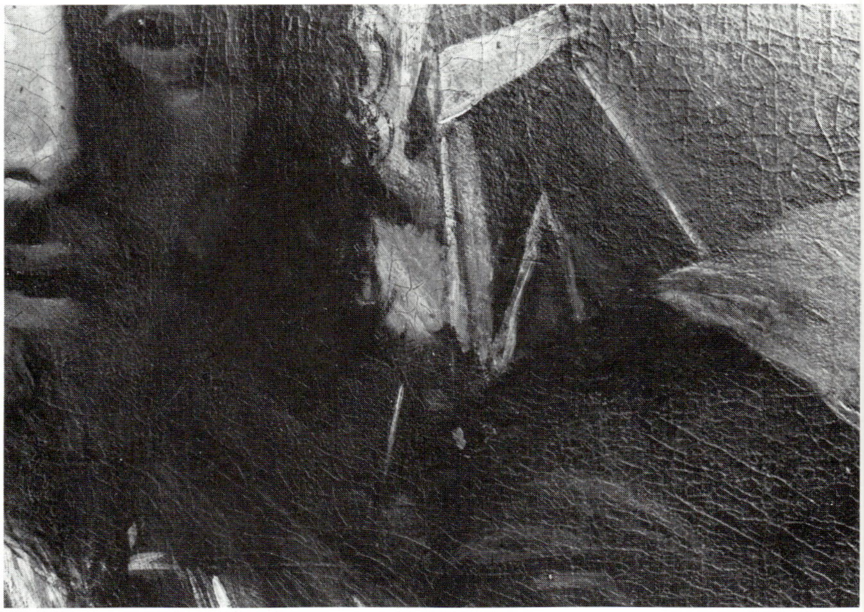

14a

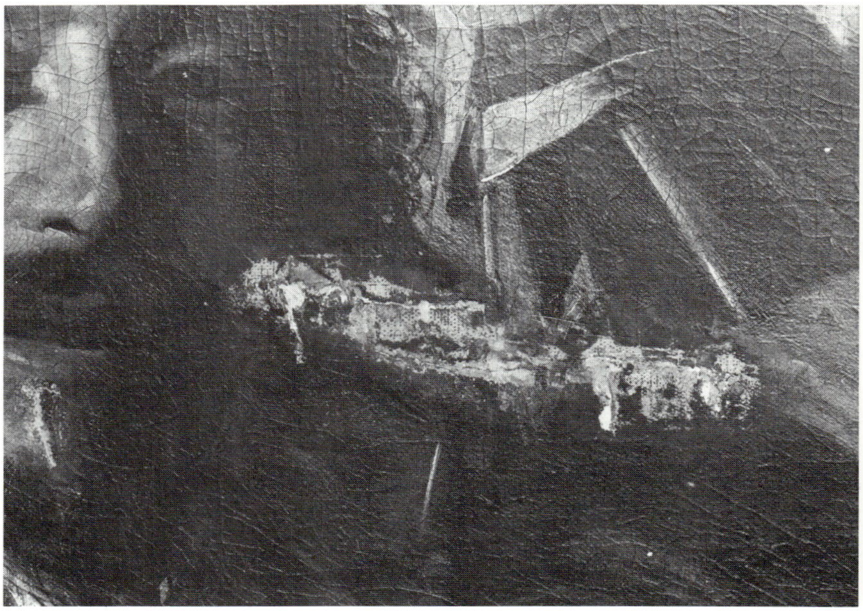

14b

The paint surface was in very good condition. Aside from a large tear in the hat and flag of fig. 9 and a tear in the hair of fig. 2, there was little damage. The painting, which still has its original edges, was put on a smaller stretcher at some point in the past and the edges were folded over. When it was relined on a later occasion, it was restretched and today, give or take a few centimetres, the size of the painting is what it originally was. The many tack holes were filled and painted over. As was the custom, the losses were broadly and creatively painted over. The right lock of hair of fig. 2, for example, was much longer than the left. That this was not Hals's intention is shown in the copy by Wybrand Hendriks.

The old varnish was removed with care and restraint. Losses were filled with a mixture of wax, chalk and pigment in the light brown tint of the ground layer. Retouches were done with dammar and dry pigment. Dammar varnish was also used for the intermediate and final layers of varnish.

Ill. 14a. Detail of the head of fig. 2 before treatment. The overpainting of the right lock of hair is longer than the left.
Ill. 14b. Detail of the head of fig. 2. After cleaning, it became apparent despite damages from sanding the filling during an earlier restoration that the hair did not extend beyond the loss. More had been overpainted than was strictly necessary. Now the hair-length is the same on both sides.
Ill. 14c. Detail after cleaning. The strip along the top contains regularly spaced tack holes. This shows that at some time in the past the painting was reduced in size by folding the upper edge around the stretcher. It was relined in the nineteenth century and this upper strip was returned to its proper place. The line of the fold is still visible. Since the folded section received less exposure to light, the colours are brighter.
Ill. 14d. Detail of the flag of fig. 9. Varnish, overpainting and filling have been partially removed. The overpainting had been more extensive than necessary.

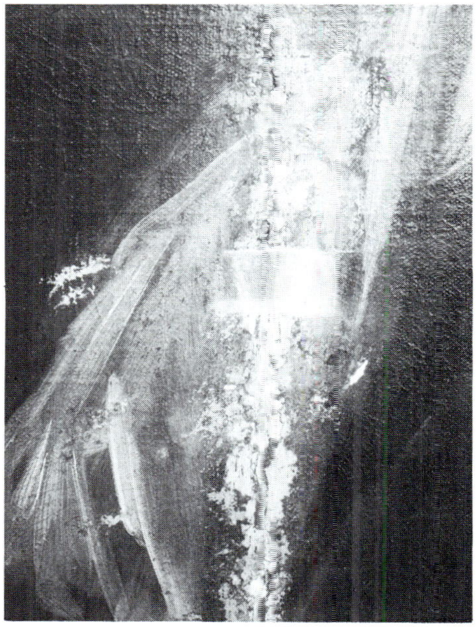

14d

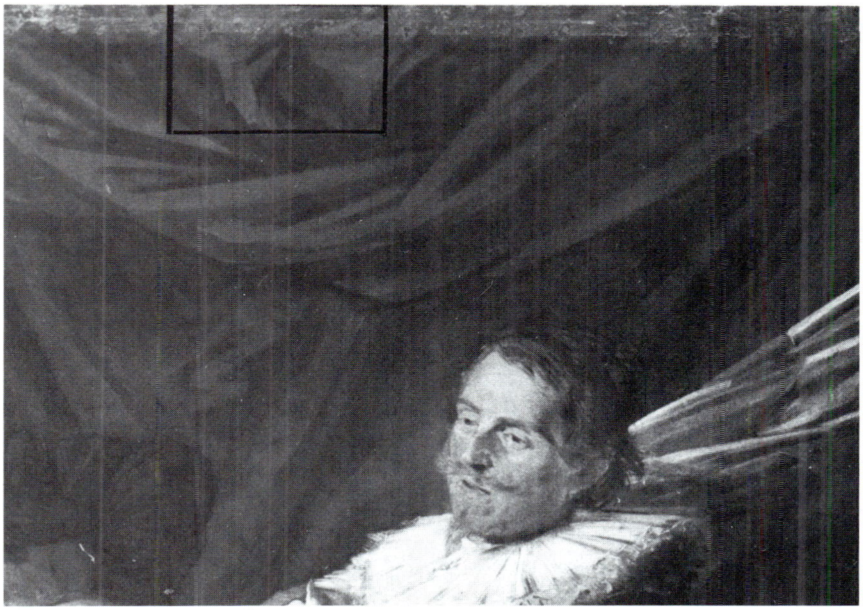

14c

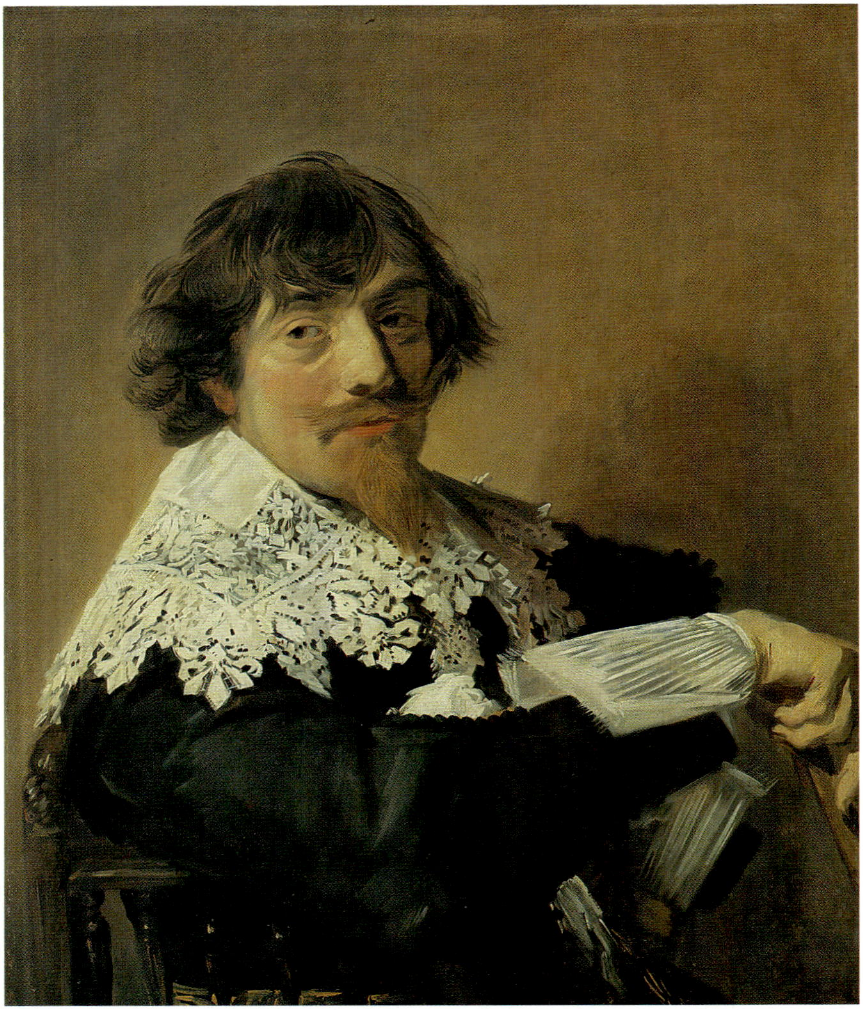

15

Plate 15. *Nicolaes Hasselaer (?),* ca. 1633. Canvas, 79.5 x 66.5 cm. Amsterdam, Rijkmuseum.
Plate 16. *Sara Wolphaerts van Diemen (?),* ca 1633. Canvas, 79.5 x 66.5 cm. Amsterdam, Rijksmuseum.
Nicolaes Hasselaer (1593-1635) had a brewery in Amsterdam. He was also captain-major of the militia and a regent of the orphanage. Like Isaac Massa, Hasselaer spent time as a diplomat in Moscow. His informal pose recalls Massa's portrait of 1626 (p. 40, ill. c). Sara van Diemen (1594-1667) was Hasselaer's second wife. She is wearing a distinctive lace cap of a type fashionable in the 1630s. The identification of the subjects, dating from the nineteenth century, is fairly uncertain; they look younger than forty, the age of Hasselaer and his wife in about 1633.

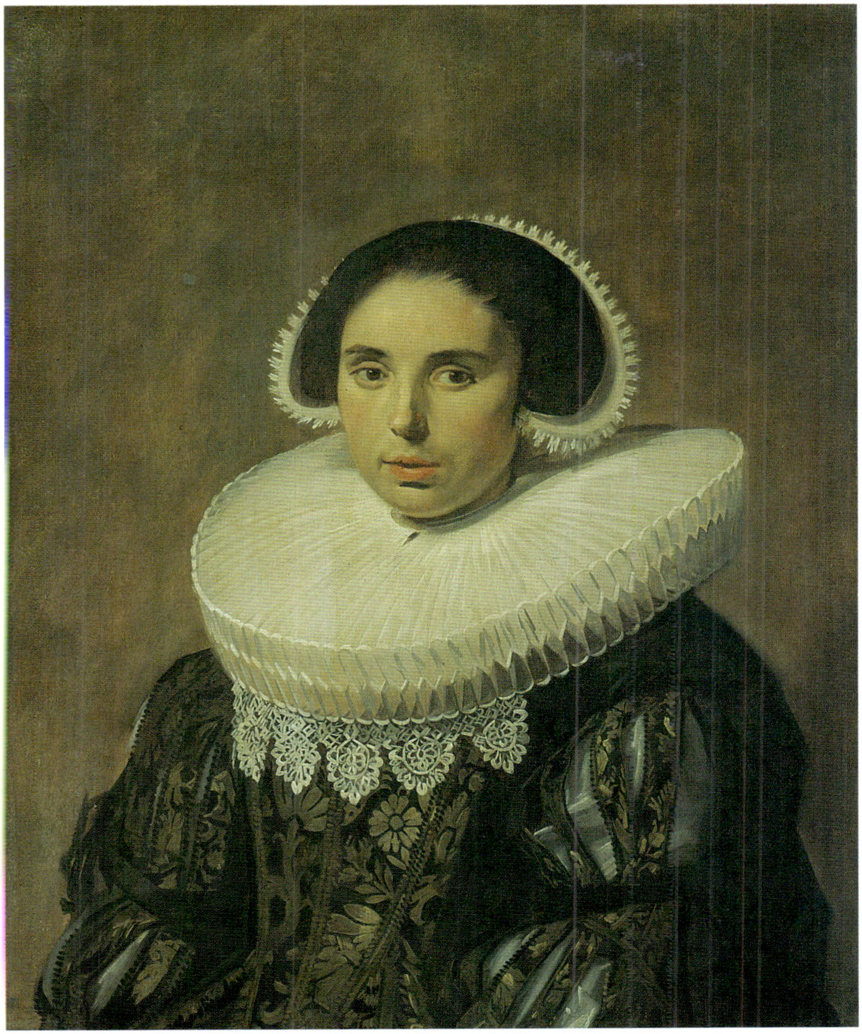

16

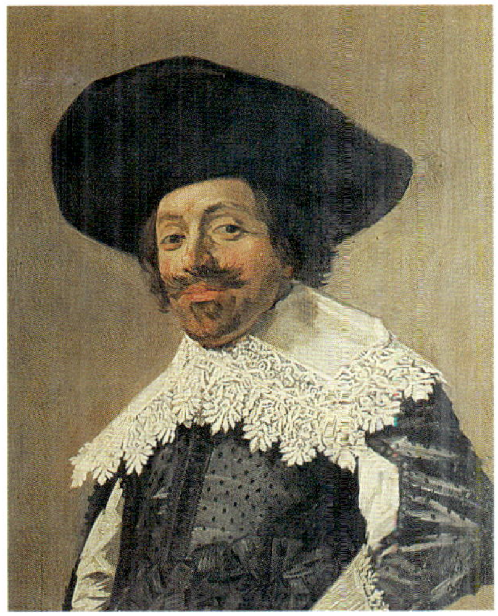

17

Plate 17. *Portrait of a man*, ca. 1633. Panel, 24.5 x 19.5 cm. The Hague, Mauritshuis. This small panel, like two similar ones in the Gemäldegalerie in Dresden, is sometimes thought to be a preliminary study for a group portrait which was never executed. But this hypothesis is questionable when one considers the fact that no preliminary studies are known for any of Hals's other group portraits. When Goethe saw the portraits in Dresden he remarked: 'Schöne kleine Bilder, nur untermalt'.

# 1630-1645

On 4 April 1634 a lottery of paintings took place in the Haarlem inn *De Bastaert-pijp*, organized by Dirck Hals and the engraver and tavern owner Cornelis van Kittensteyn. The thirty some works by Haarlem artists that were raffled included paintings by Hendrick Goltzius, Jan van Goyen and Frans and Dirck Hals. A 'Vanitas' by Frans Hals, possibly one of his child portraits, was estimated at 34 guilders, the average value of the works on offer. Two more portraits of his were estimated at 16 guilders apiece. His brother Dirck was more fortunate: his 'Five senses' - including frame - was valued at 104 guilders. Lotteries such as this were frequent and no doubt should be regarded as a kind of 'art sale in disguise', which put money in the pockets of the painters involved. The painters' guild was not enthusiastic about such practices and two months later outlawed this type of lottery.

Alongside painters, the St. Lucas Guild in Haarlem included engravers, architects, gold and silversmiths, sculptors, organ builders and even potters and plumbers. Although the painters were not in the majority - in 1634 of the 278 members only 58 were painters - they were the most strongly represented among those in charge. Each year the city council appointed four 'vinders' (deans) and a 'deken' (deacon) who saw to the daily running of the guild. The names of many Haarlem artists can be found on the list of guild directors. Frans Hals was a dean in 1644.

Not only did the guild promote the interests of its members in relation to the outside world, it also provided support for needy members, exempting them from

a. Nicolaes van Heussen (ca. 1600-after 1631) and Frans Hals, *Fruit seller,* 1630. Bridgnorth, collection of Viscount Boyne.
b. Hendrick Goltzius (1588-1617), *Tityus,* 1613. Haarlem, Frans Halsmuseum.

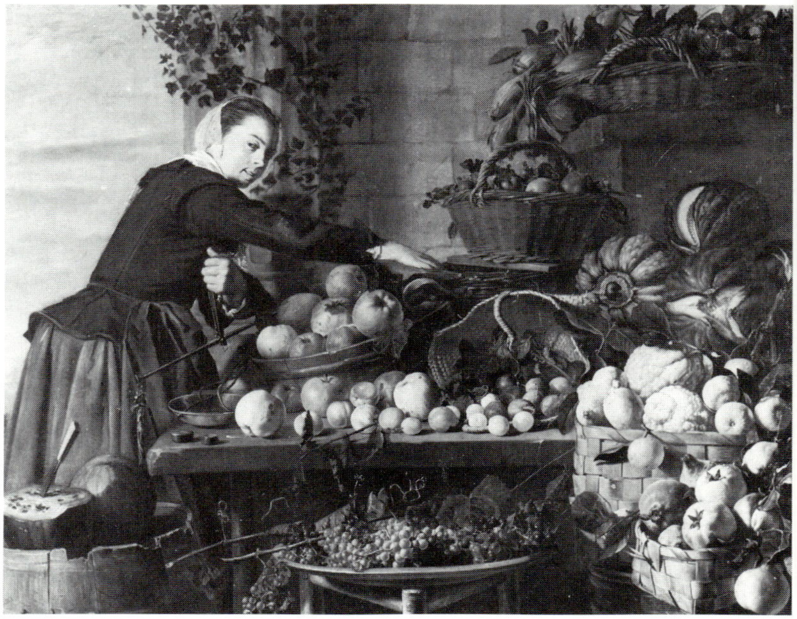

a

the yearly membership fees or contributing to their keep. In 1638 Frans Hals and two colleagues urged the guild's administration to see to the admission to the Old Men's Alms House of the painter Guilljame Polydanus. Conflicts between members were also brought before the administrators. In September 1635 Judith Leyster complained that one of her pupils had left for Frans Hals's workshop and requested that further teaching of the youth be denied the painter. The Guild's administration agreed with her.

Contacts among artists in the small town of Haarlem were intensive and productive. It was common for two painters to work on the same painting, each in his own speciality. In this way Dirck Hals provided groups of merry-makers for the interiors of Dirck van Delen (see p. 60, ill. c) and in some of his paintings, Frans Hals had the landscapes or backgrounds done by others (plate 21). He himself was probably approached by Nicolaes van Heussen for the seller in the latter's *Fruit stand* (ill. a).

The artists also joined forces in other ways. An affair which involved all painters was the art trade. In 1642 the town council elected to restrain the unbridled growth of the sale of paintings. The St. Lucas Guild spoke out against any such limitation. There was a danger that only established masters would profit from a protected market with high prices, and many painters depended on the art trade for a large part of their income. However, the town council remained firm and two years later put their proposal into effect. Frans Hals was against limiting sales. He himself dealt in paintings. In 1630 he had bought a painting by Hendrick Goltzius, *Tityus* (ill. b), for 89 guilders at an auction in Amsterdam. In the same year, he sold it through an intermediary to the city of Haarlem for 200 guilders.

It is not clear whether the town council's decision had a direct influence on Hals's income. At this time, however, it is a matter of record that the painter frequently had trouble paying his bills. His debts grew larger and multiplied, despite his great productivity. In 1631 he still owed a butcher 42 guilders for slaughtering an ox; he could pay only 29. In 1634 the baker Bouwen Fransz. held a number of paintings by Hals in security for a sum of 23 guilders, 17 stuivers and 3 cents. Two years later a certain Symon de Bray stood security for 80 guilders in back rent. Apparently the many important commissions Hals acquired, including three group portraits of Haarlem militias and regents and even a militia portrait for Amsterdam, were not enough to cover the heavy costs of raising a family, operating an atelier and dealing in the art trade.

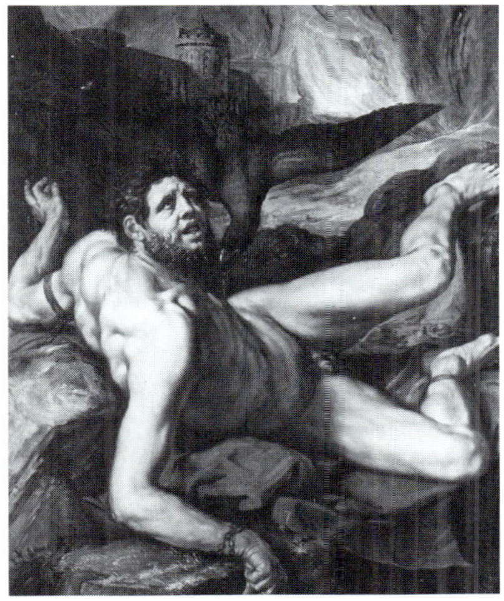

b

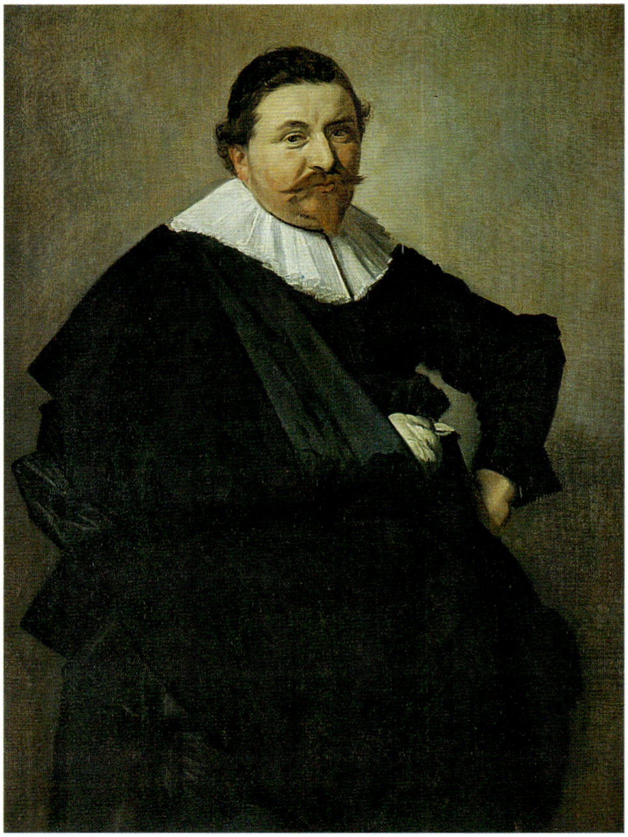

18

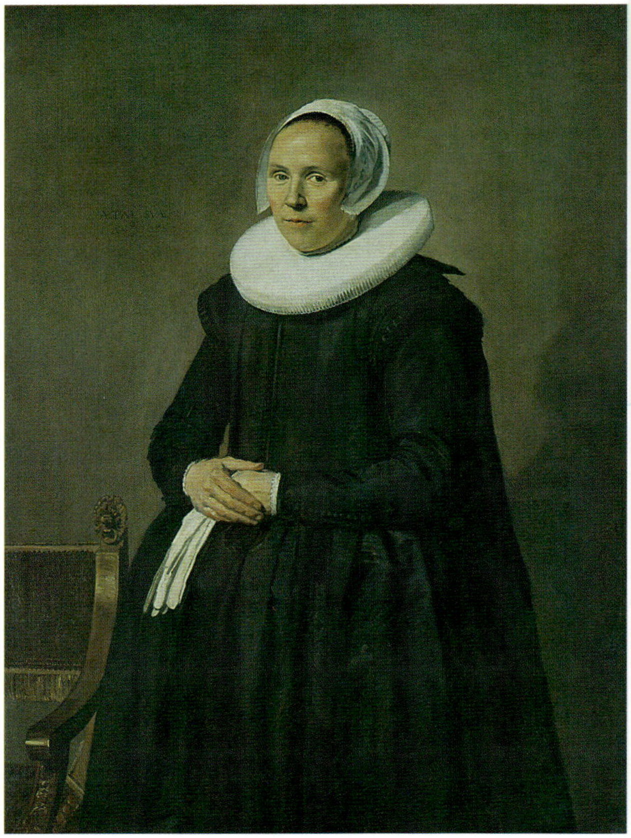

19

Plate 18. *Lucas de Clercq,* ca. 1635. Canvas, 126.5 x 93 cm. Amsterdam, Rijksmuseum.
Plate 19. *Feyntje van Steenkiste.* Canvas, 123 x 93 cm. Inscribed above left 'AETAT SVAE 31/AN° 1635'. Amsterdam, Rijksmuseum.
Lucas de Clercq (ca. 1593-1652) was a potash dealer in Haarlem. The portrait of Feyntje van Steenkiste (1603/04-before 1645) is thought by some to be painted by Judith Leyster (see p. 61). Both canvases came from the De Clercq family estate.

Plate 20. *Officers of a company of the Amsterdam Voetboogdoelen under captain Reynier Reael and lieutenant Cornelis Michielsz. Blaeuw,* 1633; completed by Pieter Codde (1599-1678) in 1637. Canvas, 209 x 429. Dated at right 'A° 1637'. Amsterdam, Rijksmuseum.
The only militia portrait painted by Frans Hals on commission from an Amsterdam militia was finished by Pieter Codde, after a difference of opinion arose about the conditions originally agreed upon (see following pages). The painting's epithet 'The Meagre Company' probably dates from J. van Dijck's description in 1760 of the art collection in the Amsterdam city hall where the painting hung. Of the militiamen portrayed he wrote: 'they are all so spare and slender that they could well be called the meagre Company'.

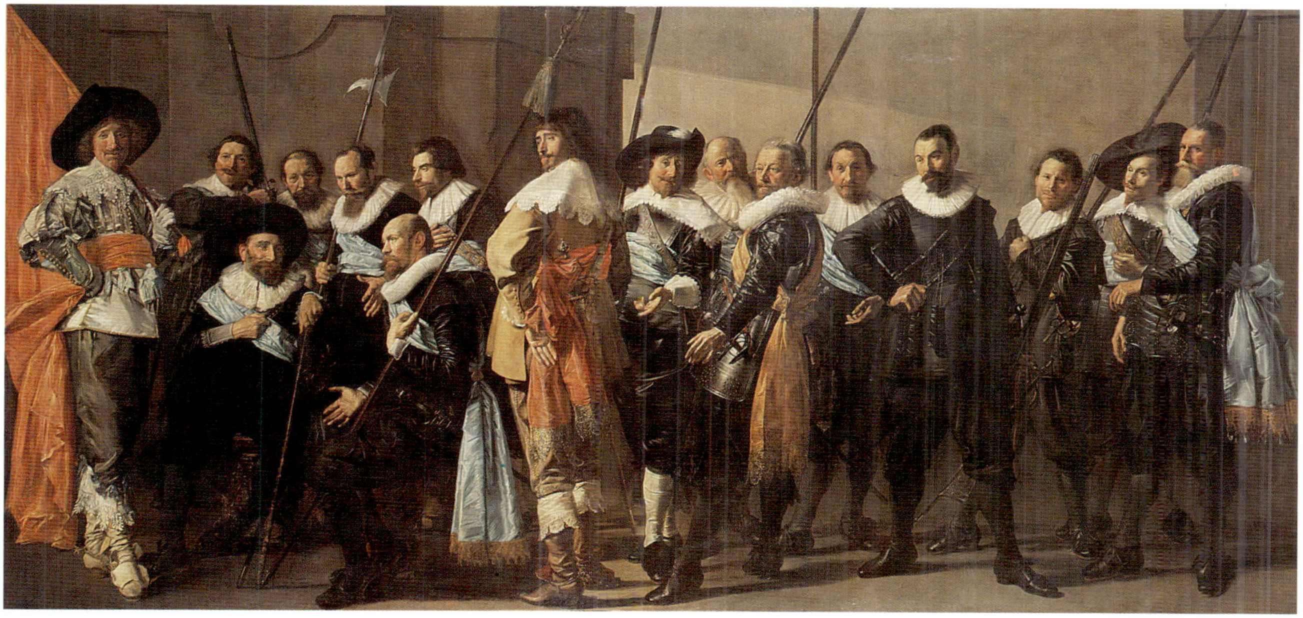

20

Plate 20a. Detail. Captain Reynier Reael and lieutenant Cornelis Michielsz. Blaeuw.

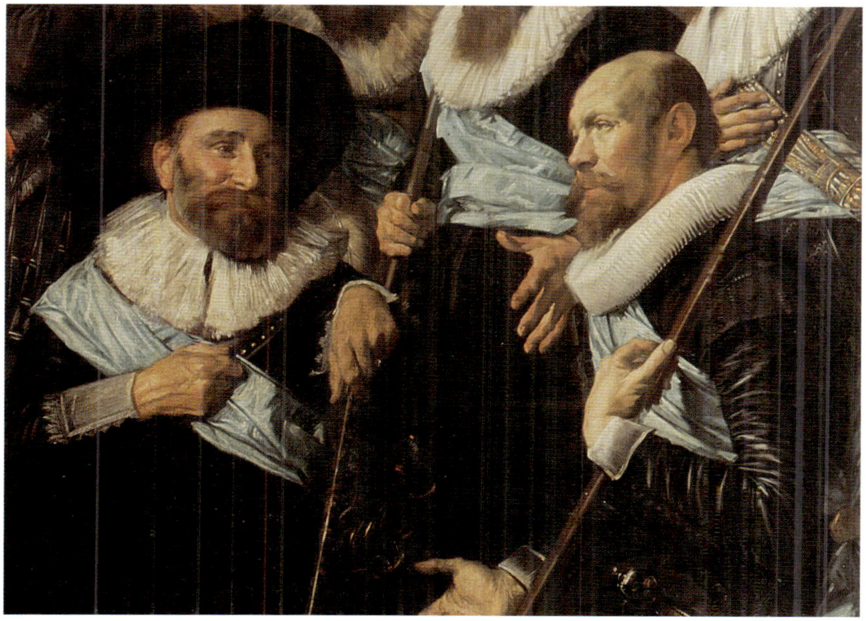

20a

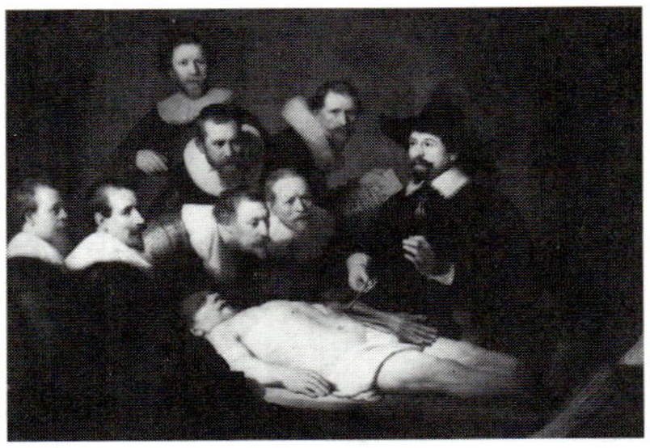

a

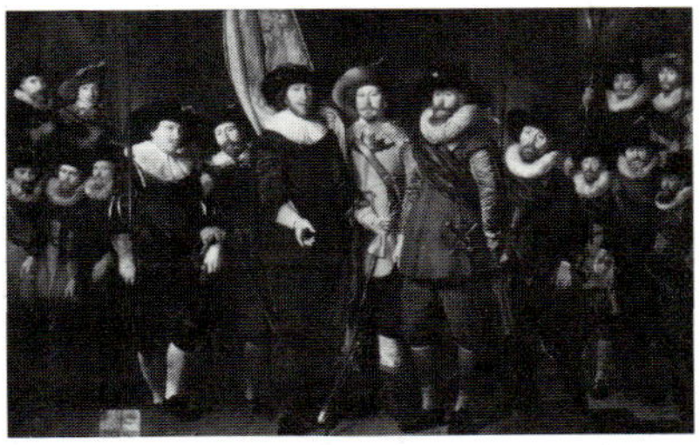

b

a. Rembrandt (1606-1669), *The anatomy lesson of Dr. Tulp*, 1632. The Hague, Mauritshuis.
b. Thomas de Keyser (1596/97-1667), *The company of Captain Allaert Cloeck,* 1632.
c. *The officers of the Amsterdam Militia under captain Reael and lieutenant Blaeuw,* 1633-37, detail.

## A commission in Amsterdam

In 1633 several officers of an Amsterdam Corporalship approached Frans Hals, asking for a portrait. It is worthy of note that they chose a painter from another town rather than from Amsterdam itself. In these years this prosperous town contained such artists as the young Rembrandt, who a year earlier had made a name for himself with *Dr. Tulp's anatomy lesson* (ill. a), and the renowned painters Nicolaes Eliasz. and Thomas de Keyser, who had a great deal of experience in executing militia portraits (ill. b). Possibly because both of these painters were already at work on similar projects, the officers went to Frans Hals, whose fame was not limited to Haarlem. Three years later they were to regret their action; the painting was still not finished.

On 10 March 1636 captain Reynier Reael and lieutenant Cornelis Michielsz. Blaeuw, representing their company, lodged a complaint with a notary that in spite of promises made, Frans Hals was 'unseemingly in default, notwithstanding declarations, both verbal and written'. Hals had completed only part of the painting and was ordered to come to Amsterdam within a fortnight 'to complete that which is still wanting from the aforementioned piece in a proper and fitting manner'. Should Hals fail to respond, the militiamen would have the painting finished 'by some other good master'.

Frans Hals's answer came ten days later. He had failed to complete the painting because it had been agreed that he 'would begin the faces in Amsterdam and carry on with them in Haarlem, as he had begun to do'. But since he 'could not get everyone together' in Amsterdam, he was unable to finish the work. In addition, he had not been reimbursed for the expenses he had run up in Amsterdam, as promised. But to show his good will, Hals proposed - providing the militia would come to Haarlem - 'that he take up the work forthwith and complete it without delay and do his duty thereby, and that to do this in Haarlem rather than in Amsterdam was more favourable to him, as he could be at home and keep an eye on his people'.

Reael and Blaeuw were not satisfied with 'the frivolous and untruthful response from Mr. Frans Halsch'. In a memorandum dated 29 April 1636, they admitted initially agreeing with Hals that he should begin the painting in Amsterdam and finish it in Haarlem. But the officers asserted that at a later date they had made a second agreement with Hals that he would complete the entire work in Amsterdam, 'both Bodies and Faces'. For this he could expect six guilders extra per portrait, bringing the payment he was to receive for each militiaman portrayed to sixty-six guilders. Reael and Blaeuw gave Frans Hals another ten days to react.

Hals's reply did not come until 26 July. He did not change his ground, but proposed 'to take the painting immediately from Amsterdam and bring it to his house in order to do the unpainted clothes'. After this, 'the gracious persons could come to Haarlem to his house' and the faces could be filled in. Hals emphasized that this would not take much time. He also undertook, 'should six or seven be unwilling' to come to Haarlem, that 'he would paint those six or seven persons in Amsterdam and complete the work properly'.

Apparently Hals's compromise did not convince the Amsterdam militia. They carried out their threat and commissioned Pieter Codde (1599-1678) to finish the painting. Codde, who did his best to adapt Hals's virtuoso technique, worked mainly on the right side of the canvas. The composition, similar to that of *The officers and subalterns of the St. Adrian militia company* of 1633 (plate 40), is probably by Frans Hals. He followed the Amsterdam tradition of portraying the sixteen militiamen from head to foot. Only the names of the two seated figures are known; they are captain Reael and lieutenant Blaeuw (plate 20a).

An interesting passage showing how the painting was appreciated in the nineteenth century occurs in the letters of Vincent van Gogh. In October 1865 Van Gogh made a special trip to Amsterdam to study the paintings of Frans Hals and Rembrandt in the newly built Rijksmuseum. He reserved his greatest enthusiasm for *'The meagre company'*, particularly for the standard-bearer on the lefthand side. In a letter to his brother Theo he wrote:

> *'I don't know if you remember, but to the left of the Nightwatch, so as a companion piece to the Staalmeesters, hangs a painting (I'd never seen it before) by Frans Hals and P. Codde of about 20 officers portrayed full-length. Did you notice it? It alone makes the journey to Amsterdam worthwhile - particularly for a colourist. There is a figure in it, the figure of the standard-bearer, all the way to the left close to the frame - the figure is grey from head to toe, let me call it pearl grey - a strange neutral tone, probably got by mixing orange and blue in such a way that they neutralize each other - by varying this basic tone, making it here lighter, there darker, the whole figure is painted with the same grey. Still the leather shoes are of another material than the leggings, which are different from the folds of the trousers, which are different from the doublet - expressing different materials, all of a different colour among themselves - yet all in a single family of grey. But wait!*
>
> *Within this grey he uses blue and orange - and some white; the doublet has satin bows of a heavenly soft blue, sash and flag orange - a white collar.*
>
> *Orange, white, blue, range the national colours at that time - orange and blue together, the most wonderful extremes, on a grey underground, expertly mixed out by uniting these two, let me call them poles of electricity (always meaning colour), so that they cancel each other against that grey and white. And carried through in the painting - other oranges with other blues, also the most beautiful blacks contrasting with the most beautiful whites; the heads - some twenty - sparkling with spirit and life! and colour! the superb aspect of all those fellows, from top to toe.*
>
> *But the orange, white, blue chap in the lefthand corner... I've seldom seen a more divinely beautiful figure. It's something wonderful and unique!'*

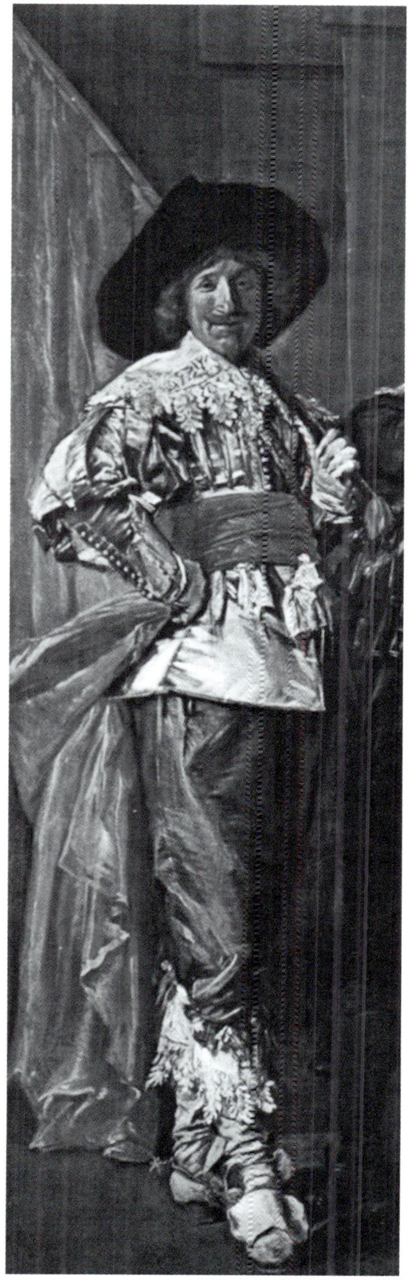

c

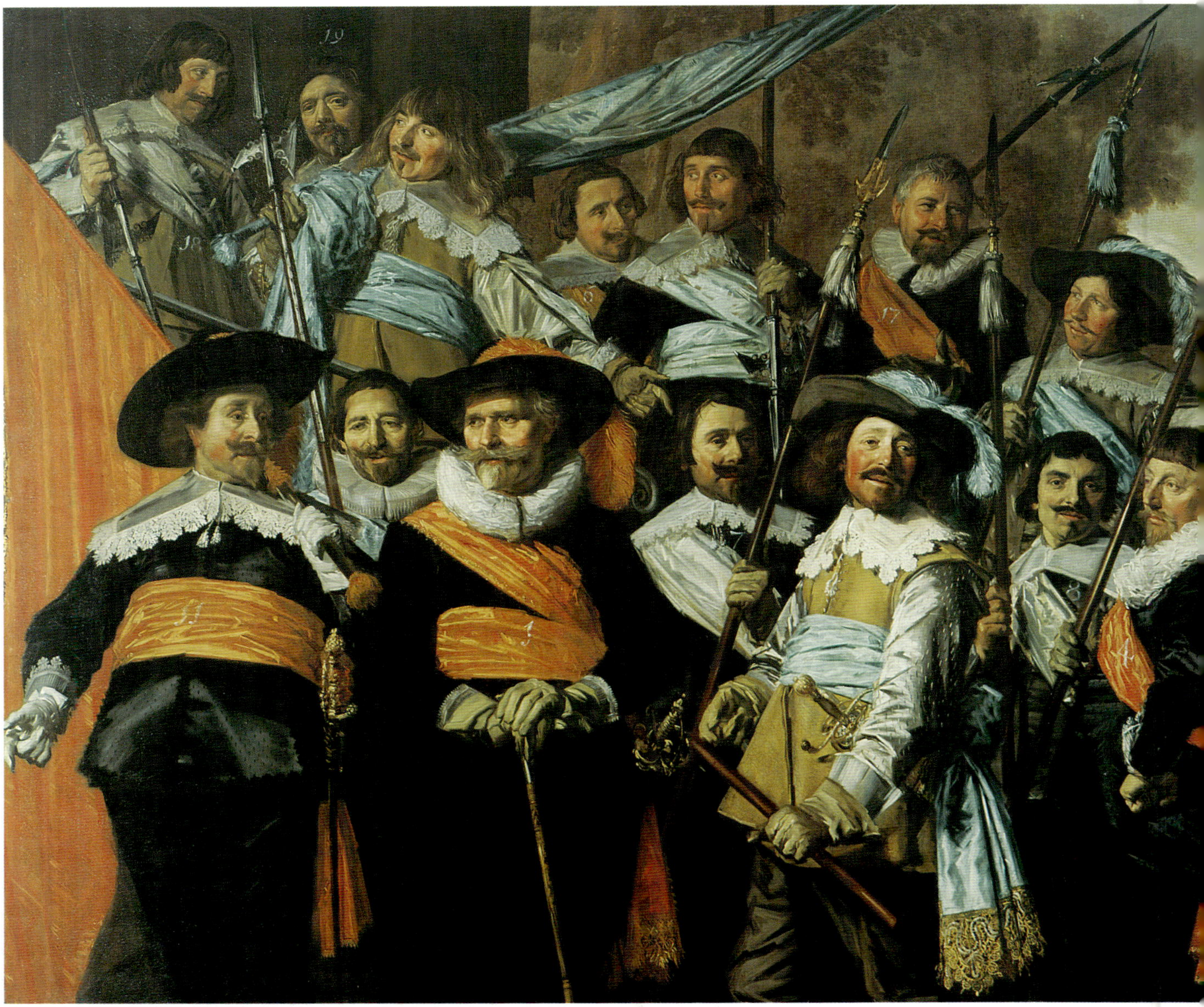

21

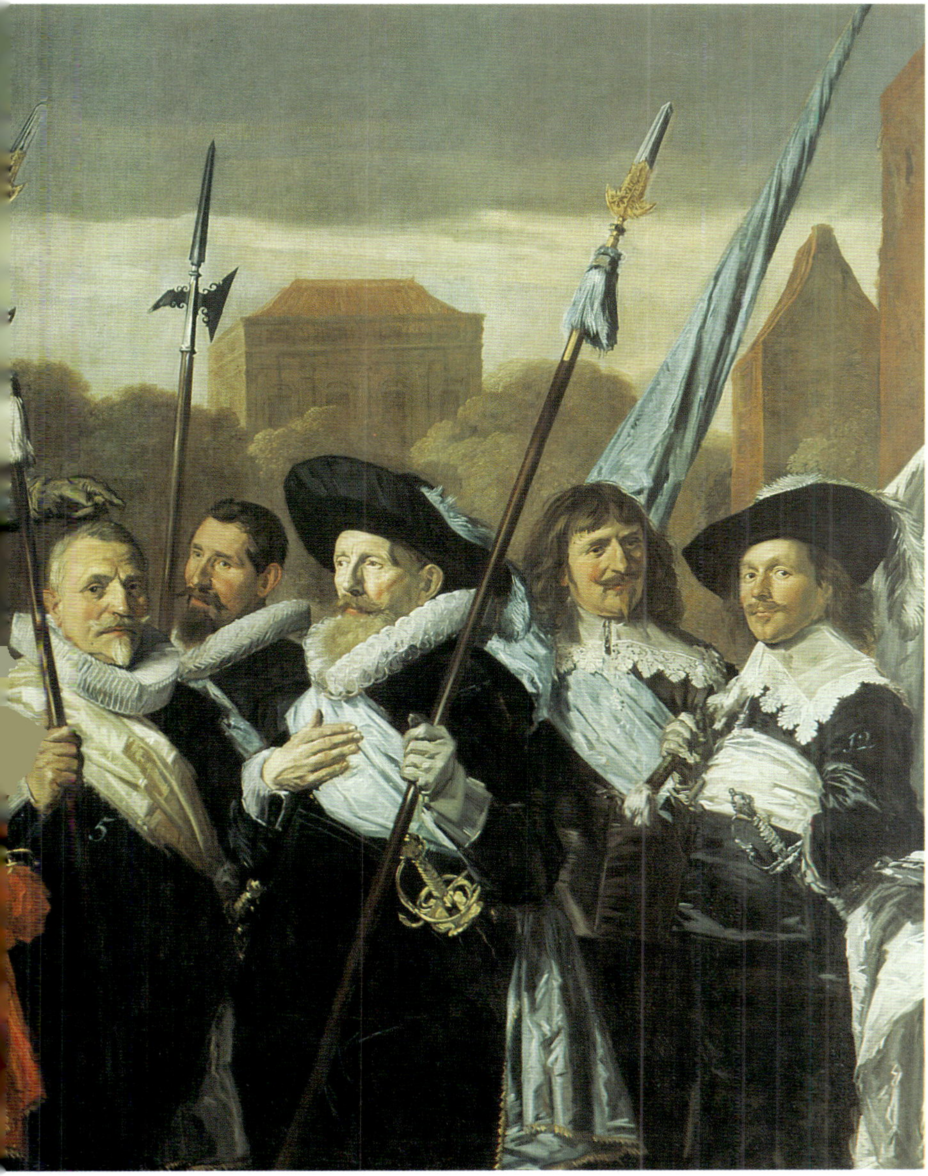

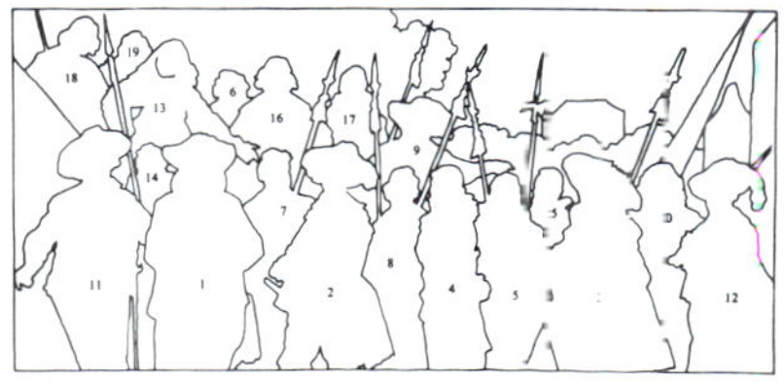

1. Johan (van) Loo, colonel (see also plate 40); 2. Michiel de Wael, fiscal (see also plate 14); 3. Quirijn Damast, captain; 4. Florens van der Hoeff, captain; 5. Nicolaes Grauwert, captain; 6. Hendrick Pot, lieutenant (see also plate 40) 7. François Wouters, lieutenant (see also plate 28); 8. Cornelis Coning, lieutenant; 9. Hendrick Coning, lieutenant; 10. Dirck Dicx, standard-bearer (see also plate 14); 11. Lambert Wouters, standard-bearer; 12. Pieter Schout, standard-bearer; 13. Jacob Druyvesteyn, standard-bearer; 14. Gabriel Loreyn, sergeant; 15. (?), sergeant; 16. Nicolaes van Loo, sergeant; 17. Abraham van der Schalck, sergeant; 18. (?), sergeant; 19. Frans Hals.

Plate 21. *The officers and subalterns of the St. George militia company*, ca. 1639. Canvas, 218 x 421 cm. Haarlem, Frans Halsmuseum.
In the eighteenth century the militiamen portrayed were given identification numbers.
The last militia portrait Frans Hals painted shows nineteen militiamen, the largest number of people in any of his paintings. The subjects include four lieutenants, four standard-bearers and five sergeants. According to the usual make-up of a militia - a colonel, a fiscal and three companies, each consisting of a captain, a lieutenant, two sergeants and a standard-bearer - there are one lieutenant and one standard-bearer too many and one sergeant too few. Each of the three companies has its own colour; orange, white, blue; the officers and under-officers wear sashes of their company's colour. Late in the seventeenth century the second man from the left in the top row was identified as Frans Hals. The background of the piece was possibly painted by Cornelis van der Schalcken.

## HISTORY OF THE OFFICERS AND SUBALTERNS OF THE ST. GEORGE MILITIA COMPANY, 1639.

*1639* Dated, based on information about the identity of the subjects.
*1701* Item of expenditure for the cleaning and 'repainting' of the paintings .
*1721* Before 1721 the painting was taken to the Cluveniersdoelen.
Item of expenditure for cleaning the paintings.
*1740* A 'Painting Commission' occupies itself with identification of the militiamen. Their names are given on a plaque below the portrait and corresponding numbers are painted on the canvas.
*1810* Mention of damage to paintings caused by soldiers at exercise.
*1819* New mention of damage, after restoration of painting two years earlier.
*1821* Request to transfer the paintings to the town hall is granted.
*1862* The painting is transferred to the Stedelijk Museum in Haarlem.
*1897* The painting is lined by F. Vos, restorer of the Stedelijk Museum.
*1906* The varnish is regenerated by F. Vos.
*1913* Taken to the Frans Halsmuseum, opened this year.
*1924* Restoration under the supervision of D. de Wild.
*1987* January-September: restoration by Anne van Grevenstein, Michaela Burek, Liesbeth Abraham, Carol Pottasch and Ella Hendriks.

## THE RESTORATION IN 1987
January-September

Except for a rather large right-angled tear in the sky to the right and a disturbing loss in the eye of fig. 5, this portrait was in good condition. Only the considerable sagging of the canvas was a problem. Adhesion between paint and canvas, as well as between canvas and lining, was good.

Old varnish and overpainting were removed with acetone and cotton swabs, except for a layer of oil-based varnish. Fillings were made in the usual way with the brown tint of the ground layer and given a surface structure. Reconstruction of the missing areas created no difficulty. As for the other four canvases, the final dammar varnish was applied carefully and with restraint.

Ill. 21a and b. One of the reasons for the decision to restore the militia portraits was concern about the sagging of the canvases. The 'bulge' of the 1639 painting in particular placed too much tension on the paint layer, threatening to raise the craquelure. Ill. 21a shows that a string hanging straight gives a curved shadow. One of the causes of the sagging was the heavy old lining. It was decided not to renew the lining but to use a less drastic, alternative treatment. In some places the tacks holding the canvas to the stretcher had been driven directly through the original paint. These were removed along the bottom edge and for about 30 cm. up each side. In order to prevent paint sticking to the heads of the tacks, the old varnish around them was soaked with solvent. The old lining was secured with extra tacks along the upper side of the stretcher to support the canvas when hanging. After the canvas was loosened, the string produced a fine straight shadow (ill. 21b). The 'bulge' had been reduced sufficiently to make further treatment unnecessary. After the canvas had hung for several months, the bottom edge could be reattached.

Ill. 21c. Detail of the eye of fig. 5. Was the loss so obvious because it was in an eye? Not improving missing parts may well give a feeling of integrity, but damage like

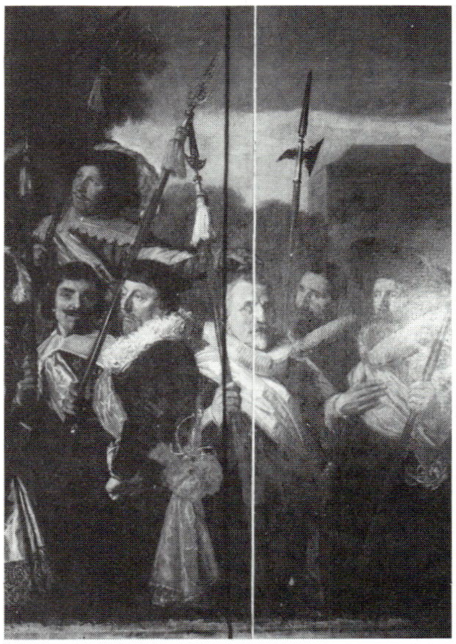

21a

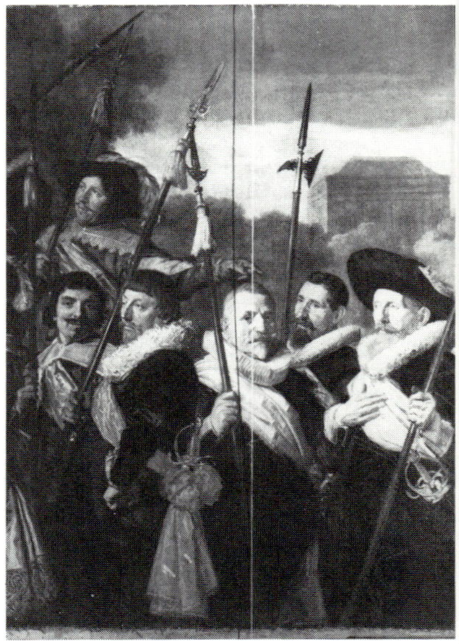

21b

this can distract and lessen enjoyment. Ill. 21d. The eye of fig. 5 after filling the loss with a mixture of wax and pigment. The filling was treated with a silicone mould in order to reproduce the surface structure of the craquelure (compare also ill. c and ill. d). The loss is now almost invisible. Photographs taken before retouching make it possible to discuss the acceptability of such a step. Was it truly called for or only the whim of the restorer? Every restoration is a product of its time. When the next one takes place, the discussion will no doubt be reopened. For this reason, types of paint,

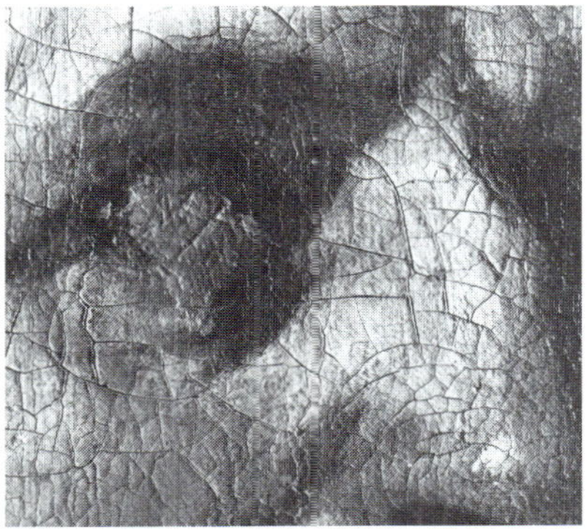

21d

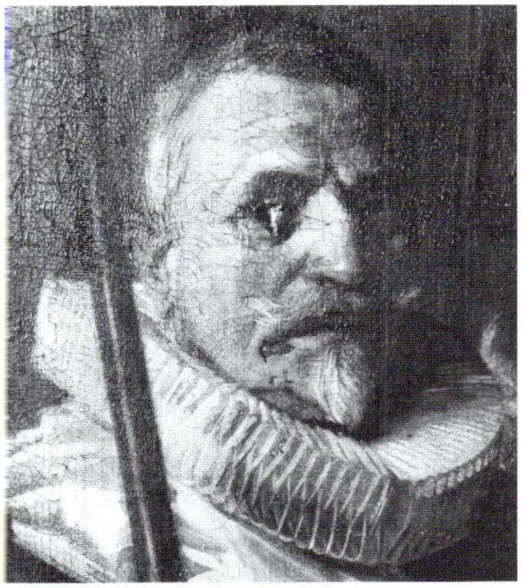

21c

filling medium and varnish were used which could be dissolved and removed without affecting the original paint.

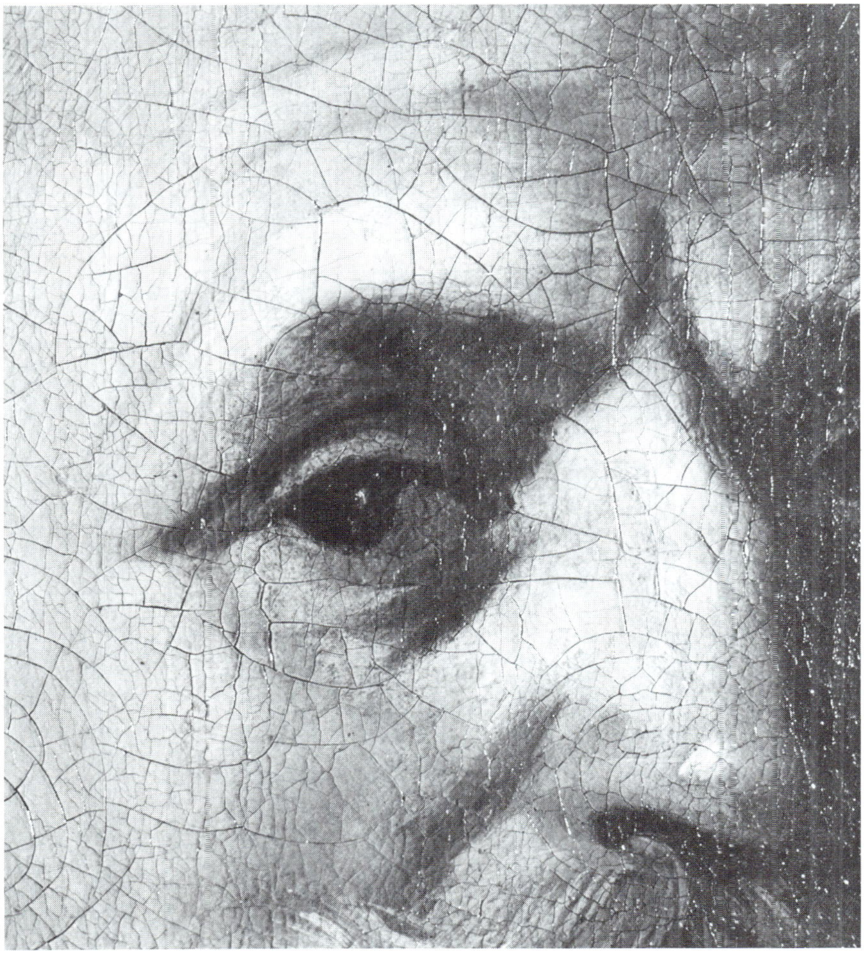

21e

Ill. 21f. Detail of the right side of the painting.
All four edges of the canvas are intact. The seam with the cord protecting the edges from tearing and the original cusping show that the canvas is still entire. In some places - unfortunately - the tacks attaching the canvas were driven through the original paint, making loosening of the canvas hazardous. Essentially, every $mm^2$ of paint is irreplaceable.

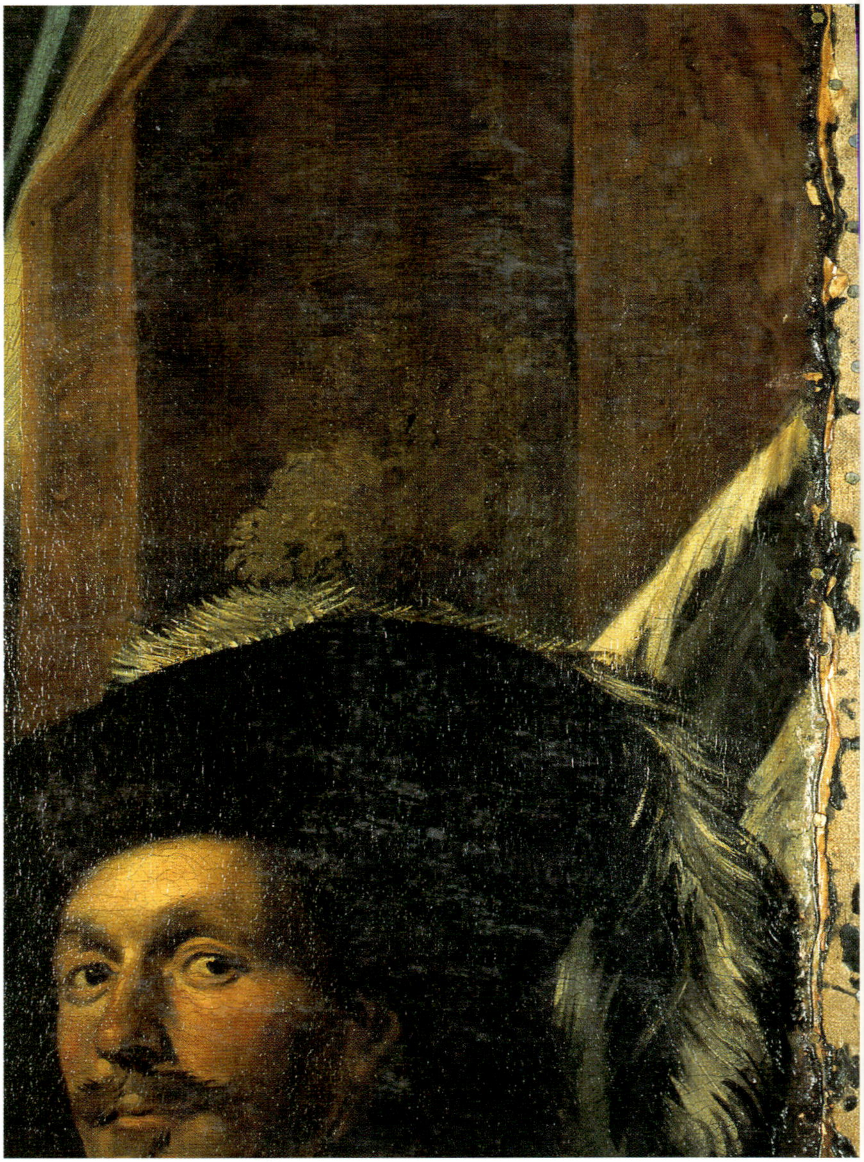

21f

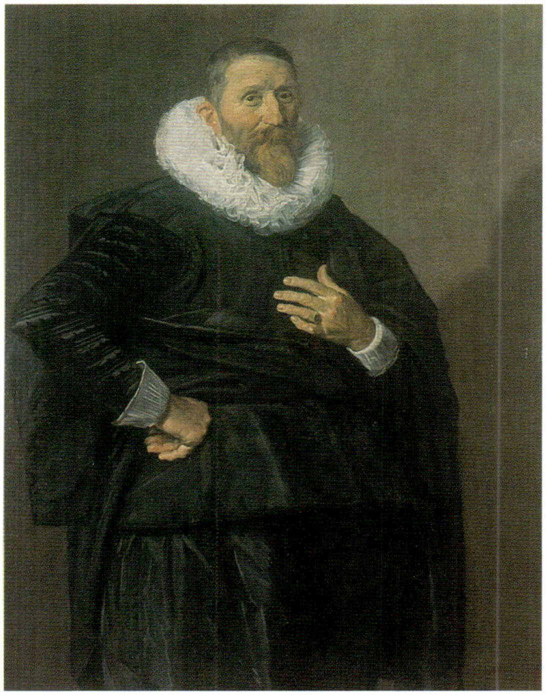

22

Plate 22. *Portrait of a man*, ca. 1637. Canvas, 125 x 95.5 cm. Rotterdam, Museum Boymans-van Beuningen.
Plate 23. *Hendrick Swalmius,* Panel, 27 x 20 cm. Inscribed right 'AETAT 60/1639'. Rotterdam, Museum Boymans-van Beuningen.
Plate 24. *Portrait of a woman.* Panel, 29.5 x 21. Inscribed left 'AETAT 57/1639'. Detroit, The Detroit Institute of Arts.
The portrait of the Haarlem preacher Hendrick Swalmius (ca. 1579-1649) was not discovered until 1934. The identity of the subject was determined from an engraving of the work. The panel was evidently larger originally; this could be determined not only from the engraving but also from the female portrait, considered to be its pendant. The book Swalmius holds in his hand is probably a Bible.

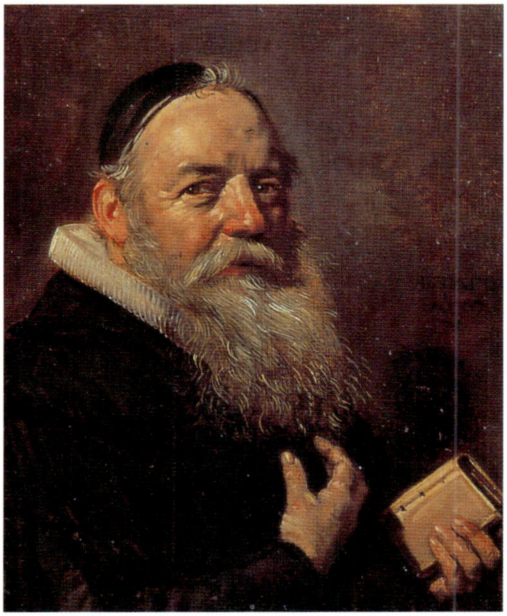

23

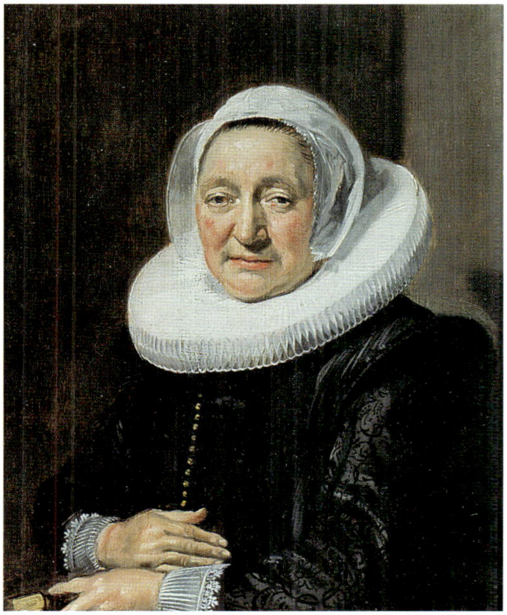

24

## Pupils

Master painters had pupils who during their apprenticeship helped the master in his atelier, preparing canvas and mixing pigments. Part of their instruction involved copying their teacher's works (ill. a). Alongside commissions and trading in art, teaching pupils was a welcome source of income for the artist. Usually a pupil stayed with the painter for a number of years and paid for his or her instruction, room and board. When the apprenticeship was over, the 'new' painter was eligible to join the St. Lucas Guild.

Most of the information about the pupils of Frans Hals is to be found in *De Groote Schouburgh der Nederlantsche Konstschilders en Schilderessen* by Arnold Houbraken. This collection of artists' biographies, published in 1718, can be regarded as a follow-up to Carel van Manders *Schilder-boeck*, though not always as reliable. In *De Groote Schouburgh* Dirck van Delen, Adriaen Brouwer, Adriaen van Ostade, Vincent van der Vinne and Pieter van Roestraten are named as pupils of Hals. According to Houbraken, Frans Hals used a somewhat unconventional approach with his pupils and 'was wont to say: Use plenty of paint; once you are an Artist the proper measure will come of itself'.

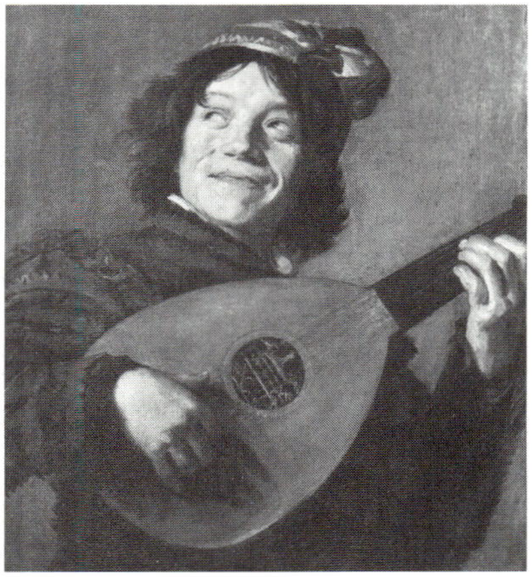

a

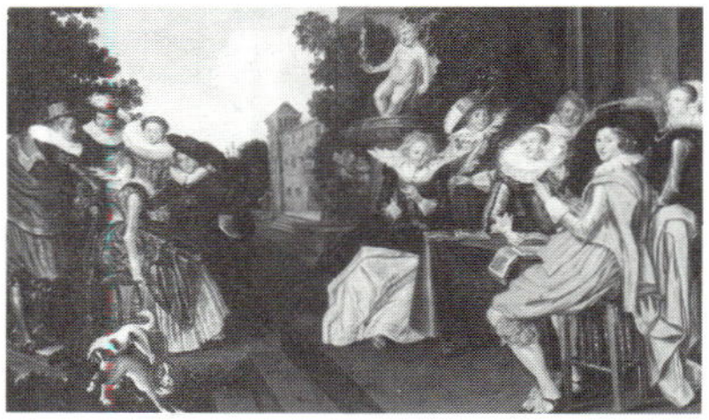

b

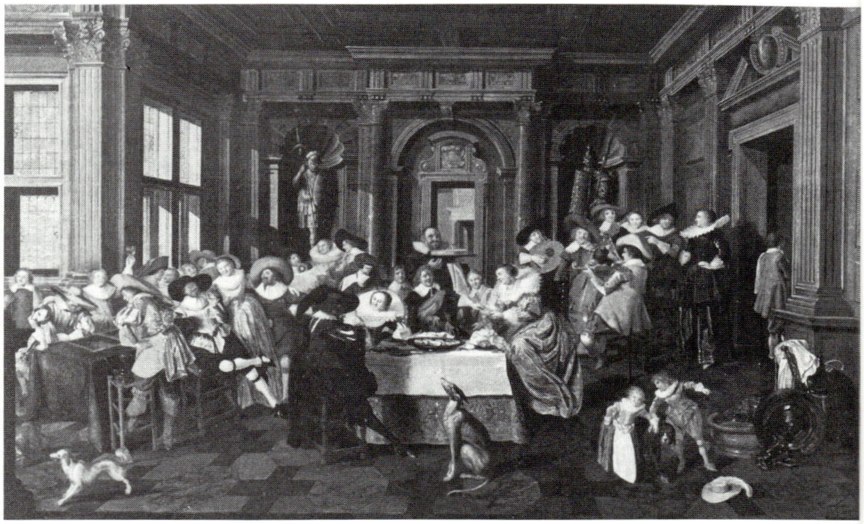

c

a. Judith Leyster? (1609-1660), *The lute player,* ca. 1626. Copy after Frans Hals (p. 25, ill. c). Amsterdam, Rijksmuseum.

b. Dirck Hals (1591-1656), *Merry Company,* ca. 1620. Haarlem, Frans Halsmuseum.
Like Willem Buytewech, Dirck Hals made many paintings of festive groups. He filled his scenes with all sorts of details warning the observer of the worldly pleasures of drinking and

sensuality. This type of painting can be considered a precursor of genre painting. Not surprisingly, Dirck Hals's artistic development was influenced by his older brother Frans.

c. Dirck van Delen (1604/05-1671) and Dirck Hals (1591-1656), *Merry company in an interior,* 1628. Haarlem, Frans Halsmuseum.
Dirck van Delen specialized in painting architecture. He frequently had the people in his pictures painted by others. His apprenticeship with Frans Hals must have taken place before 1626, the year in which he moved to Zeeland.

d. Adriaen Brouwer (1605/06-1638), *The smoker,* ca. 1634. The Hague, Mauritshuis.
The Fleming Adriaen Brouwer was probably apprenticed to Hals between 1623 and 1626. Brouwer is known principally for his tavern scenes and influenced many later painters.

e. Adriaen van Ostade (1610-1684), *The contented drinker,* ca. 1650-55. Haarlem, Frans Halsmuseum.
Adriaen van Ostade was probably a pupil of Frans Hals at the same time as Brouwer. The many similarities between paintings by Brouwer and Van Ostade seem to indicate that they knew each other. As teacher to the painters Cornelis Dusart and Jan Steen, Adriaen van Ostade was an important figure in the development of Dutch 'genre painting'.

f. Jan Miense Molenaer (ca. 1610-1668), *Family making music,* ca. 1635. Haarlem, Frans Halsmuseum (in loan from the Rijksdienst Beeldende Kunst).
Jan Miense Molenaer was possibly a pupil of Frans Hals in about 1630. He painted peasant and tavern scenes as well as portraits. In his *Family making music* there are many references to the transitory nature of life, such as the boy blowing bubbles, the clock, the (Frans Hals-like) portraits on the wall and the musical instruments. The sound of music is as fleeting as life.

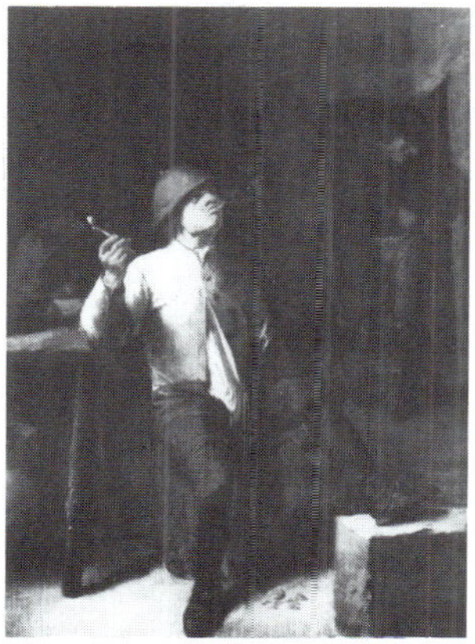

d

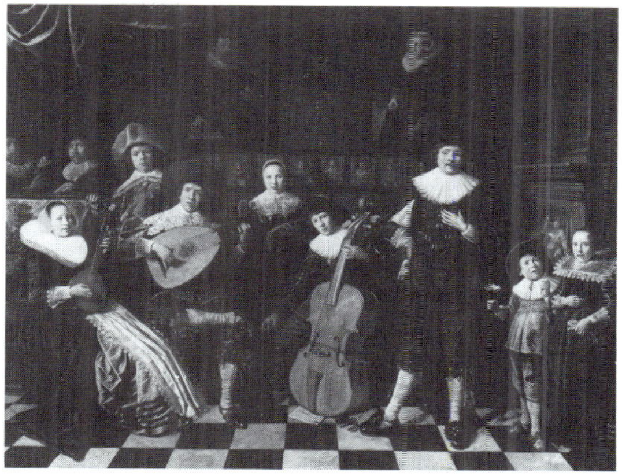

f

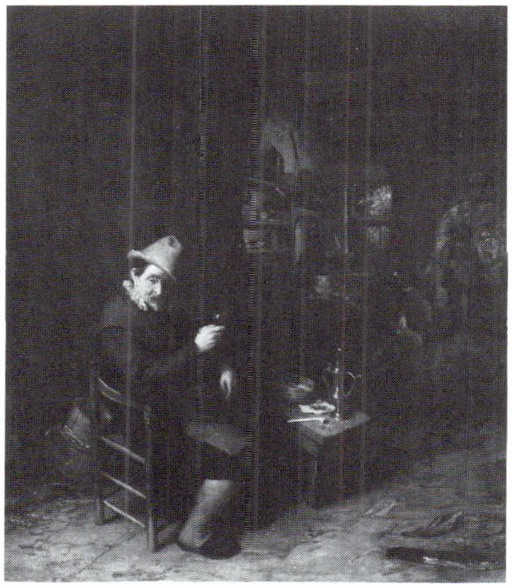

e

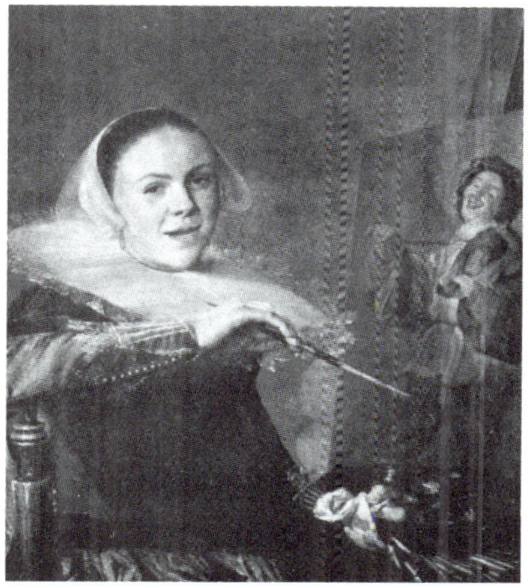

g

g. Judith Leyster (1609-1660), *Self-portrait,* ca. 1635. Washington, National Gallery of Art.
In 1633 Judith Leyster became the first woman to be admitted to the St. Lucas Guild in Haarlem. Some of her paintings, like this portrait for example, were admired long before the work of Frans Hals. She was probably his pupil in about 1630. In 1631 Judith Leyster was one of the witnesses at the baptism of Hals's daughter Maria. She married Jan Miense Molenaer in 1636.

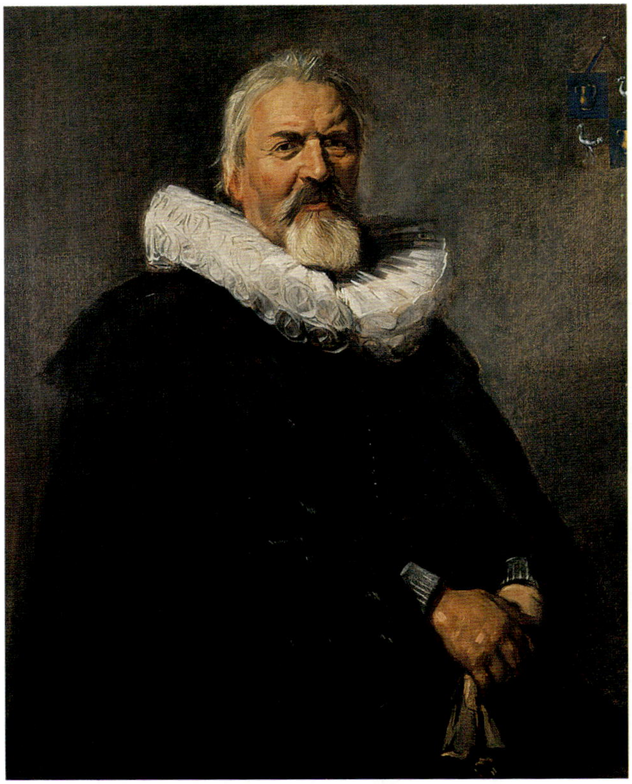

25

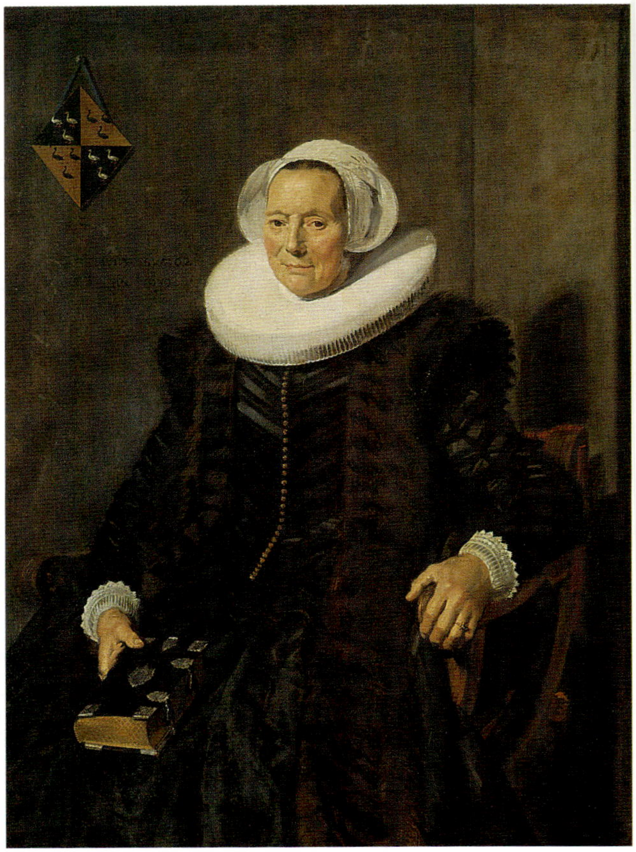

26

Plate 25. *Pieter Jacobsz. Olycan,* 1639. Canvas, 111.1 x 86.3 cm. Sarasota, The John and Mable Ringling Museum of Art.

Plate 26. *Maritge Vooght Claesdr.* Canvas, 128 x 94.5 cm. Inscribed left 'AETAT SVAE 62/AN° 1639'. Amsterdam, Rijksmuseum.

Pieter Olycan (1572-1658) had a brewery in Haarlem. He was also burgomaster and a member of the States General in The Hague, the highest governmental body in the Republic. His portrait - the paint surface is in poor condition in places - was probably cut down on all four sides at some point; the portrait of his wife is somewhat larger. Maritge Vooght (1577-1644) was the sister of Cornelia Vooght, portrayed by Frans Hals in the same pose eight years earlier (plate 2).

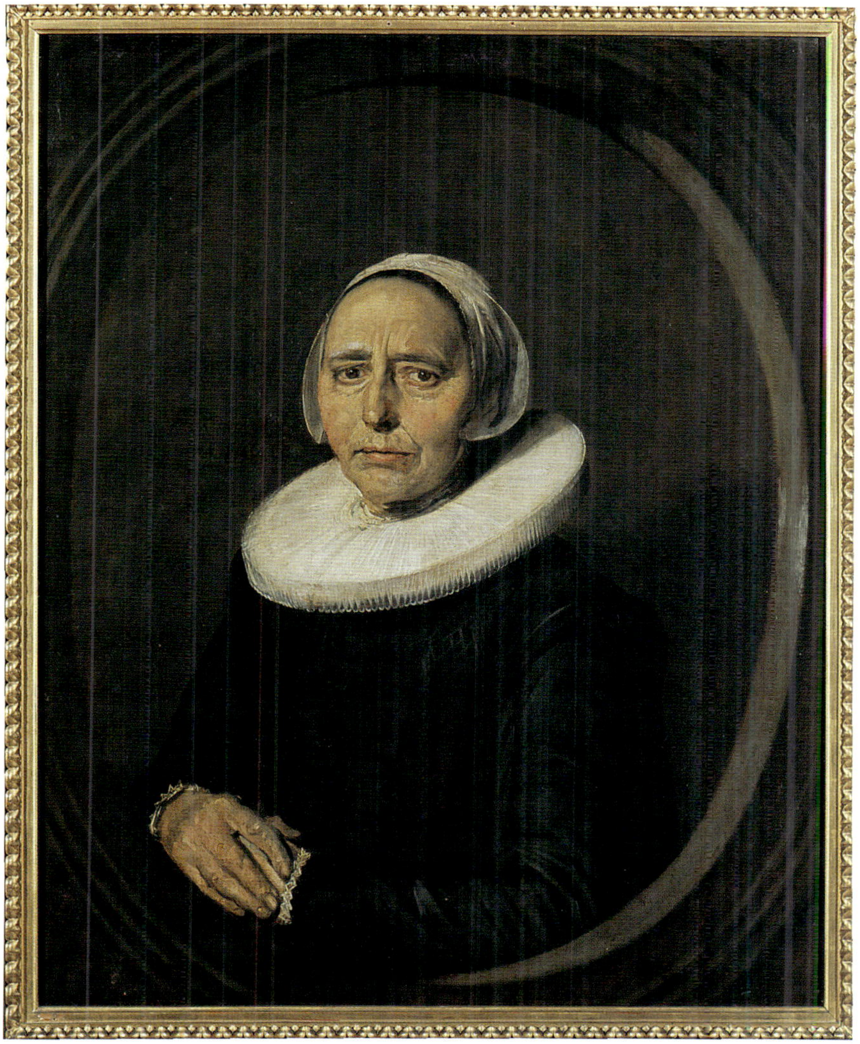

27

Plate 27. *Portrait of a woman.* Canvas, 84.5 x 67.5 cm. Inscribed left 'AETAT SVAE 53/...1640' and signed with the monogram 'FH'. Ghent, Museum voor Schone Kunsten.
This sober but impressive female portrait seems to be surrounded by a stone frame. As far as is known, this is the last portrait that Frans Hals made inside such an oval.

## Pupils; the sons of Frans Hals

Remarkably, none of the pupils of Frans Hals on record later acquired a reputation as a portraitist. Most of them devoted themselves to 'genre painting', landscapes and still lifes. A reasonably large number of portraits survive only from the hand of Frans Hals's son Jan. In the past his work gained recognition before that of his father. Jan's monogram 'IH' could easily be altered to 'FH' and it is not impossible that still some of the portraits attributed to Frans Hals are actually by Jan Hals. This is also possible in the case of Frans Hals II, who possibly signed his portraits like his father with the monogram 'FH'. Presumably Jan and Frans II learned painting from their father, as did Harmen, Reynier and Nicolaes. However, little is known about the life and work of the sons of Frans Hals.

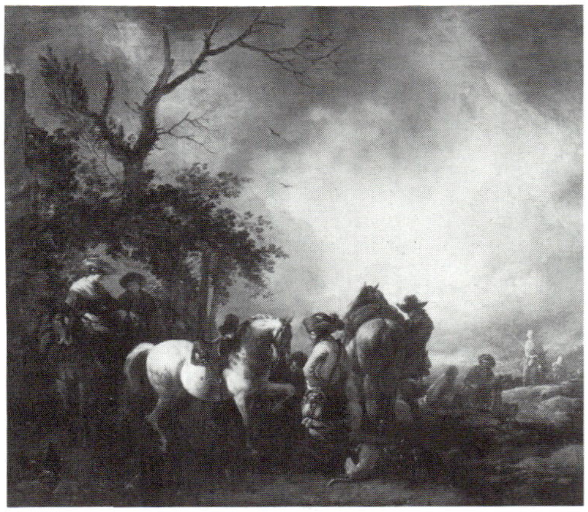

a

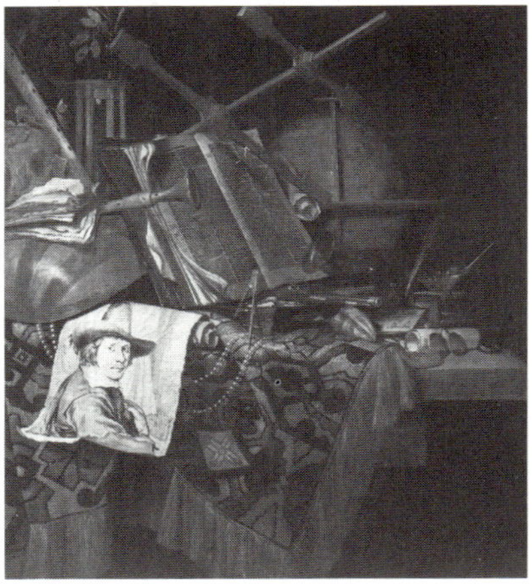

b

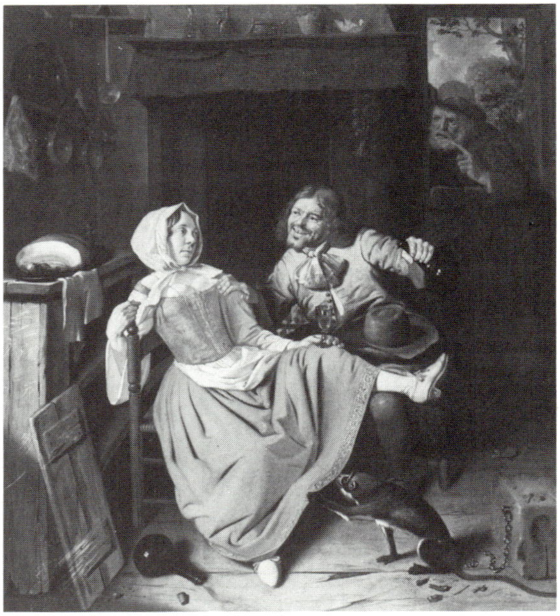

c

a. Philips Wouwerman (1619-1668), *Halt at the farrier's*, ca. 1655. Haarlem, Frans Halsmuseum.
Philips Wouwerman is named among the pupils of Frans Hals by Cornelis de Bie in his *Gulden Cabinet van de Edele Vrij Schilder Const* of 1661. This book dates from the time that both Hals and Wouwerman were still alive and is therefore more dependable than Houbraken's biography. Wouwerman was a painter of landscapes and hunting scenes, usually with the horse as the central feature. His apprenticeship must have taken place before 1638. Wouwerman's paintings were very popular during his lifetime. In the eighteenth century he was even considered to be Haarlem's most famous painter.

b. Vincent Laurensz. van der Vinne (1628-1702), *Still life with portrait of the artist* (by Leendert van der Cooghen), ca. 1670. Haarlem, Frans Halsmuseum.
Vincent van der Vinne was a pupil of Frans Hals from 1646 to 1649. According to Houbraken, as a child he was a playmate of the Hals children. Van der Vinne must have been a versatile painter, but unfortunately little of his work is known.

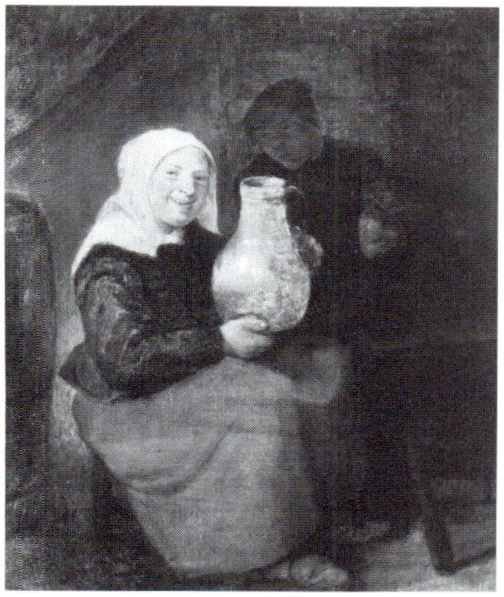

d

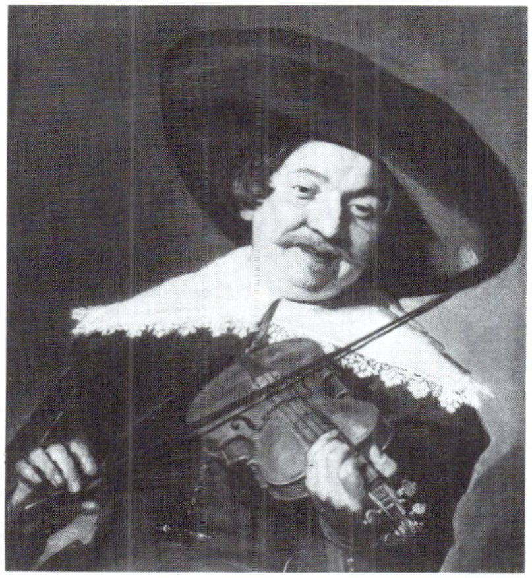

f

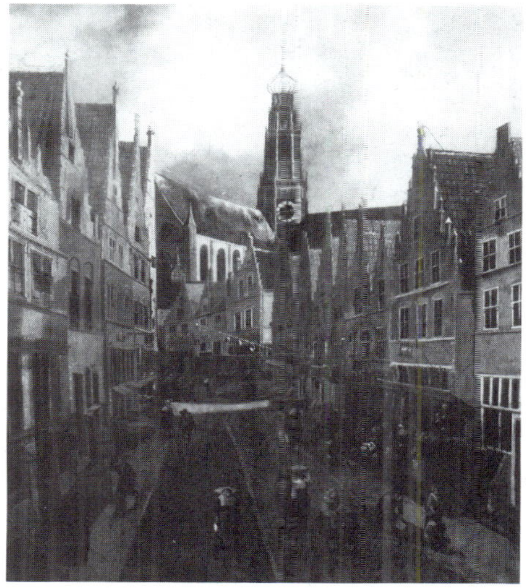

h

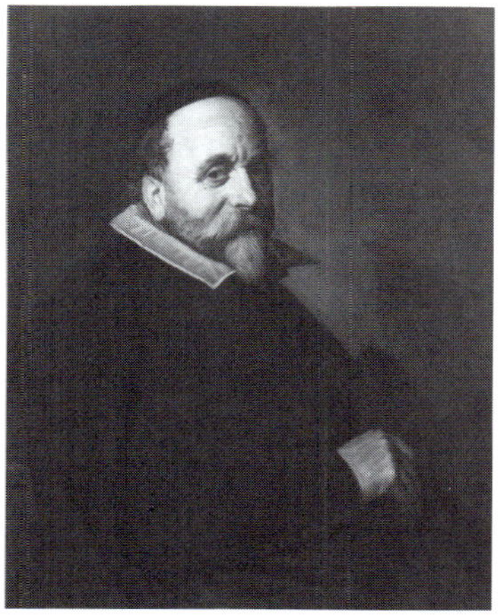

e

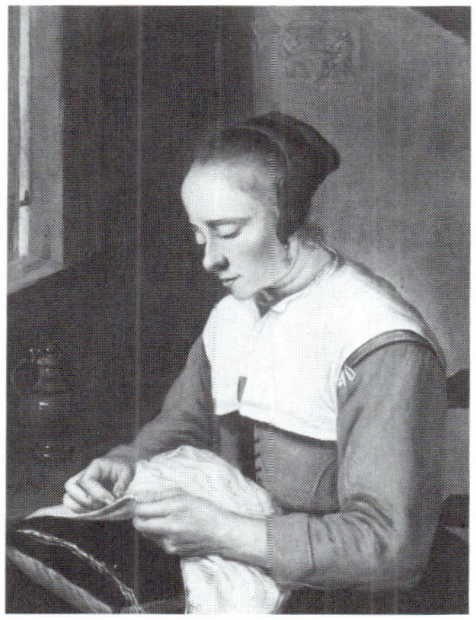

g

c. Pieter Gerritsz. van Roestraten (ca. 1630-1700), *Declaration of love,* ca. 1665. Haarlem, Frans Halsmuseum.
Pieter van Roestraten was a pupil of Frans Hals between 1646 and 1651. He is known for his still lifes, but he also produced some 'genre paintings'. In 1654 Van Roestraten married Hals's daughter Adriaentgen. Years later he settled in London.

d. Harmen Hals (1611-1669), *Peasant company,* ca. 1650. Haarlem, Frans Halsmuseum.

e. Frans Hals?, Frans Hals II? (1618-1669), Jan Hals? (ca. 1620-1674), *Portrait of a man,* 1640. The Hague, Rijksdienst Beeldende Kunst.

f. Frans Hals?, Frans Hals II?, *Daniël van Aken,* ca. 1640. Stockholm Nationalmuseum.

g. Reynier Hals (1627-1671), *Woman with handiwork,* ca. 1650. Haarlem, Frans Halsmuseum.

h. Nicolaes Hals (1628-1686), *The Grote Houtstraat at Haarlem,* ca. 1655. Haarlem, Frans Halsmuseum.

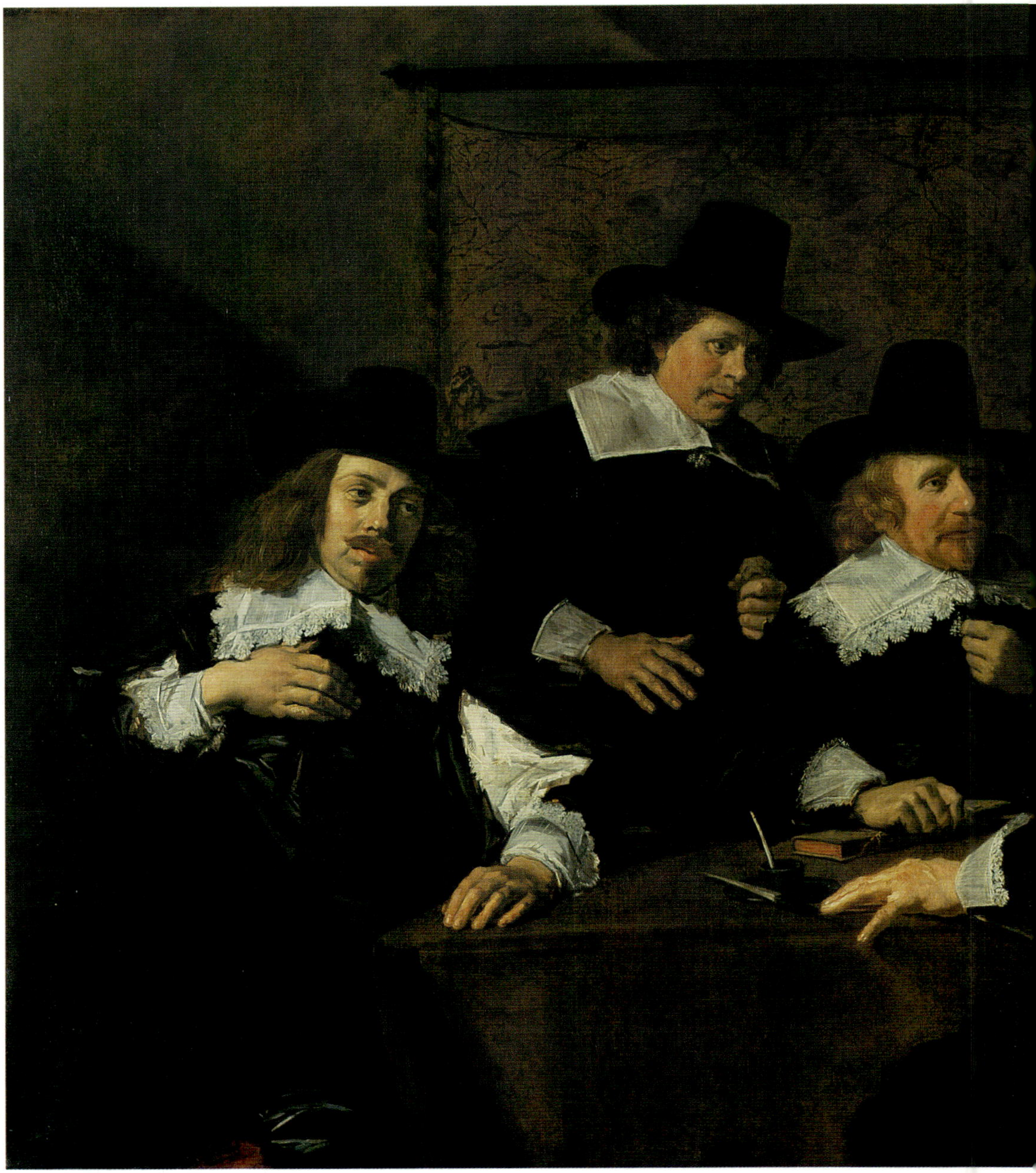

28

Plate 28. *Regents of St. Elisabeth's Hospital*, ca. 1640. Canvas, 153 x 252 cm. Haarlem, Frans Halsmuseum (in loan from the trustees of St. Elisabeth's Hospital). Compared to the militia portraits by Frans Hals, this regents portrait radiates a striking tranquillity, almost a blessedness. The sunlight shining down from the left bathes the room in a warm glow. The identities of the black-clad men are unknown. However, the regent at the extreme right can be recognized as François Wouters, regent of the hospital between 1637 and 1654. In about 1639 Hals portrayed him in the portrait of the St. George militia company (plate 21). The map on the wall perhaps refers to one of the regents' tasks: supervision of the properties held by the St. Elisabeth's Hospital. The regents also managed the finances. The lady-regentesses of the hospital also had themselves painted, not however by Frans Hals but by Johannes Verspronck (see following pages).

## Regents and regentesses

Frans Hals's *Regents of St. Elisabeth's Hospital* (plate 28) is the first regents portrait painted in Haarlem. Various models for the unforced composition were available to Hals in Amsterdam where the genre had existed for some time. The regentesses of the hospital also had a portrait made of themselves. However, the commission went not to Frans Hals but to Johannes Verspronck (ill. a). Like Hals, Verspronck was a portrait painter and many of Haarlem's citizens were among his subjects. Before his admission to the St. Lucas Guild in 1632, he was possibly a pupil of Hals; his early work definitely shows Hals's influence. Verspronck's portraits reflect a high degree of expertise. They are painted in a very refined style, altogether different from Hals's much freer brushwork. Apparently unity of style was not a consid-

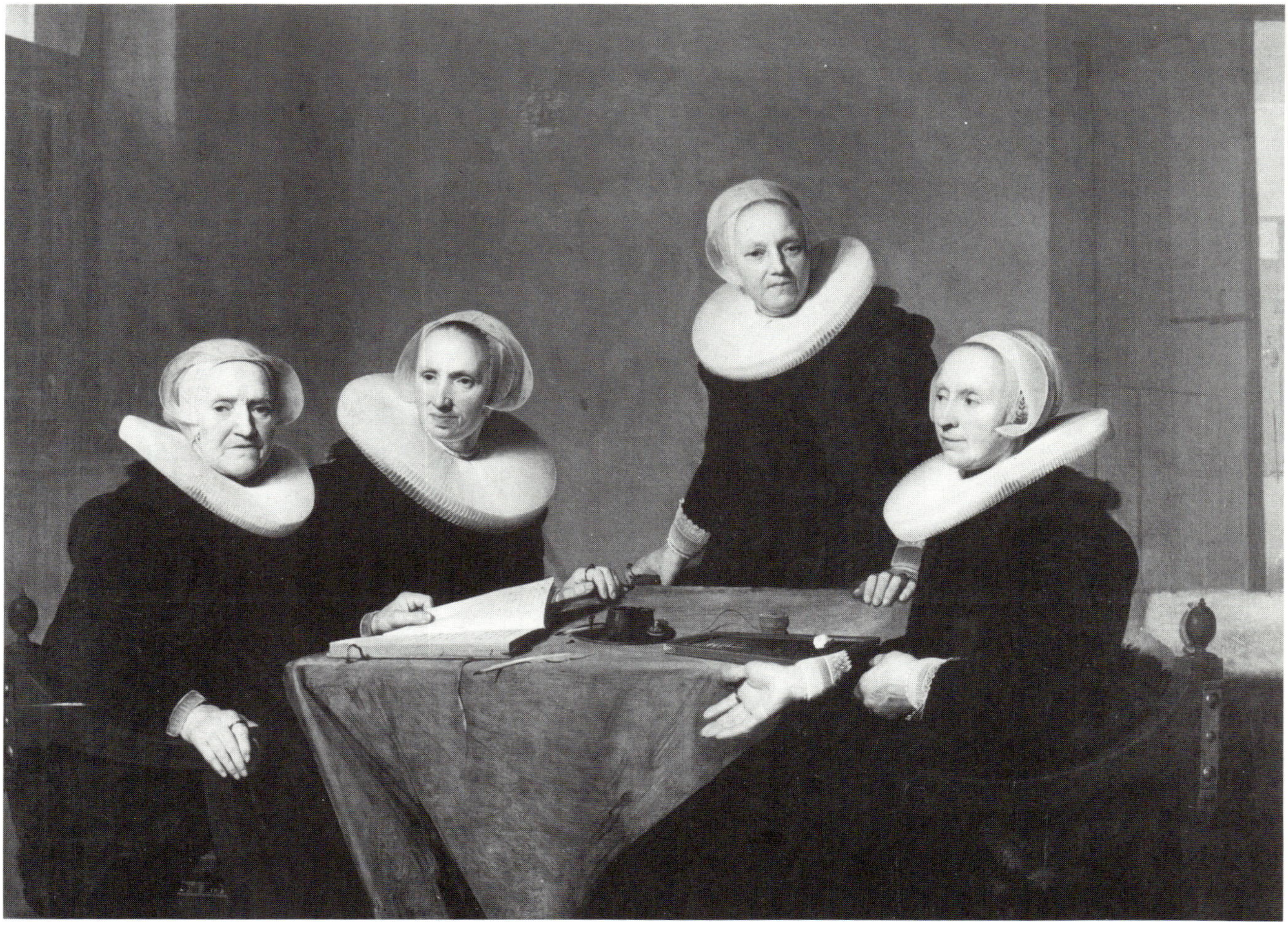

a

eration for the regents and regentesses of the St. Elisabeth's Hospital, but the two group portraits were in fact destined for two different rooms in the hospital.

In the seventeenth century, councils of regents administered all sorts of institutions for needy citizens, the sick, orphans and old people. In Haarlem, for example, there were the St. Elisabeth's Hospital, the Leprosarium, the orphanage (ill. b), the Old Men's Alms House and 'hofjes' for old women. There was also a Workhouse where beggars, idlers and other 'undesirables' were put to work (see p. 9, ill. a).

On 31 March 1642, Hals's wife Lysbeth submitted a request to the town council that their daughter Sara be sent to the Workhouse 'in hope of betterment', evidently because of her less than uplifting life-style. The burgomasters replied that Frans Hals should make further arrangements with the regents of the Workhouse, preparatory to taking the girl into custody. In May of the same year, Sara gave birth to an illegitimate child; she asserted that the father was Abraham Potterloo, but admitted having had relations with other men as well. Several years later Sara married Sieuwert Eebes from Friesland.

In the same year as Sara, Frans Hals's feeble-minded son Pieter was placed in the Workhouse, 'in a separate place outside the community of men', on order to 'labour if capable of such'. At that time the Leprosarium, the Schael (the poor relief) and the St. Elisabeth's Hospital already provided his keep for five years. These institutions continued to contribute to his livelihood for a long time; in the hospital's books the sum of 52 guilders and ten stuivers paid out semi-annually was last recorded in 1667.

The two regents portraits for the St. Elisabeth's Hospital were not lent to the city of Haarlem at the same time. In 1862 the city authorities found Hals's *Regents* indispensable for the projected museum, as they would provide a stately counterweight to the militiamen 'in their colourful costumes'. Considerable pressure was applied and at last the regents of the St. Elisabeth's Hospital consented to lend the coveted Hals to the city. Verspronck's *Lady-Regentesses* was apparently less important to the museum; it was not acquired until 1928.

In 1913 the Stedelijk Museum, henceforth called the Frans Halsmuseum, was housed in the former Old Men's Alms House. Two years before his death, Frans Hals portrayed both the regents and regentesses of this institution (plate 34 and 38). The two group portraits now hang in their original surroundings, albeit in a newly built wing.

a. Johannes Cornelisz. Verspronck (1606/09-1662), *Lady-Regentesses of the St. Elisabeth's Hospital*, 1641. Haarlem, Frans Halsmuseum (in loan from the trustees of the St. Elisabeth's Hospital).
b. Jan de Bray (ca. 1627-1697), *Regents of the Orphanage*, 1663. Haarlem, Frans Halsmuseum. The influence of Frans Hals can also be seen in the work of Jan de Bray.
c. Rembrandt (1606-1669), *'De Staalmeesters': the wardens of the Amsterdam drapers' guild*, 1661/62. Rembrandt's celebrated regents portrait is similar in composition and the fall of light to Hals's *Regents of the St. Elisabeth's Hospital*. Whether or not there was a direct influence can not be ascertained.

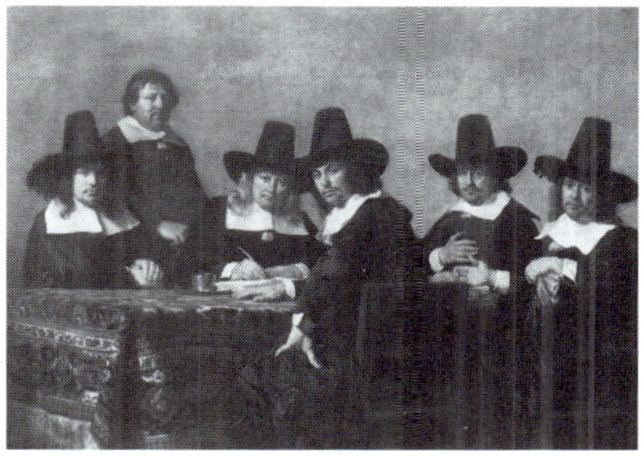

b

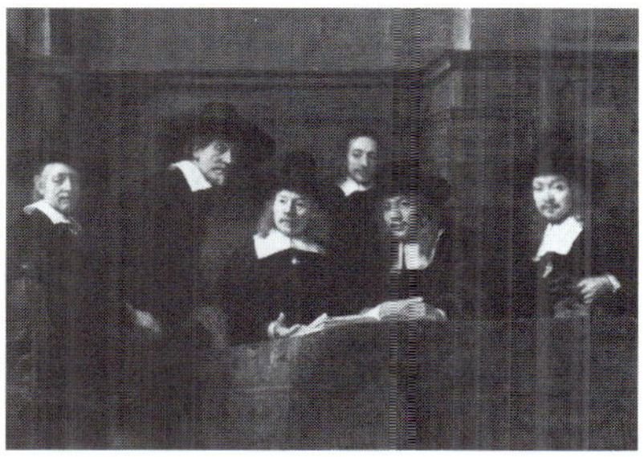

c

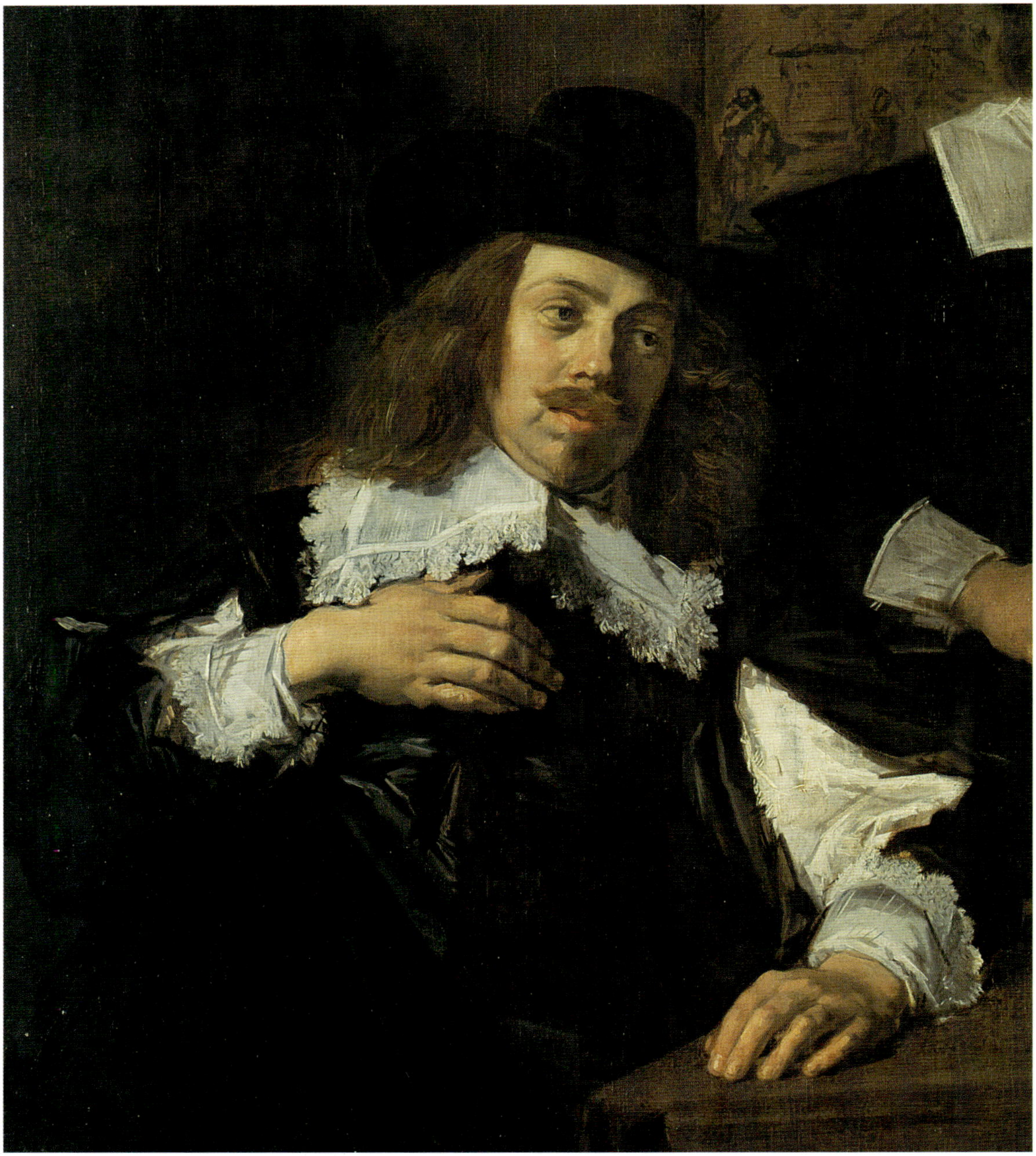

28a

Plate 28a. *Regents of the St. Elisabeth's Hospital*, ca. 1640. Detail.

Plate 29. *Portrait of Nicolaes Tulp.* Oval panel, 74.5 x 60.8 cm. Signed on back 'A 16(4)4/den 12 august', Amsterdam, Collectie Six. This man may be the Amsterdam doctor Nicolaes Tulp (1593-1644). The portrait bears a similarity to the portait of Tulp in Rembrandt's *Anatomy lesson* (p. 52, ill. a) and a painting by Frans Hals is listed in an old inventory of the Tulp family's possessions. The year given on the back of the painting has been changed from 1634 to 1644; the portrait was probably painted over ten years later. X-rays show that initially the hat was missing and the collar was larger. The panel was recently restored.

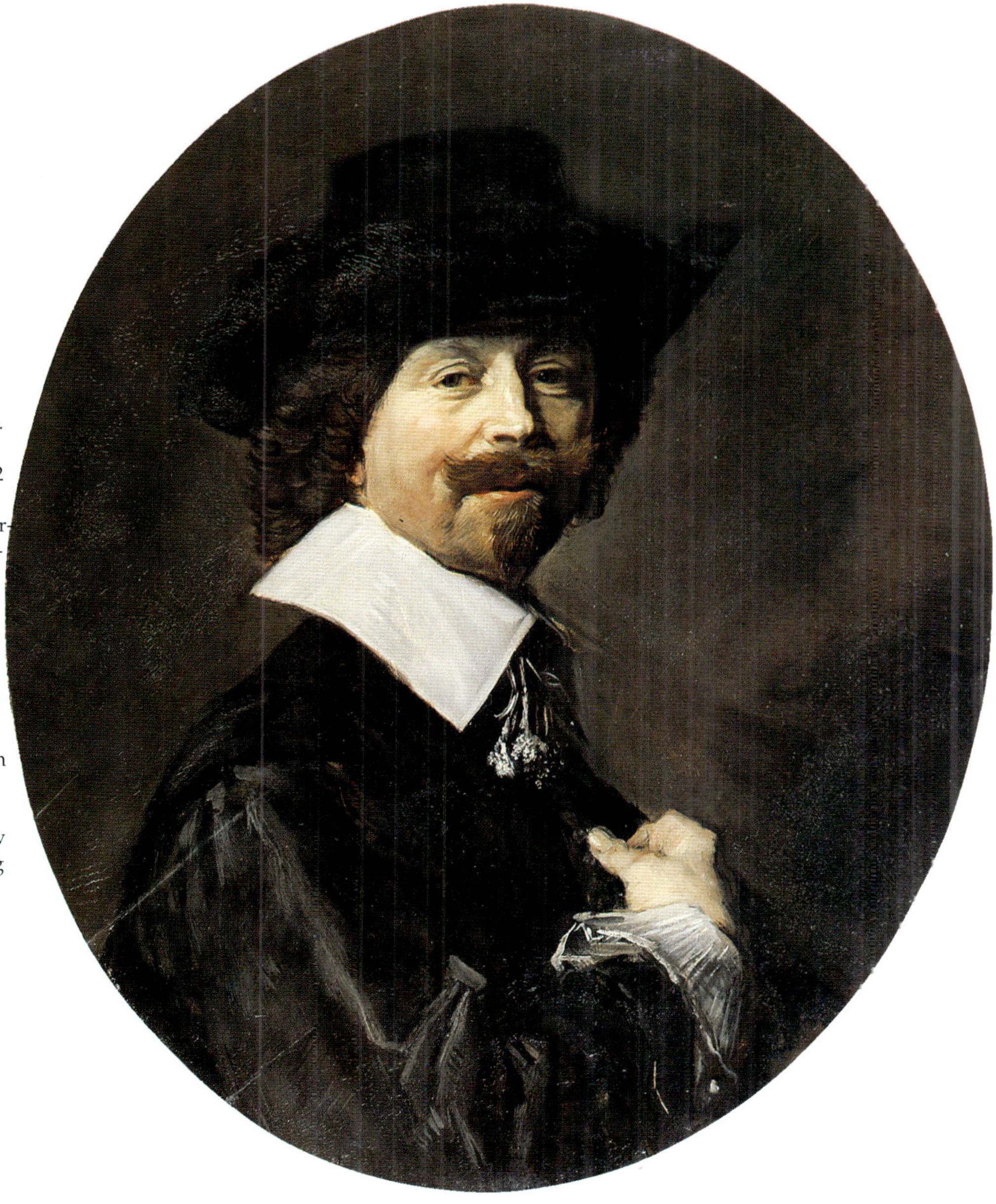

29

# 1645-1655

a. Anthonie van Dyck (1599-1641), *The painter Quintyn Simons,* ca. 1634. The Hague, Mauritshuis.
b. *Theodorus Schrevelius*, 1617. Dusseldorf, Kunstmuseum (loan).
c. *René Descartes,* ca. 1648. Copenhagen, Statens Museum for Kunst. There are several versions of this portrait, the Copenhagen panel generally thought to be the original. Damages, retouching and small size (19 x 14 cm) indicate substantial past restoration, hence the present dimensions.
d. *Adriaen van Ostade,* ca. 1650. Washington, National Gallery of Art.
e. *Vincent van der Vinne,* ca. 1658. Toronto, The Art Gallery of Ontario.
f. *Frans Post,* ca. 1655. Evanston, Mrs. David Corbett.

Dutch portraits from the beginning of the seventeenth century are characterized by a sober, realistic reproduction of the subject. After 1630 portrait painting in the Republic took on an increasingly international style whose main features were the idealization of the person portrayed and an elegant composition. Pieter Paul Rubens and Anthonie van Dyck in particular contributed to the development of this style of portraiture in Holland (ill. a). Both worked at various European courts where this type of portrait was favoured. Van Dyck painted for the English court along with several other Dutch painters who were influenced by him. They brought the international style back to the Netherlands where it became very popular in the 1640s.

Portraits by Frans Hals from this period show that he adapted to some extent to the new taste; by painting with small brush strokes he achieved more detailed representations than in some of his portraits from the preceding decade. But after 1645 the number of commissions Hals received dropped off dramatically, if his surviving work is any indication. Apparently other painters were better equipped to satisfy the wishes of their 'customer'. Despite the decline in commissions, Hals's style acquired high praise. In his *Harlemias* of 1648, the Haarlem historian Theodorus Schrevelius (ill. b) wrote:

> *'About the brothers Frans and Dirck Hals / I can not be silent / of whom the first by his unique manner of painting / for in his paintings / there is such force and life / that he seems to challenge nature herself with his brush./ This is seen in all his portraits, unbelievable many / which are painted in such a way / that they seem to breath and live.'*

Schrevelius's words of praise indicate that the lifelike quality of Frans Hals's portraits was greatly admired while he was still active.

In the late 1640s the colours of Hals's palette became more austere. Backgrounds in his portraits are darker - gold-brown or olive-green - and black dominates in the clothing of the subjects themselves. A number of Hals's most striking works date from this period: the portrait of the French philosopher René Descartes (ill. c), his

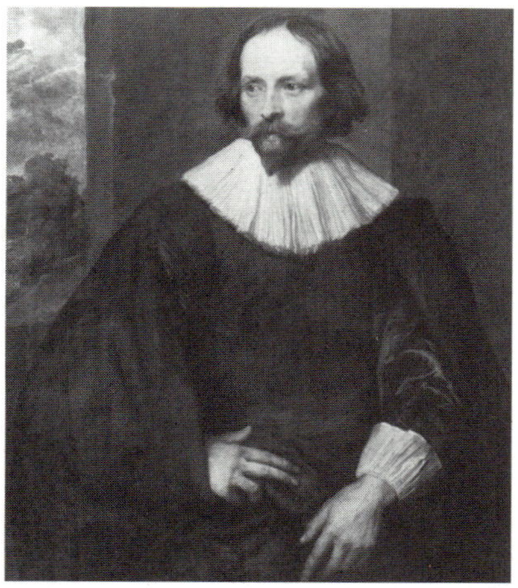

a

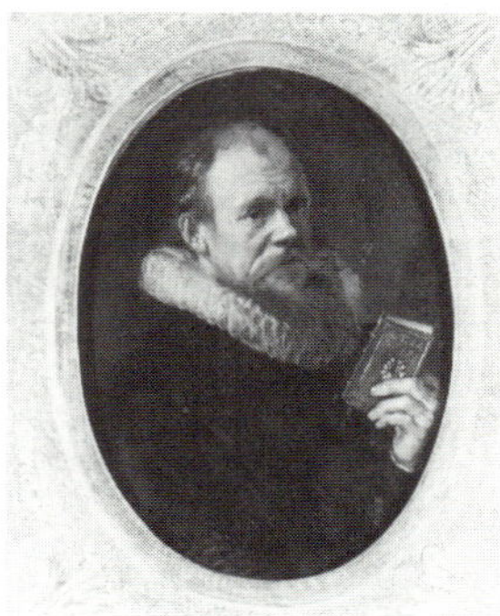

b

most famous model, and the impressive pair of portraits of Stephanus Geraerdts and Isabella Coymans, which figure among the high points of the art of portraiture (plate 32 and 33). A remarkable number of Hals's fellow artists posed for him. The subdued - but relaxed - models include his former pupils Adriaen van Ostade and Vincent van der Vinne, as well as the landscape painter Frans Post (ill.d, e, f) and possibly Jan Asselyn. Portraits of Thomas Wyck and Jacob van Campen survive in copies and an inventory shows that Frans Hals also painted portraits of Jan Miense Molenaer and Judith Leyster (see p. 37, ill. b). In about 1650 the artist must have painted a self-portrait which has unfortunately been lost, although many copies survive (see p. 93, ill. c).

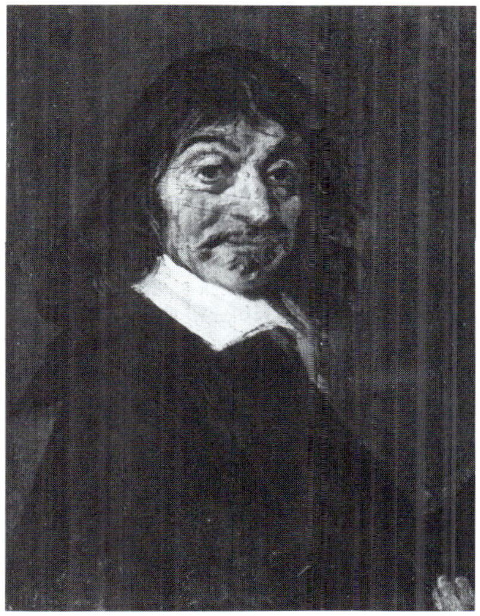

c

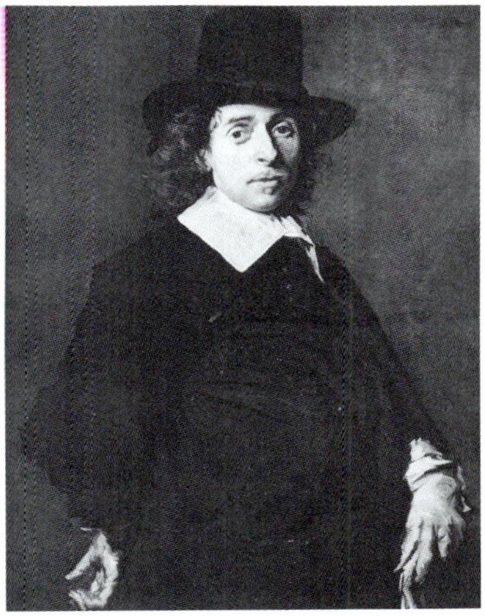

d

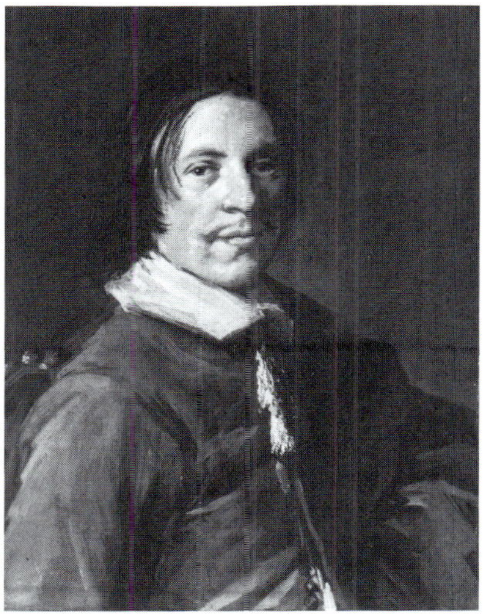

e

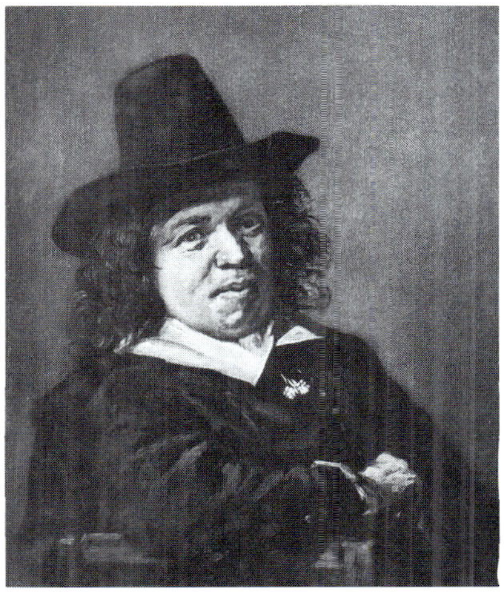

f

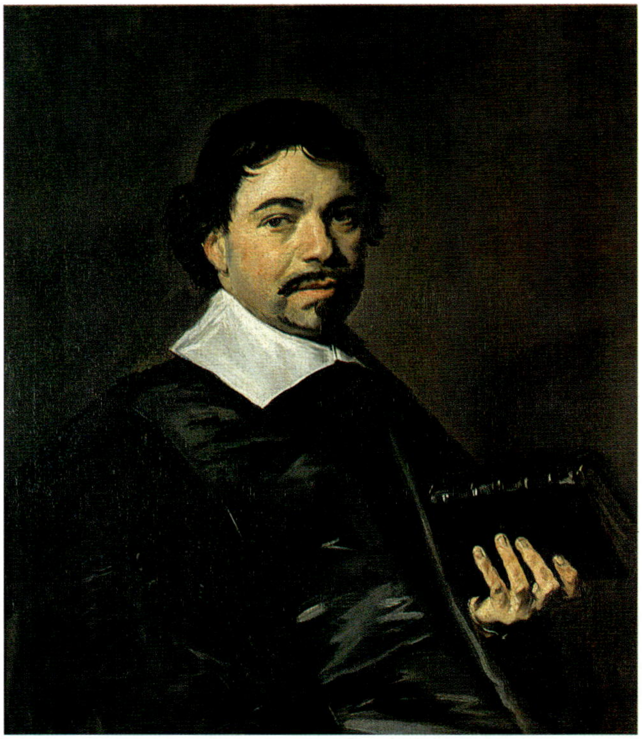

30

Plate 30. *Johannes Hoornbeeck.* Canvas, 79.5 x 68 cm. Inscribed below right 'AET.SVAE/27./1645'. Brussels, Koninklijke Musea voor Schone Kunsten.
This man was identified from an engraving of the portrait. Johannes Hoornbeeck (1617-1666) was a theologian and preacher from Haarlem and taught at the universities of Utrecht and Leiden. The book in his hand is probably a Bible.

31

Plate 31. *Nicolaes Stenius.* Canvas, 100 x 75.5 cm. Inscribed above left 'AETA SVAE 45/AN° 1650' and signed with the monogram 'FH'. Utrecht, Rijksmuseum Het Catharijneconvent.
Nicolaes Stenius was a Roman Catholic priest at Akersloot. At the end of the last century his portrait was discovered in the attic of the parish church in that town. An intensive restoration was necessary to make it presentable. The portrait has also been attributed to Jan Hals, Frans's son (see pp. 64-65).

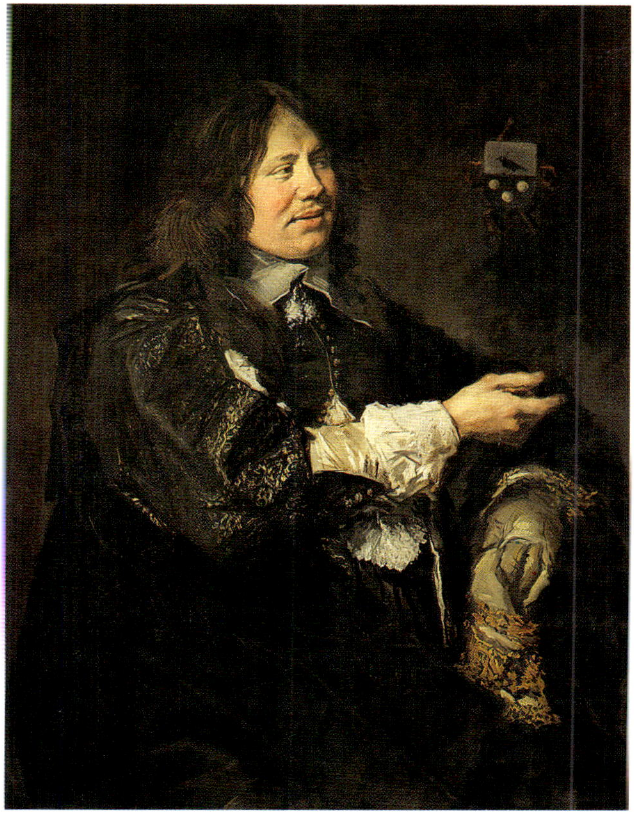

32

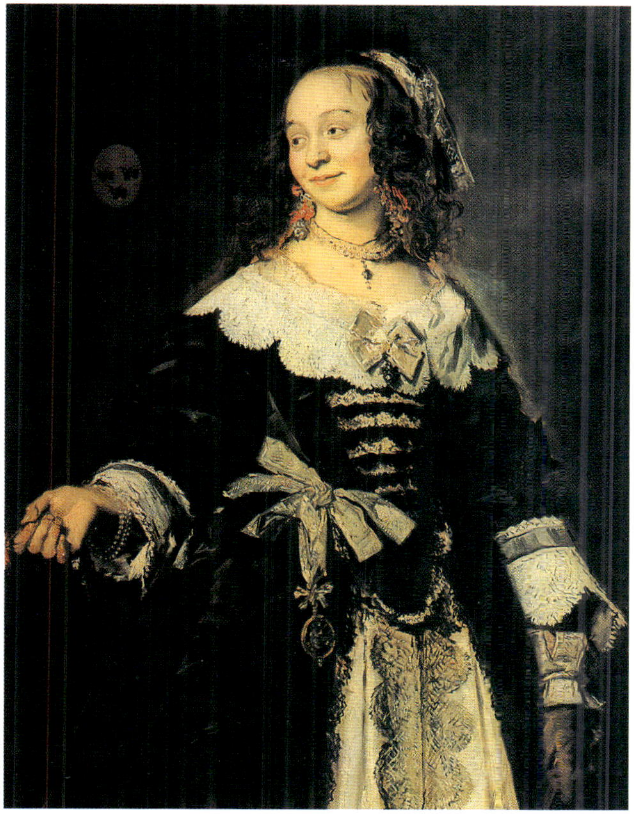

33

Plate 32. *Stephanus Geraerdts,* ca. 1650. Canvas, 115.4 x 87.5 cm. Antwerp, Koninklijk Museum voor Schone Kunsten.

Plate 33. *Isabella Coymans,* ca. 1650. Canvas, 116 x 86 cm. Private collection.

The portraits of Stephanus Geraerdts and Isabella Coymans are the saddest example of separated pendants in Hals's *oeuvre*. Their graceful pose - Stephanus is stretching out his hand towards a rose that Isabella holds out to him - forms a unique composition, part of it made up by the space between the paintings. However, this Baroque effect can be experienced only when both canvases are viewed together. Stephanus Geraerdts († 1671) was an alderman and member of the town council in Haarlem. He married Isabella Coymans († 1689) in 1644. She came from an Amsterdam banker's family. Her parents had their portraits commissioned from Hals in 1644. The rose in her hand symbolizes the transitory nature of earthly love.

## The portrait in the seventeenth century

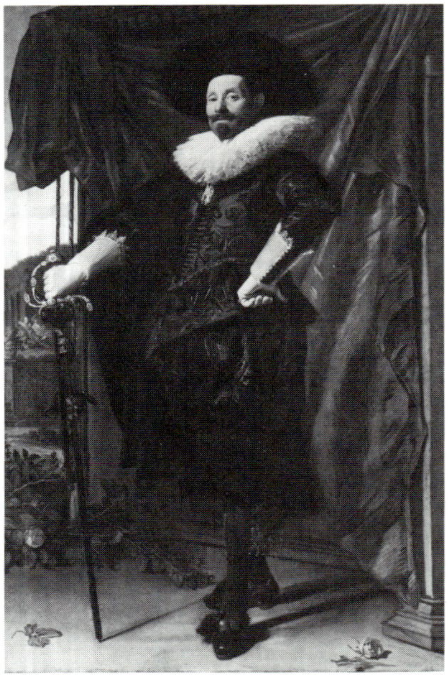

a

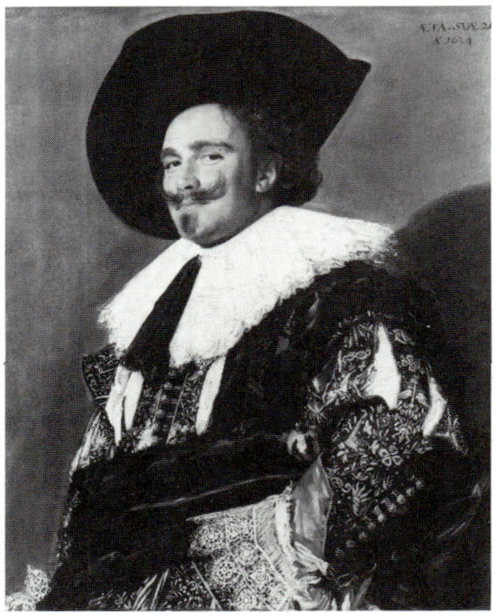

b

Unlike family photographs today, seventeenth-century portraits rarely show people smiling. A successful citizen behaved with dignity, and even in a painting felt obligated to obey the principles of decorum prescribed by his or her social class. Needless to say, being immortalized in a portrait was not something everyone could afford. Only rich citizens, the nobility and the clergy had sufficient funds at their disposal. Portraits were commissioned to commemorate special occasions, such as serving in a militia, sitting on a regents' council or getting married. A frequent type of portraiture in the seventeenth century consist of portraits in pairs: two separate paintings of husband and wife. Traditionally, the man was pictured on the right, the woman on the left. In Jan Miense Molenaer's *Family making music,* such 'pendants' can be seen in a Dutch interior (p. 61, ill. f).

The genre was immensely popular. A portrait lent emphasis to one's status in life and could even raise it. The Haarlem merchant Willem van Heythuysen had himself portrayed by Frans Hals in about 1625 in a manner previously reserved for noblemen (ill. a). The other portrait of Van Heythuysen, painted by Hals more than ten years later, makes a much more informal impression (see pp. 94-95). Frans Hals always succeeded in giving his portraits an outspoken character. He frequently pictured his models smiling, most unusual for the time, as has been said. By departing from the current norm, Hals and his subjects slightly 'ruffled' the seventeenth-century viewer, who knew the social codes through and through. The ironic smile of the man renowned as *'The laughing cavalier'* shows that he is aware of the role he is playing; he boldly exhibits his richly worked sleeve with its symbols of gallantry (ill. b). The restless attitude of the Haarlem brewer Michiel de Wael, painted by Hals at least three times (ill. c), and the unconventional poses of Isaac Massa (see pp. 39-40) make it clear that they too took their portraits not that seriously.

A small portion of Hals's work consists of miniature portraits probably used as models for engravers, such as the portraits of Schrevelius (p. 72, ill. b), Ampzing (p. 25, ill. g), Massa (p. 40, ill. a and b) and Swalmius (plate 23). Thanks to engravings, a number of Hals's paintings can be identified; but at the same time they give rise to a painful awareness of how many originals by Hals have been lost!

Although there was an enormous demand for portraits in the seventeenth century, the genre was by no means considered worthy of the highest respect. At the beginning of the century Carel van Mander called it 'a side-road of Art' and exhorted painters to devote themselves primarily to subjects taken from history, mythology and the Bible. That there was little change in this feeling as the century wore on can be seen when the words praising Frans Hals by Samuel Ampzing and Theodorus Schrevelius (pp. 25 and 72) are taken in their full context: both writers pay more attention to Haarlem's history painters than to the portraitist Hals (ill. d). He was indeed highly valued by Ampzing and Schrevelius, both of whom he painted, but his inclusion in their histories of the town was due mainly to his virtuoso brushwork.

One wonders why Frans Hals painted no history pieces. There is no reason to believe that he could not have done if he so chose. Grouping people in a composition was never a problem for him and his portraits show his mastery at portraying the human figure in all kinds of attitudes and moods. The chief reason for Hals's absence in the genre of history painting was perhaps his lack of funds, something that got in his way more than once. Often Hals was obliged to come up with money quickly. History painting required profound study; portrait painting was more lucrative. Frans Hals was capable of delivering a portrait in a short time. The money he thus earned helped him out of need for the moment.

Frans Hals does not seem to have had much ambition to extend his clientele to other towns. In contrast to some of his fellow citizens, Hals preferred to stay in Haarlem in order to 'be at home and keep an eye on his people', as he wrote to the Amsterdam militia in 1636 (see pp. 52-53). He was kept busy enough caring for his wife, his many children and the pupils in his atelier. Things might have been very different for Frans Hals if he had given the militia its wish and gone to Amsterdam. But probably he had no choice...

a. *Willem van Heythuysen*, ca. 1625. München, Alte Pinakothek.
b. *'The laughing cavalier'*, 1624. London, Wallace Collection.
c. *Michiel de Wael*, ca. 1735. Cincinnati, Taft Museum. See also plate 14 and 21.
d. Pieter Fransz. de Grebber (ca. 1600-1653?), *Emperor Frederik presenting the sword for the Haarlem coat of arms*, 1630. Haarlem, Town Hall.
'Pieter de Grebber is both gifted in invention and adept at painting / that he deserves to be set among the best Painters of our century', wrote Schrevelius about this history painter from Haarlem. He prizes not only De Grebber's technique but also his inventiveness, a fitting judgment for a painter who was successful in depicting subjects from the Bible, from mythology, - or as here - from the town's history.

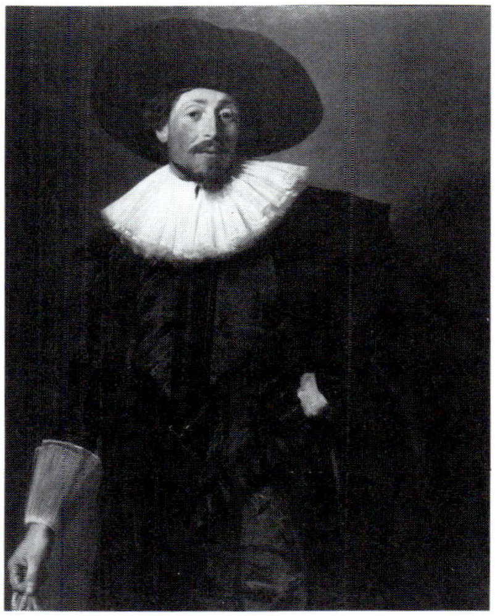

c

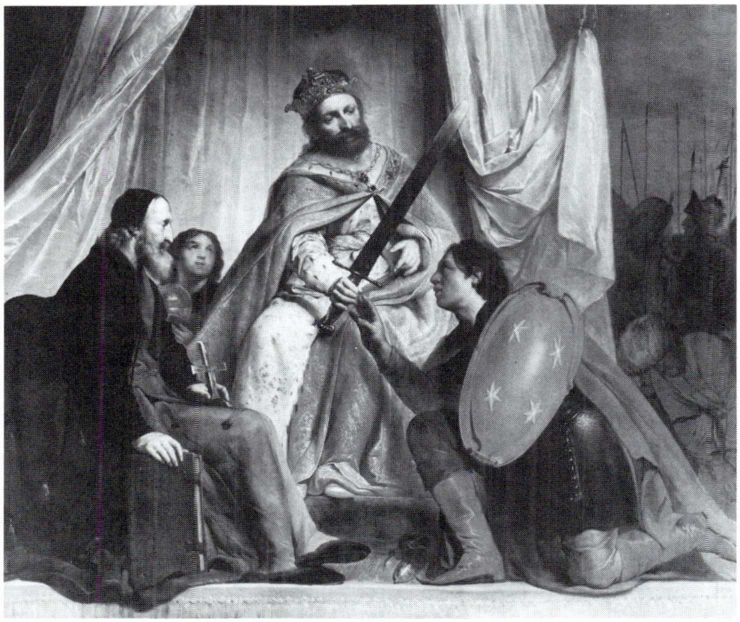

d

Plate 34. *Regents of the Old Men's Alms House,* ca. 1664. Canvas, 176.5 x 256 cm. Haarlem, Frans Halsmuseum.
The identities of the regents in this impressive group portrait are uncertain. A list of regents of the Old Men's Alms House gives the names of those who served between 1662 and 1665 and it is probably they who are pictured: Jonas de Jong, Mattheus Everswijn, Cornelis Westerloo, Daniel Deinoot and Johannes Walles. The second regent from the right possibly suffered from an eye disease, hence the dullness of his look. The man in the background is the housemaster who, together with the housemistress, was responsible for the daily running of the Old Men's Alms House.
In the course of the centuries, the paint has probably darkened considerably. The original composition shows with more clarity in a water-colour by Wybrand Hendriks (p. 84, ill. a).

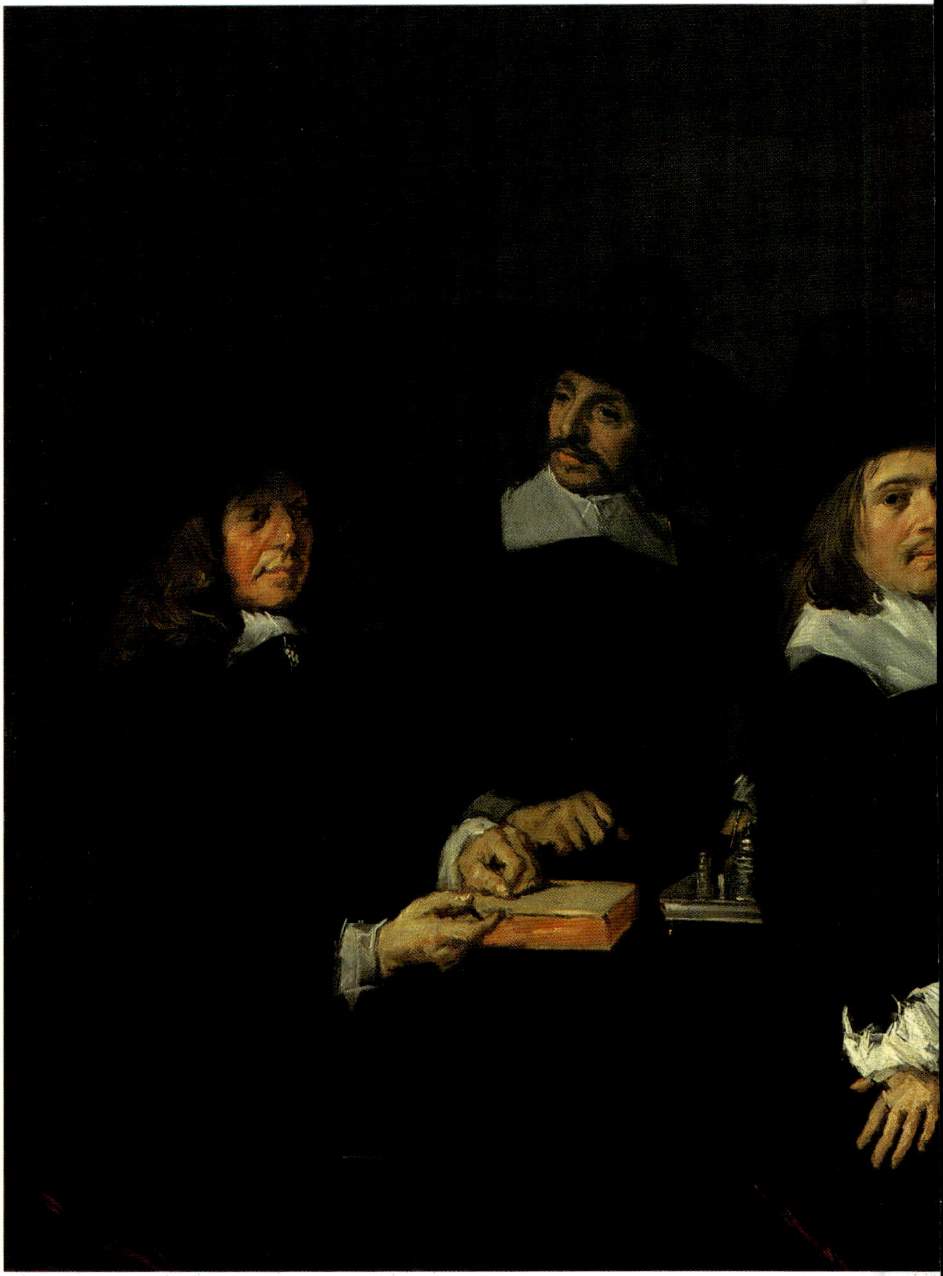

34

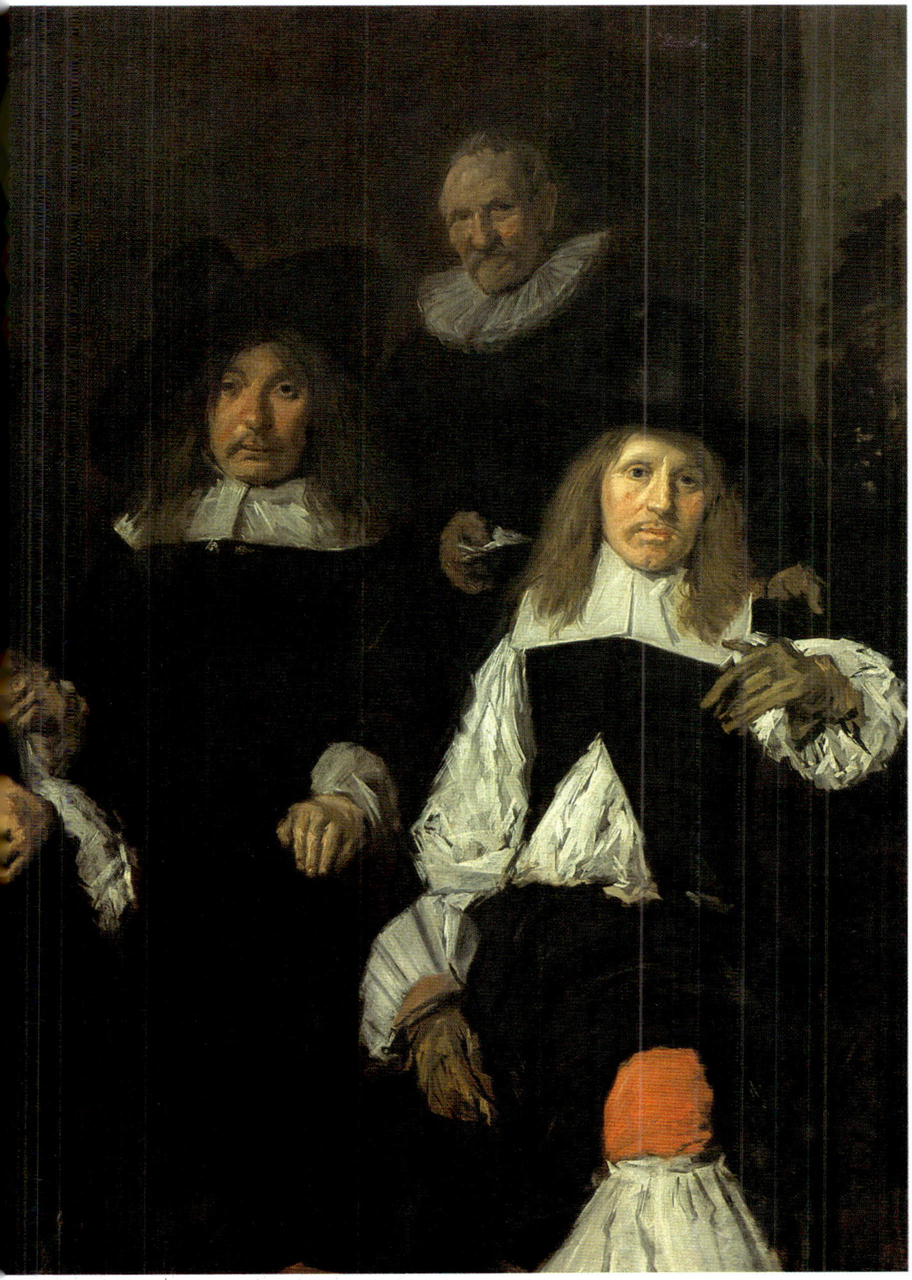

# 1655-1666

a. *Portrait of a man*, ca. 1664. Cassel, Hessisches Landesmuseum.
b. Cornelis van Noorde (1731-1795), *Apotheosis of Frans Hals*, 1754. Water colour. Haarlem, Gemeente-archief.

Creditors continued to haunt Frans Hals. Not only the baker, the butcher, the shoemaker and the landlord, but also the innkeeper and the supplier of painter's canvas. They got little satisfaction for their pains. Although Hals had earlier been able to pay off his debts with the income from his work, now the number of commissions was on the decline and he was less able to do so. In 1654 the baker Jan Ykessz., to whom Frans Hals owed 200 guilders for bread and a loan of money, seized three beds, a chest, a table and five paintings, including one by Carel van Mander. Ykessz. agreed to let Hals keep the items in his house, providing he could lay claim to them whenever he saw fit. Frans Hals's last recorded debt dates from December 1661: for paintings purchased, an amount remained unpaid of 21 guilders and 16 stuivers. Interestingly enough, Hals's first recorded debt, in 1616, was also for the purchase of paintings. A first-rate art dealer! In 1661 the St. Lucas Guild exempted Frans Hals from the payment of his annual membership fees by reason of his advancing age. For his younger colleagues the painter must have been something of a living legend, one of the few in their circle who had personally known Hendrick Goltzius, Cornelis van Haarlem and Carel van Mander. According to the French nobleman Balthasar de Monconys, who travelled through the Low Countries and visited Haarlem in 1663, Frans Hals was 'rightfully admired' by the greatest painters of his time.

Late works by Frans Hals show an extremely sketchy style: with direct, almost unmixed touches of paint the old painter captured the essence of his models (ill. a). Portraits are now reduced to an assemblage of strokes and patches determined by light and shade. Cornelis de Bie probably had this later work in mind when in his *Gulden Cabinet van de Edele Vrij Schilder Const* of 1661 he wrote that Frans Hals:

> *'is still alive and residing in Haarlem, who miraculously excellent at painting portraits very rough and bold / nimbly brushed and well done / pleasant and tasteful to see from afar as nothing of life appears to be absent.'*

De Bie expresses his admiration for Hals's skill and shows an appreciation for his manner of painting. His claim that the portraits are 'pleasant and tasteful' when viewed at a certain distance sounds strikingly modern!

Not everyone was taken with Hals's imprecise style. In a satirical poem written in 1660, the Amsterdam poet Herman Frederik Waterloos ridicules Hals's portrait of Herman Langelius (plate 35):

> *'Old Hals, why do you try to paint Langelius?*
> *Your eyes are too weak for his learned vision;*
> *Your stiff hand too rude and lacking art*
> *To express the superhuman and matchless*
> *understanding of this man and teacher*
> *Haarlem may boast of your art and early masterpieces,*
> *Our Amsterdam will now witness with me that*
> *You have not half captured the essence of this light.'*

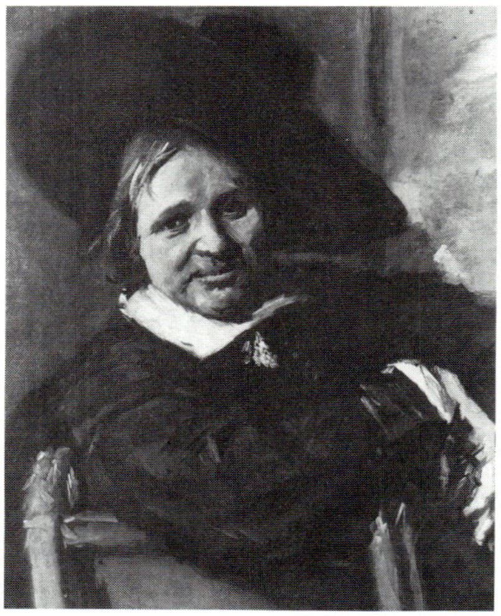

a

The verse suggests that Waterloos's negative feeling had more to do with the fact that an Amsterdam clergyman was portrayed by a Haarlem painter than with Hals's skill. His preconceived opinion would have been the same in any event. A very different point of view is shown in a poem from 1680 by Arnold Moonen in praise of the preacher Jan Ruyll and his untraceable portrait by Frans Hals. But Ruyll was from Haarlem.

*'This is the Portrait of your faithful Ruyll*
*O Haarlem, your hero, your churchpillar and column*
*Of temple peace, as naturally as if he lived,*
*Thanks to Hals, whose brush moved so inspired*
*High and low. But if the man's spirit has ever charmed you,*
*Retain the Lessons you hear from his golden mouth.'*

On 9 September 1662, Frans Hals asked for financial aid from the burgomasters of Haarlem. The request was granted. Hals was given 50 guilders straightaway and from 1 October, 150 guilders a year, divided into four payments. In the winter of 1664 he received three loads of peat. His financial support was increased to 200 guilders annually, '50 guilders to come from the hands of the treasurers every fourth part of the Year for as long as he shall live, as from the first of October 1663'.

In January 1665, suddenly Frans Hals was in possession of a considerable sum of money. He stood security for a debt made by his son-in-law Hendrick Hulst in the amount of 458 guilders and 11 stuivers. Probably the money came from Hals's last large commission: the *Regents* and *Lady-Regentesses of the Old Men's Alms House at Haarlem* (plate 34 and 38). Legend has it that Hals himself spent his last years in this hostel. This persistent misconception probably grew out of the establishment of the Frans Halsmuseum in the former Old Men's Alms House in 1913. In any case, the two canvases can be considered the apotheosis of Hals's art. There was much more to these works than painting colleagues or friends in relaxed and amused attitudes; they represented an official commission, portraying a council of regents. It is not known why the regents approached Hals. Perhaps out of respect for the old painter or because he was less expensive than the younger generation of artists. Much has been written about Hals's merciless vision of the governing councils. Admittedly the impressive canvases invite such an interpretation. However, each viewer must decide for himself if the master truly captured the character of his subjects rather than simply reproducing their portraits faithfully.

Frans Hals died on 29 August 1666, more than eighty years old. He was buried three days later in a simple grave at St. Bavo. His wife Lysbeth survived him for many years. 'Having reached an advanced age and having fallen into poverty', from 1675 onwards she was given 14 stuivers a week by the poor relief.

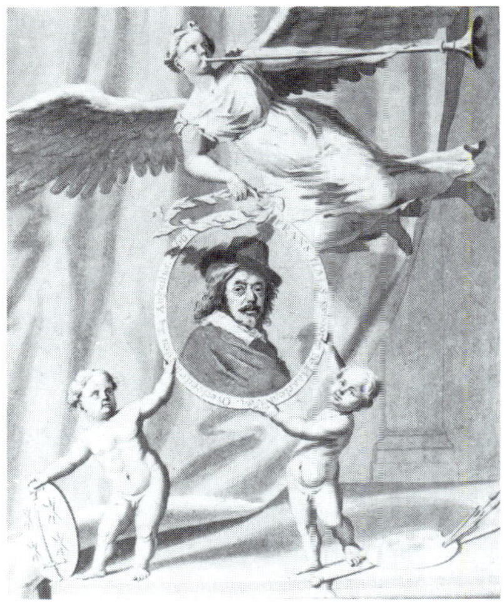

b

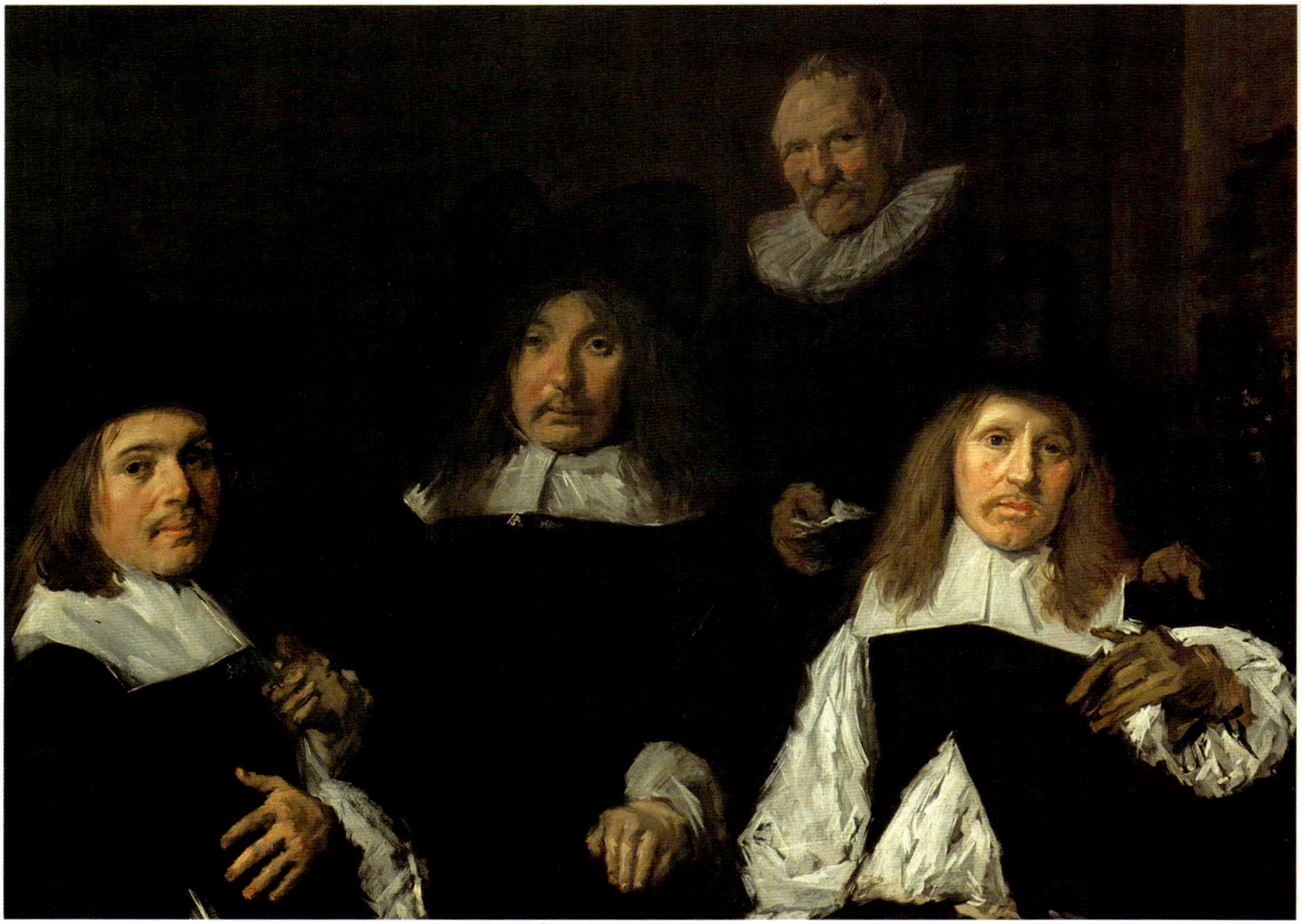

34a

Plate 34a. *The Regents of the Old Men's Alms House,* ca. 1664. Detail.

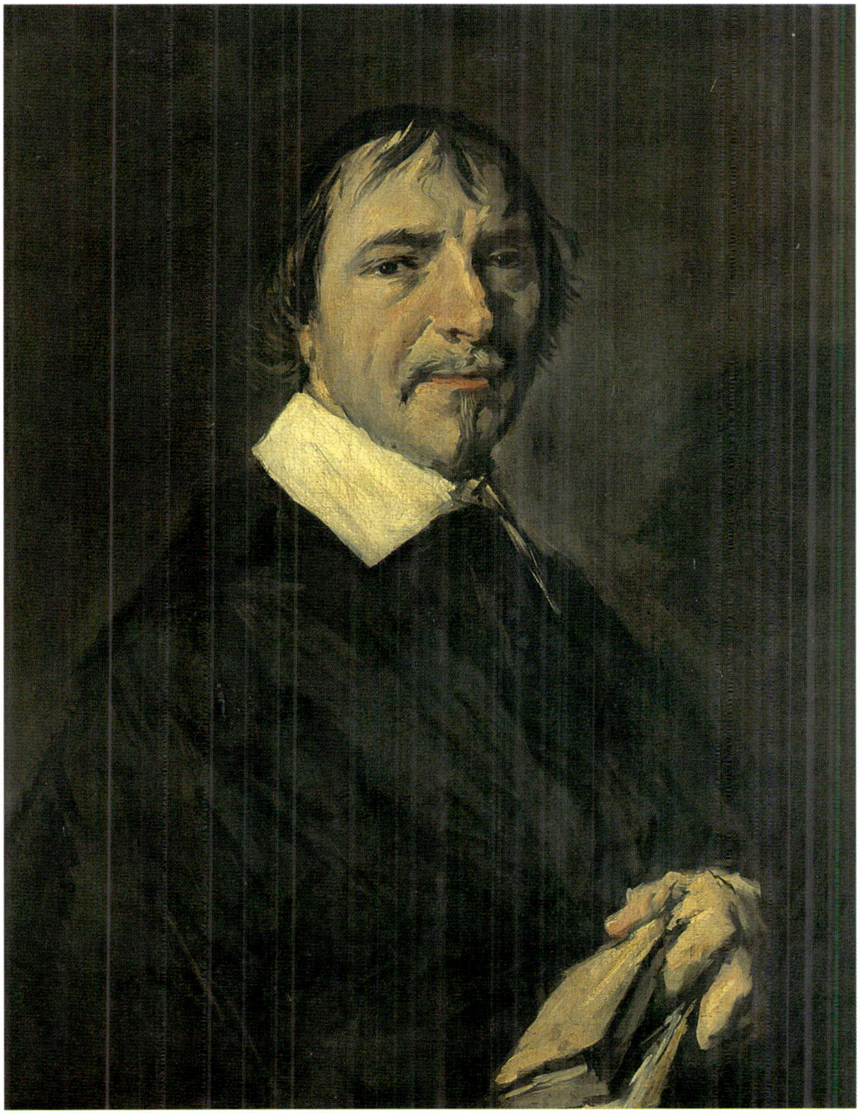

35

Plate 35. *Herman Langelius,* ca. 1659. Canvas, 76 x 63 cm. Signed right with the monogram 'FH'. Amiens, Musée de Picardie.
Herman Langelius (1614-1666) was an Amsterdam preacher. His portrait was satirized by the poet Herman Frederik Waterloos in 1660 (see p. 80) and so must have been painted by Frans Hals before this year.

a. Wybrand Hendriks (1744-1831), *Regents of the Old Men's Alms House,* ca. 1800 (?). Haarlem, Teylers Museum. Copy after Frans Hals (plate 34).
b. Gustave Courbet (1819-1877), *Malle Babbe,* 1869. Hamburg, Kunsthalle. Copy after Frans Hals (p. 37, ill. e).

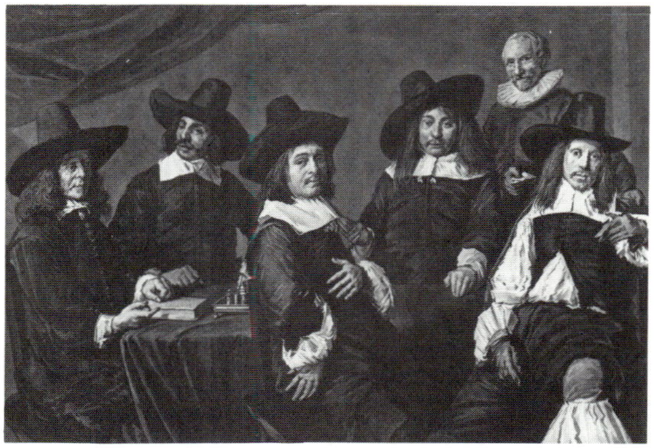

a

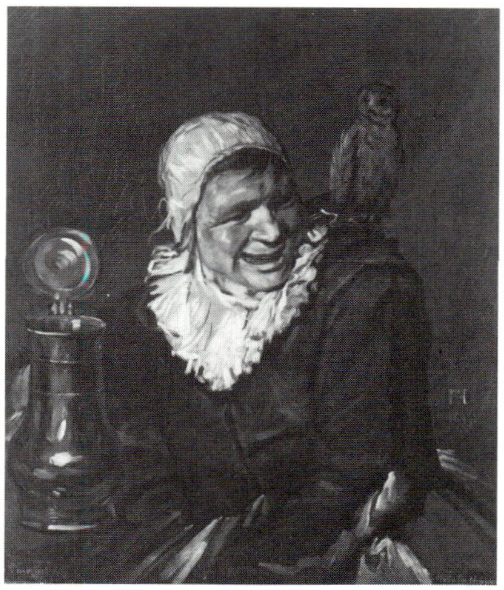

b

## The fame of Frans Hals

Frans Hals was by no means forgotten after his death. In a New Year's greeting, spoken before the St. Lucas Guild on 1 January 1686, Raphel Adamsz. van Hessel spoke of him in an enumeration of Haarlem's great painters:

*'It was Love for Art that moved Vermander,*
*And brought him from Flanders to Haarlem:*
*Where with the brush he flourished twenty years:*
*He passed his skill to Frans Hals, the proud Prince Apelles.*
*But when this Phoenix outgrew him in Glory,*
*He left the town and went to Amsterdam.'*

Throughout the eighteenth century there were artists who admired Hals's work, imitated his style and copied his paintings. Wybrand Hendricks, for example, painted several water-colours after the militia portraits (see p. 108) and the last regents portrait (ill. a). But in the matter of historiography, things were somewhat different.

In 1718 Arnold Houbraken published his collection of artists' biographies in *De Groote Schouburgh der Nederlandsche Konstschilders en Schilderessen.* Though this work is an important source of information about the history of art in the Netherlands in the seventeenth century, Houbraken appears to have often got things wrong, and Frans Hals was one of his 'victims'. He expresses admiration for Hals's style of painting, but sketches his life as that of a drinker for whom art took second place. There is, however, no documentary evidence to support Houbraken's allegations of Hals's drunkenness and except for the Amsterdam affair (pp. 52-53), Frans Hals was never charged with neglect of his work. Houbraken's fictions probably have their roots in the preconceptions of the period in regard to painting: portraiture was still considered inferior to historical painting and only artists whose works included more than portraits could be counted among the great masters, such as Rubens, Van Dyck and to some extent Rembrandt. The era of great expansion in the Republic, both culturally and economically, was at an end and new impulses in painting came from France: a classicism, bound to strict rules and harkening back to the authority of the Italian Renaissance and its followers. Frans Hals was far from corresponding to the good taste of the enlightened art-lover. To the latter's refined imagination, Hals's unpolished style was almost certain proof that the painter usually stood at his easel in a state of intoxication.

Art criticism's negative image of Frans Hals survived for a long time. In 1774 Sir Joshua Reynolds praised Hals's virtuoso brushwork but at the same time expressed regret for the lack of finishing of his work:

*'If he had joined to this most difficult part of the art, a patience in finishing what he had so correctly planned, he might justly have claimed the place which Vandyck, all things considered, so justly holds as the first of portrait painters.'*

In about 1855 the tide turned for Frans Hals. At this time art history became a true science and the first attempts were made to catalogue the work of many artists. Particularly in the Netherlands, it was difficult to bring order to the artistic inheritance which had been so long neglected. Disconcerted, the French researcher Theophile Thoré noted in 1856:

*'Il n'y a point de catalogues, que notes insignifiantes, et pour tant de trésors! Ils ne connaissent point du tout eux-mêmes leurs maîtres, ni les oeuvres les plus célèbres de leurs maîtres.'*

It was Thoré who was first to place Frans Hals among the great masters. In enthusiastic articles he emphasized the importance of Frans Hals for the development of painting in the Netherlands. In line with Thoré's systematic approach, by researching records in Haarlem historians made an effort to erase all blame attaching to Hals's name. They discovered that he was a dean of the St. Lucas Guild and a member of the militia. In their enthusiasm, they even portrayed Frans Hals - erroneously - as having descended from a distinguished family! In 1862 the Municipal Museum opened its doors in the town hall in Haarlem. A central place was given to Frans Hals's group portraits, gathered from various public buildings in the town. Gradually there grew up again an appreciation of the rich past and an admiration of the nation's Golden Age. Admiration for Dutch painting also arose abroad. Every self-respecting museum in Europe began building a collection of Dutch masters and Frans Hals could not be omitted. At the same time his paintings found their way into the hands of many collectors who were willing to pay handsomely for them.

The rediscovery of Frans Hals is also connected with the rise of Realism, a cultural current which manifested itself from 1840 onwards, particularly in France. As its name implies, Realism centred on the visible world. The use of symbols, allegorical figures and exaggerated dramatic effects was felt to be fundamentally wrong. History painting fell from the pedestal it had occupied for centuries. Scenes of everyday life gained supremacy. In seventeenth-century Dutch art the Realists found a historical justification for their principles. Frans Hals's modern style was not lost upon them. The most important representative of Realism, Gustave Courbet, copied Frans Hals's *Malle Babbe*, after seeing it in an exhibition in Munich (ill. b). He called it one of the great masterworks in the history of art. Many painters followed his example, copying and imitating the work of Frans Hals - not always with the purest of motives.

In 1875 Eugène Fromentin visited the museum in Haarlem and became fascinated with Hals's paintings. In his famous book *Les Maîtres d'Autrefois* he advised his fellow-painters to learn from Hals's example. Two pioneers of modern painting, however, were ahead of Fromentin: Claude Monet saw Hals's group portraits during a trip through Holland in 1871 and a year later Edouard Manet visited the museum in Haarlem (ill. c).

In 1885 years of effort to establish a national art collection in the Netherlands resulted in the opening of the Rijksmuseum in Amsterdam. Among the first visitors was Vincent van Gogh (ill. d). In a letter to his brother Theo he exclaimed:

*'What a pleasure to see a Frans Hals, what a difference from the paintings - and there are so many of them - where everything is smoothed out in the same way.'*



c. Edouard Manet (1832-1883), *The plum*, 1877. Washington, National Gallery of Art.
d. Vincent van Gogh (1853-1890), *Skull with cigarette*, 1886. Amsterdam, Rijksmuseum Vincent van Gogh.

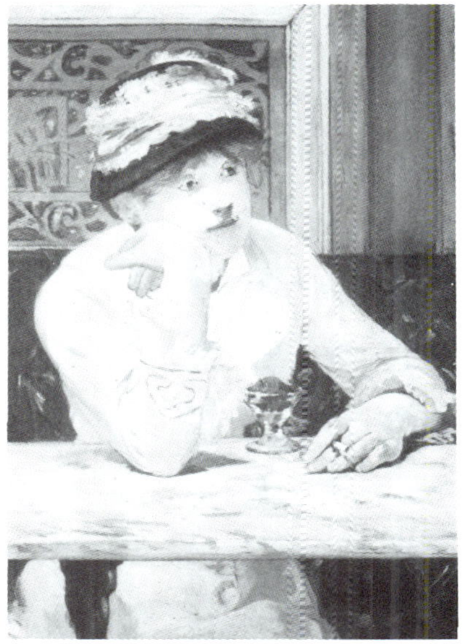

c

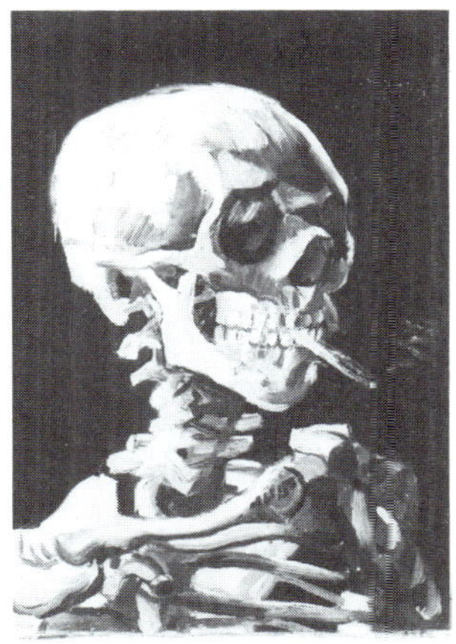

d

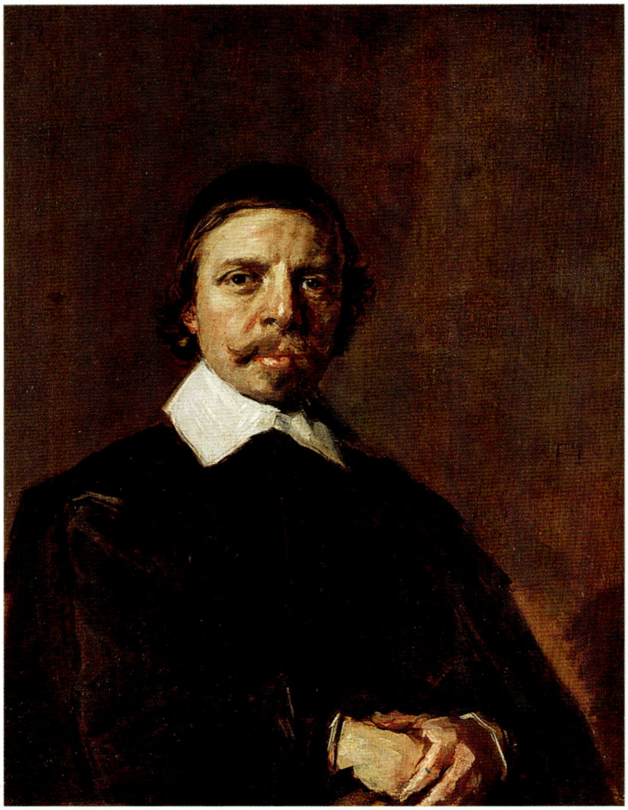

36

Plate 36. *Portrait of a man,* ca. 1656. Panel, 37 x 29.8 cm. Amsterdam, Rijksmuseum. In the past this portrait has been connected to the one of Jan Ruyll mentioned in the poem by Arnold Moonen (see p. 81), but it is impossible to establish if this is indeed the preacher Jan Ruyll.

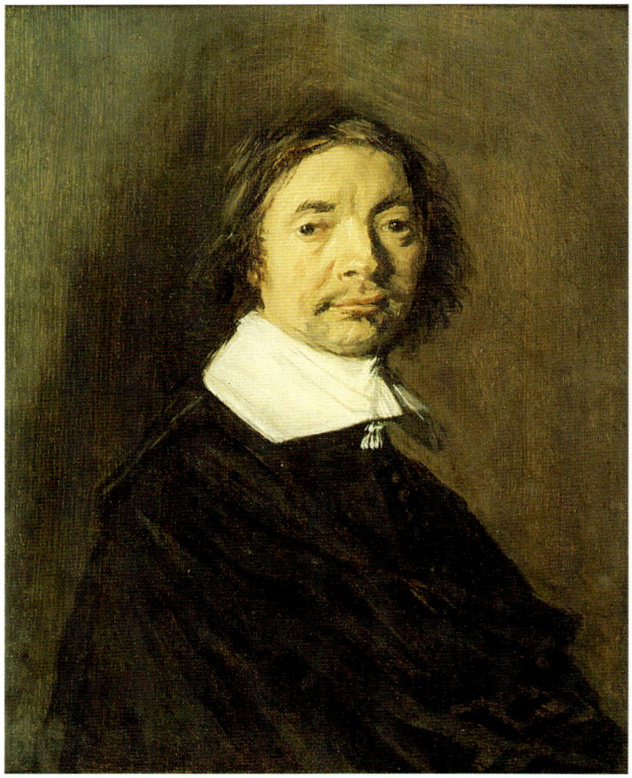

37

Plate 37. *Portrait of a man,* ca. 1660. Panel, 31.6 x 25.5 cm. The Hague, Mauritshuis. During the restoration of this panel at the beginning of the century, several original white paint specks were removed from the black clothes; they were felt to be disruptive!

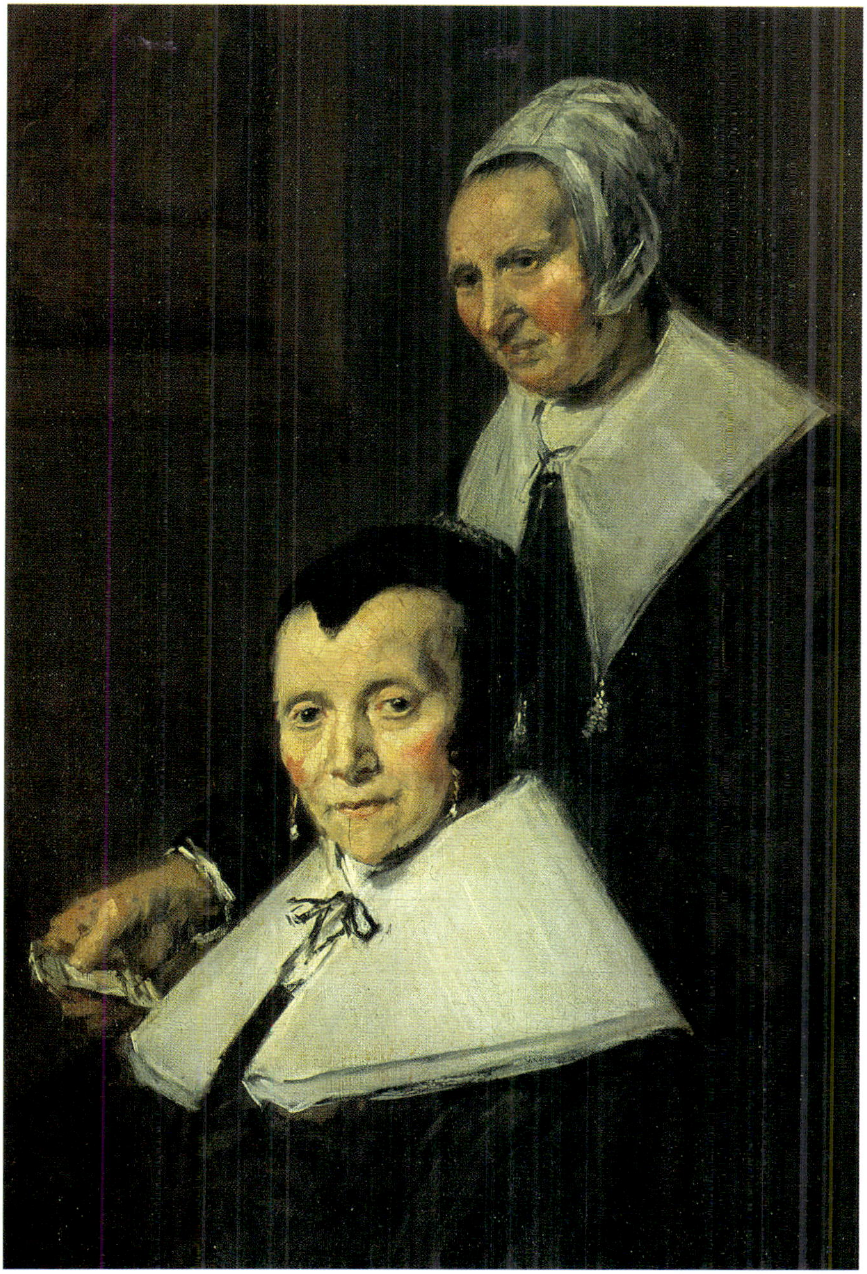

38a

Ill. 38a. *Lady-Regentesses of the Old Men's Alm House,* ca. 1664. Detail.

a. Pieter Paul Rubens (1577-1640), *The Way of the cross*, ca. 1635. Amsterdam, Rijksmuseum.
b. Titian (Tiziano Vecelli, ca. 1490-1576), *Self portrait*, 1562 (?). Berlin, Dahlem, Gemäldegalerie.

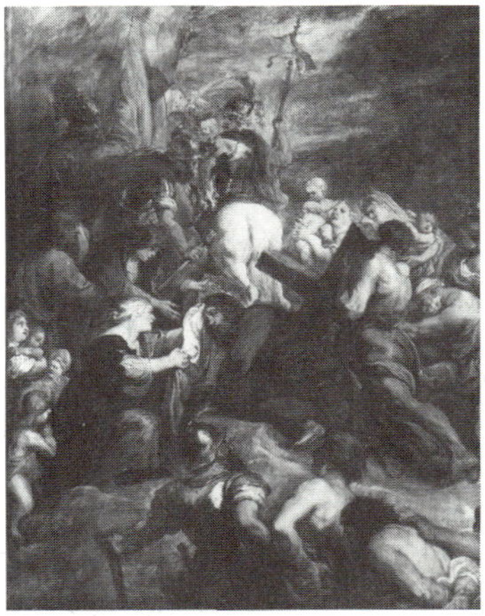

a

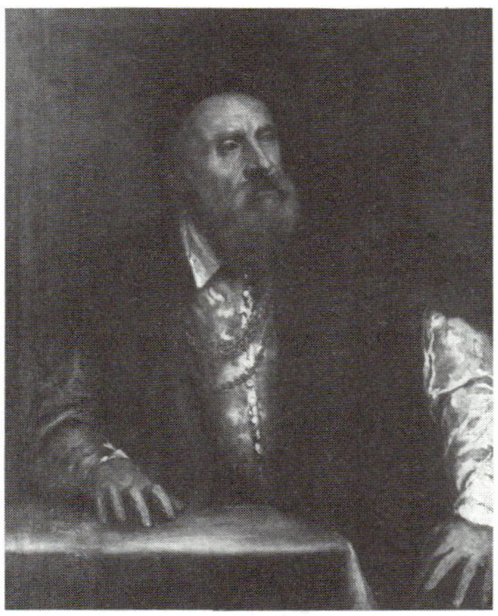

b

## 'Frans Hals est un moderne' *(L'Art Moderne 1883)*

'He led a merry life in his younger days,' wrote the German painter Matthias Scheits (1625/30-ca. 1700) about Frans Hals in his copy of Carel van Mander's *Schilder-boeck*. The discovery of this remark at the end of the last century contributed to the persistence of Hals's negative image as it had existed since Houbraken. However, the notation by Scheits, a pupil of Hals's pupil Philips Wouwerman, can just as well be taken as a positive comment - at third hand - about the youth of Frans Hals.

As long as no documents are found which shed more light on Hals's early life, it must be assumed that in about 1600 he was indeed a pupil of Carel van Mander. The years between 1603 and 1610 remain a mystery. Possibly Hals worked for his father during this time; his good eye for the texture of various kinds of cloth may have been acquired in his father's weaving-mill. Who taught Frans Hals his characteristic brushwork is a complete riddle. The work of the two foremost painters in Haarlem before 1610, Hendrick Goltzius and Cornelis van Haarlem, displays little of the unpolished style of Hals's work. Yet both may have contributed to the artistic development of Frans Hals; Cornelis, for example, in the practical area of the painter's trade and Goltzius, who took up painting late in life, in the area of studying from nature.

A painter who possibly had a direct influence on Hals's style was Pieter Paul Rubens, who had returned to Antwerp from Italy in 1608. His preliminary studies particularly show similarities with Hals's sketchy technique (ill. a). In 1616 Hals stayed in Antwerp where he may have met Rubens; a visit to the town of his birth may also have taken place earlier. Many members of Frans Hals's family lived in Antwerp. Rubens himself visited Haarlem in 1613, in search of an engraver. The contact between the two painters may have been more intensive than has previously been thought. The theory that Frans Hals perhaps spent several years away from Haarlem between 1603 and 1610 is supported by the fact of his late marriage, in about 1610, and the absence of any document whatsoever regarding him before his registration with the St. Lucas Guild in that same year.

The above speculations about Hals's youth do not alter our conception of Frans Hals as a prodigy, an extraordinary painter for his time, with a uniquely personal viewpoint. In his biography, Houbraken describes Frans Hals as the painter *par excellence*, someone who could capture with his brush anything he saw. Ironically, despite the dubious stories it contributed to the history of art, Houbraken's *Grote Schouburg*, is the only old source which makes mention of the painter's work methods:

> *'It is said that he was in the habit of setting down his Portraits*
> *thickly and softly fusing, bringing in it the brushstrokes afterwards,*
> *saying: Now the master's touch.'*

Research has shown that here Houbraken was right. Frans Hals quickly painted a portrait in its entirety, then added visible strokes in the wet paint, 'the master's touch'. Probably Hals worked directly on the canvas or panel, with little advance study and only a composition sketch as an aid. This is not to say that Frans Hals worked haphazardly; the poses of his models betray a thorough knowledge of the tradition of portrait painting.

The sixteenth-century Venetian painter Titian greatly influenced the art of portraiture. He developed compositional precedents that formed the basis for portrait painting in the following centuries. Frans Hals's work exhibits points of resemblance with Titian's portraits, not only in the matter of composition but also in style and the use of colour (ill. b). Titian worked in a similar, thickly painted style. His influence may have reached Hals through Rubens, who was a great admirer of Titian.

Frans Hals himself also brought innovations to the portrait genre. He painted people as though they were scarcely posed; the originality of the compositions, a simple gesture, the tilt of a head and above all the smiling faces give Hals's portraits their extraordinary lifelikeness (ill. c and d).

Frans Hals's subtle renewal of the art of the portrait was not lost on other painters. Yet it is not his contribution to the tradition which won him a prominent place in the history of art. This he owed to the storm of enthusiasm for his work in the last century. His striking, impressionistic style was 'recognized' and conformed perfectly with developments in painting at that time. It is by no means an exaggeration to say that Frans Hals was more important for the history of art in the nineteenth century than in his own.

At present there is a tendency not only to appreciate Hals's style of painting, but also his influence on seventeenth-century portrait art. However, what was true a century ago is true today: Frans Hals painted his portraits in a way which appeales strongly to the eye of modern man; capturing his subjects in natural attitudes, with spontaneous facial expressions, catching the moment as in a photograph. It is as though he viewed his contemporaries with the eyes of our time. This is the reason why Frans Hals's reproduction of people in the seventeenth century seems more faithful than any other.

c. *Boy with a flute (hearing)*, ca. 1627. Berlin-Dahlem, Gemäldegalerie.
d. *The Merchant Pieter van den Broecke*, ca. 1633. London, Kenwood House.

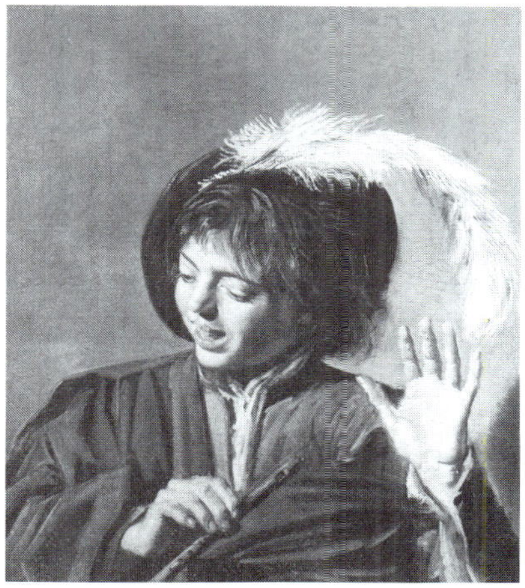

c

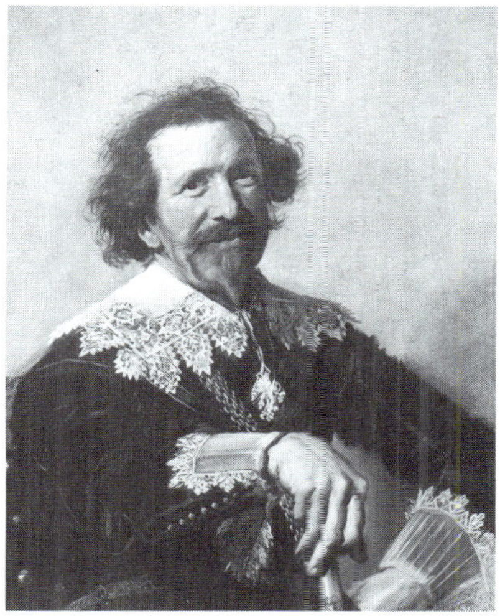

d

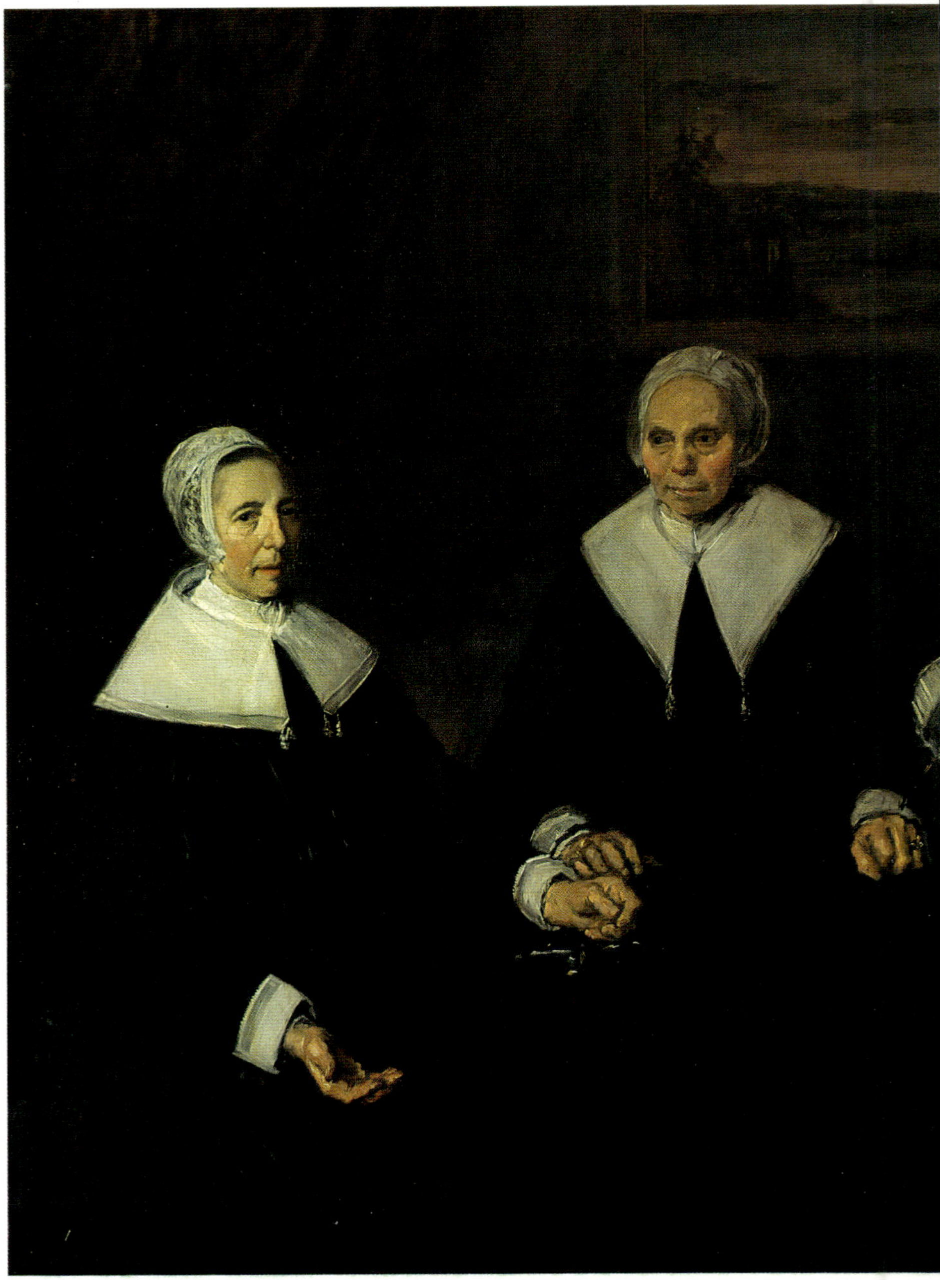

38

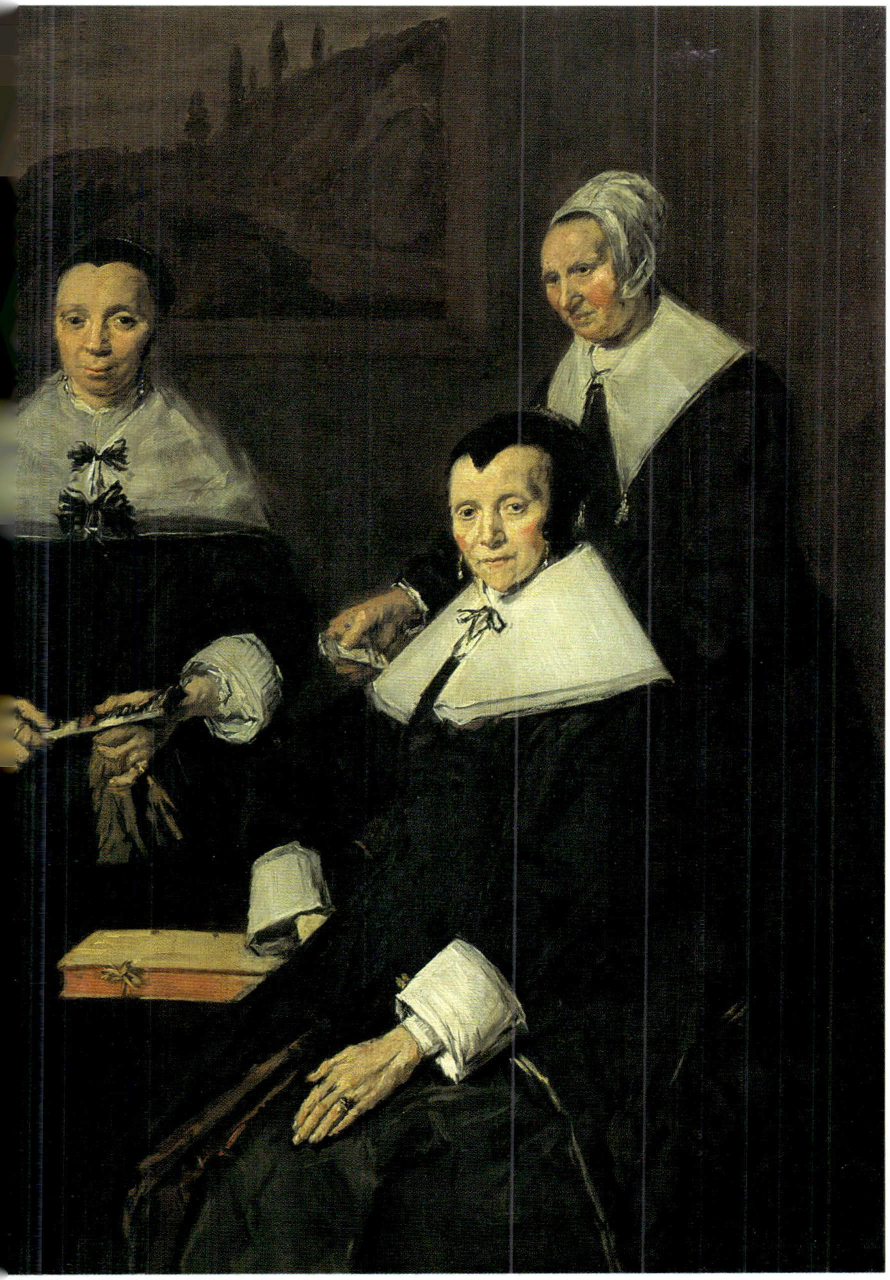

Plate 38. *Lady-Regentesses of the Old Men's Alms House,* ca. 1664. Canvas, 170.5 x 249.5 cm. Haarlem, Frans Halsmuseum. Like the *Regents of the Old Men's Alms House* (plate 34), these severe-looking women can not be identified with any certainty. But the regentesses during the appropriate years were Adriaentje Schouten, Marijte Willems, Anna van Damme and Adriana Bredenhof and it is probably they who are portrayed. The housemistress stands behind them. An eighteenth-century description of the Old Men's Alms House indicates that the *Regents* and *Lady-Regentesses* hung in different rooms. In the nineteenth century both works were taken to the Haarlem town hall where they were seen by the French writer and painter Eugène Fromentin. According to Fromentin, Hals began painting in a more abstract manner in his later years due to failing eyesight and an unsteady hand. However, today Hals's reduction of the portrait to its essentials is considered, on the contrary, to be a sign of his masterly skill.

# Hals's own portrait

a. Unknown artist. *Frans Hals.* Canvas, 69 x 55 cm. Lepke Auction, Berlin, 18 March 1918, No. 10.
b. Self-portrait in *The officers and subalterns of the St. George militia company,* 1639 (plate 21)
c. *Self-portrait,* copy of a lost original of about 1650. Indianapolis, Indianapolis Museum of Art, The Clowes Fund.
d. David Coster (active 1696-1749), *Frans Hals.* Engraving, 22 x 16.3 cm.
e. Unknown seventeenth-century artist (Anthonie van Dyck?), *Frans Hals,* ca. 1630? White and black pastel on blue paper, 26.4 x 18.5 cm. Amsterdam, Rijksprentenkabinet.

Arnold Houbraken begins his controversial biography of Frans Hals with an anecdote. He states that the painter Anthonie van Dyck, before his trip to England in 1632, visited the master in Haarlem:

> *'Anthony van Dyk, the Phoenix of his time, before sailing to England in the service of Charles the first, desirous of seeing him , came to Haarlem and went to his House. But he found him in a tavern, which he refused to leave before emptying his pint. Van Dyk waited patiently, his hat on his head, telling him only that he was a stranger and that he had no other time but that time and that he wished to have his Portrait painted. F. HALS consented without further question. He took the first canvas he laid his hands on and set to work. While posing, van Dyk said little in order to keep his identity a secret. In a short time it was done and FRANS asked him to stand and see if it pleased him. Van Dyk praised it and made some conversation, but in such a way that he did not reveal who he was. Among the things he said were: Is that how one paints? Could I not do it myself? He took an empty canvas which was standing there, set it upon the Easel and asked him to sit. FRANS saw from the way he handled the palette and brushes that this was not the first time and waited for the disguised Ulysses to reveal himself, not suspecting it was van Dyk, but thinking it must be some eccentric Painter who wanted to show his Art by this example. Before long van Dyk asked him to get up and view the work. As soon as he saw it he said: You are van Dyk, for none other could do such a thing, then fell on his neck and kissed him.'*

Although Houbraken's anecdote is no doubt romanticized, it is possible that the two artists did in fact meet and paint each other's portrait. The portrait of Van Dyck has not been located among Frans Hals's unidentified portraits, but the portrait the anecdote says Van Dyck painted of Frans Hals may exist.

In 1910 a portrait of Frans Hals, attributed to Van Dyck, was exhibited in Brussels (ill. a). It was auctioned eight years later. In those years questions arose as to the identity of the painter at the easel. The youthful face does not correspond with Hals's age at the time of the supposed meeting. In about 1630 Hals was between forty-five and fifty years old, whereas the painter in the portrait looks no older than twenty-five. The clothing also poses a problem. The small collar and high hat did not come into fashion before the 1640s and since Van Dyck died in 1641, it is unlikely that he painted the portrait. The work is not mentioned anywhere in the modern literature about Van Dyck. Perhaps it came into being in this way: an unknown painter, active in about 1700, wanted to give substance to the anecdote by painting a portrait of Frans Hals in the style of Van Dyck. For the figure of Hals, he took as a model the self-portrait of Frans Hals among the militia-men of St. George, reproducing the pose and face in reverse (ill. b). He dressed the painter in old-fashioned - for his time - clothes; maybe he also had in mind the other self-portrait by Frans Hals, now known only from several copies (ill. c).

Completely different in composition from this painting is another portrait of Frans Hals, an engraving. According to the inscription, the print was made after a painting by Anthonie van Dyck (ill. d). The engraver, David Coster, is not well-known; he was active between 1696 and 1744 and specialized in map-making. The

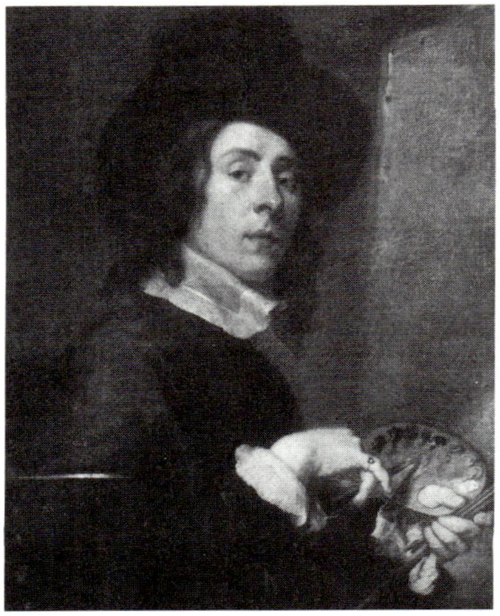

a

credibility of this painting is also questionable. The forced composition is in no way reminiscent of Van Dyck, and in addition, the subject's clothes seem to date from the sixteenth century (compare p. 28, ill. a and b). Possibly Coster too wanted to give support to the veracity of Houbraken's anecdote.

For lack of evidence, the meeting between Hals and Van Dyck could be considered another of Houbraken's fictions, were it not for the existence of a seventeenth-century drawing which can not be ignored in this context (ill. e). It is the portrait of a man, done in white and black pastel on blue paper. The original sheet was probably larger; it appears to have been cut down - unevenly - in the eighteenth century, framed and provided with an inscription. 'Frans Hals' is written in pencil on the back, writing that may well date from the seventeenth century. It is not known who made the portrait, but he was obviously a skillful artist. The interplay of black and white, the effective fall of light and the strong composition of the face make the portrait one of high quality.

It is tempting to regard this portrait as the one mentioned in the anecdote, all the more so as the style of execution bears similiarities to other drawings by Van Dyck. In addition, it could well have been made in about 1630 when large hats, such as the man is wearing, were fashionable. And even Houbraken's anecdote provides some substantiation of the suggestion: Frans Hals painted quickly and so could have fulfilled the stranger's wish. Van Dyck would have been more likely to use pastels and paper in order to make a portrait of Frans Hals in a short time.

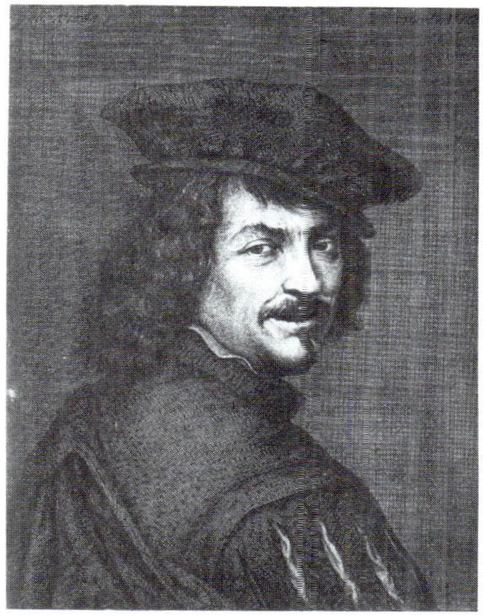

d

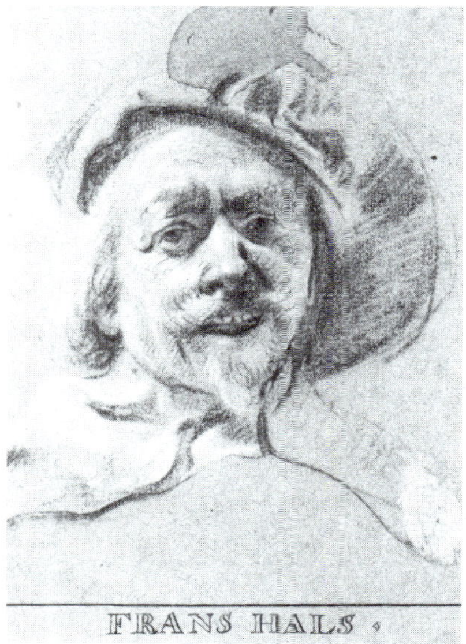


e

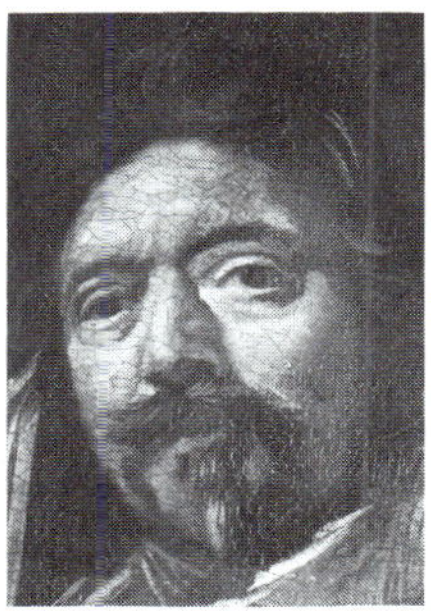

b

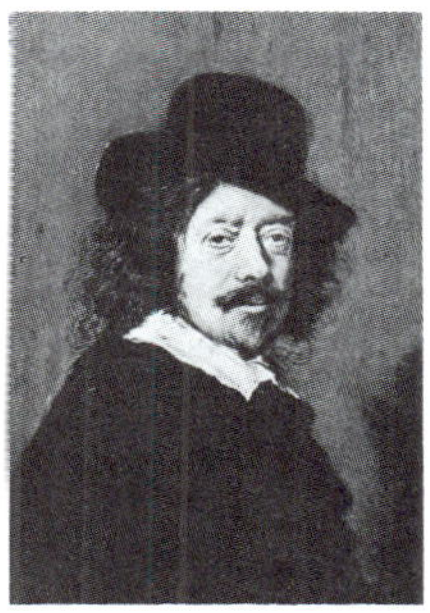

c

# Van Heythuysen times three

In about 1638, ten years after he had commissioned a portrait by Frans Hals (p. 76, ill. a), the Haarlem merchant Willem van Heythuysen again posed for the artist. This portrait, of a much more intimate character than the early one, exists in three versions, each with its own particularities. Together they pose a question for art historians (plate 39, 39a and 39b).

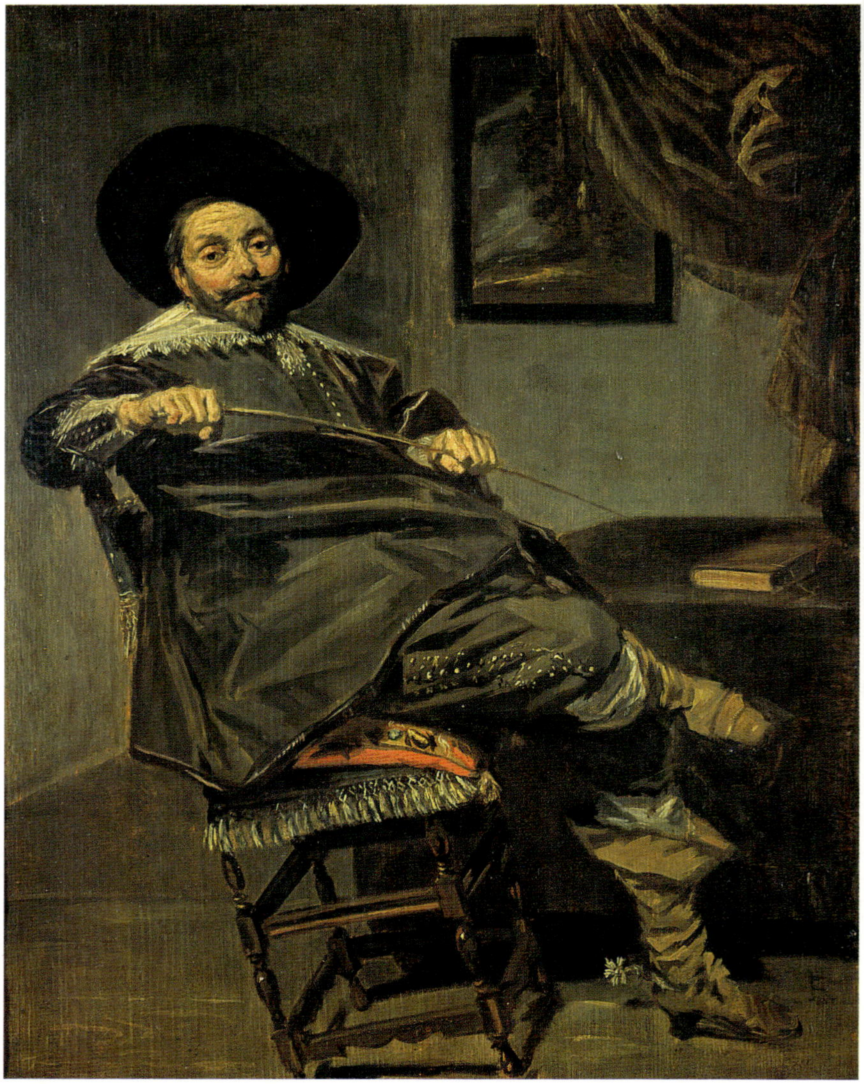

39

Plate 39. *Willem van Heythuysen.* Panel, 46.5 x 37.5 cm. Signed bottom right with the monogram 'FH'. Brussels, Koninklijke Musea voor Schone Kunsten.
Ill. 39a. *Willem van Heythuysen,* 'Rothschild version' (so called after a former owner). Panel, 46 x 36 cm. Signed bottom right with the monogram 'FH'. Present location unknown; in 1963 it was in the Schuller collection in São Paolo.
Plate 39b. *Willem van Heythuysen,* 'Mildmay version' (so called after a former owner). Panel, 46.5 x 36 cm. Private collection.

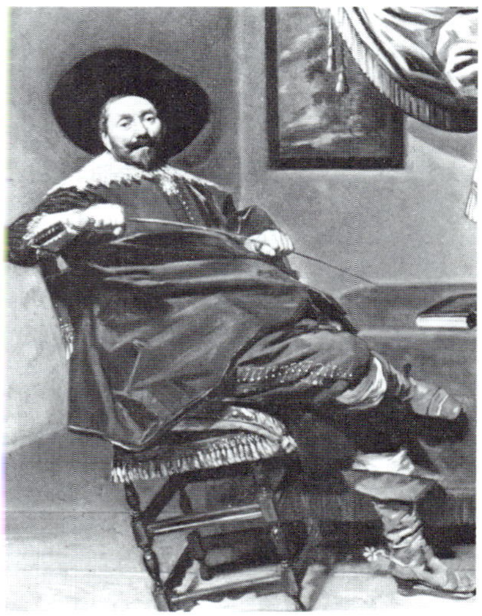

39a

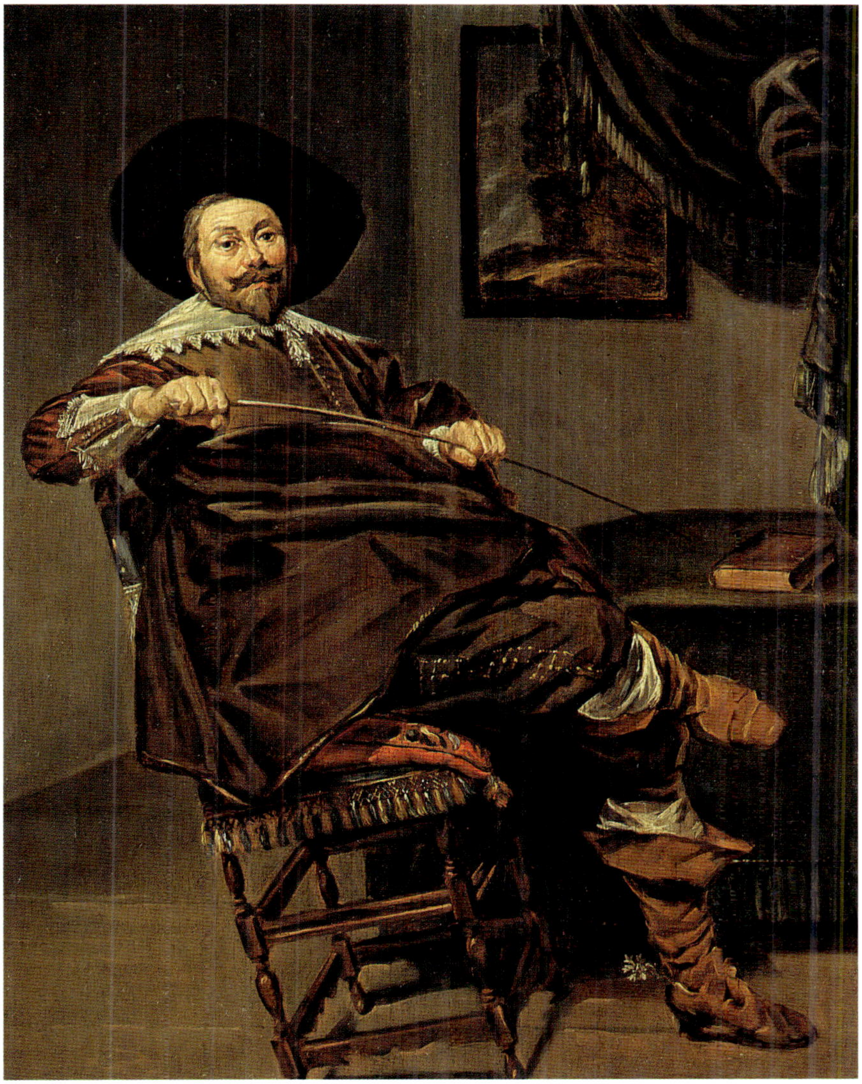

39b

Willem van Heythuysen came from Limburg originally and settled in Haarlem where he dealt in thread and yarn. He was a rich man and owned several houses in Haarlem. After Van Heythuysen's death in 1650, in accordance with his wishes his estate in the 'Haarlemmerhout', south of the city, was made into a home for the needy (see p. 9, ill. a). This 'Hofje van Heythuysen' still exists. An inventory was made of his many possesions; in addition to an extensive library, there were costly pieces of furniture, maps, clothing and jewels - and many paintings. Two of these were probably portraits Hals painted of him: 'Effigy or Portrait of Willem van Heythuysen with a black cloth' and 'Portrait of the deceased in miniature in a black frame'.

But which of the three known versions of Van Heythuysen's small portrait is the original? Or, as is often asserted, are all three copies of a lost original? In the case of the 'Rothschild version' (ill. 39a), no reliable judgment can be made since its present location is unknown and it can only be studied from a black and white photograph. Yet the work makes a satisfying impression; the subject sits in a relaxed pose and the style of painting appears to conform to Hals's work in about 1638 (see for example p. 7, ill. d). However, the curtain in the background is of an inferior quality, probably an instance of overpainting.

The 'Mildmay version' of the Heythuysen portrait (plate 39b) was recently subjected to a thorough examination in order to determine if it was painted in the seventeenth century. Paint samples were taken and the panel itself was inspected. This last was particularly spectacular: the structure and thickness of the rings in oak give a reasonable indication of the year in which the tree that provided the wood may have been cut down. It was established that the 'Mildmay version' was painted on wood from a tree cut down in or after 1599, making it quite plausible that it was used by Frans Hals. The results of the study of the paint were also positive in situating the portrait in the seventeenth century; no pigment was found which was not yet known at the time.

Despite the valuable information to be gained from this type of examination, the question remains as to whether or not this portrait is indeed by Frans Hals. The human eye must decide for itself. In the case of the 'Mildmay version' (the only unsigned version), it must be established that the painting, qualitatively speaking, falls short of Frans Hals's typical work. Compared with the two other versions of the portrait, the subject's pose is rather stiff and the vacant facial expression creates a forced impression. Although everyone is free to make up his or her own mind, probably the 'Mildmay version' should be regarded as a seventeenth-century copy of the original.

In the past, the portrait of Willem van Heythuysen in Brussels was attributed by most experts to Frans Hals. To be sure, the brushwork is strong and convincing, as is the way in which the subject perches on his chair. This version was also examined to determine the age of the panel. This was done by Dr. Peter Klein of Hamburg, who also examined the 'Mildmay version'. He established that the tree from which the panel came was cut down in about 1642. Logic would thus indicate that Frans Hals painted the portrait between 1642 and 1650, the year of Van Heythuysen's death. Yet this is unlikely; not only are the clothes quite old-fashioned for the second half of the 1640s, the style of painting does not conform with other work by Hals done at this time. Given the fact that the style of the 'Rothschild version' fits in better with

Hals's other portraits from the late 1630s. it would be reasonable to question the authenticity of the Brussels portrait.

However one factor invites an hypothesis: the provenance of the panel. Before it was bought by the Brussels museum in 1870, it hung in the Hofje van Heythuysen. It is inscribed on the back: 'Willem van Heythuysen. Founder of this Hofje. Deceased 6 July 1650'. The inscription probably dates from the seventeenth century. It is therefore not impossible that the portrait was made after the home was founded in 1651, thus after Willem van Heythuysen's death. Possibly Frans Hals was commissioned to make a copy of the portrait which he himself had painted in the 1630s. If the Brussel's version is dated at about 1655, the problematic panel fits in perfectly with Hals's stylistic development (see plate 36). The face of the subject betrays the work of a copyist with his own mind: in this portrait Willem van Heythuysen looks considerably older than in the 'Rothschild version'.

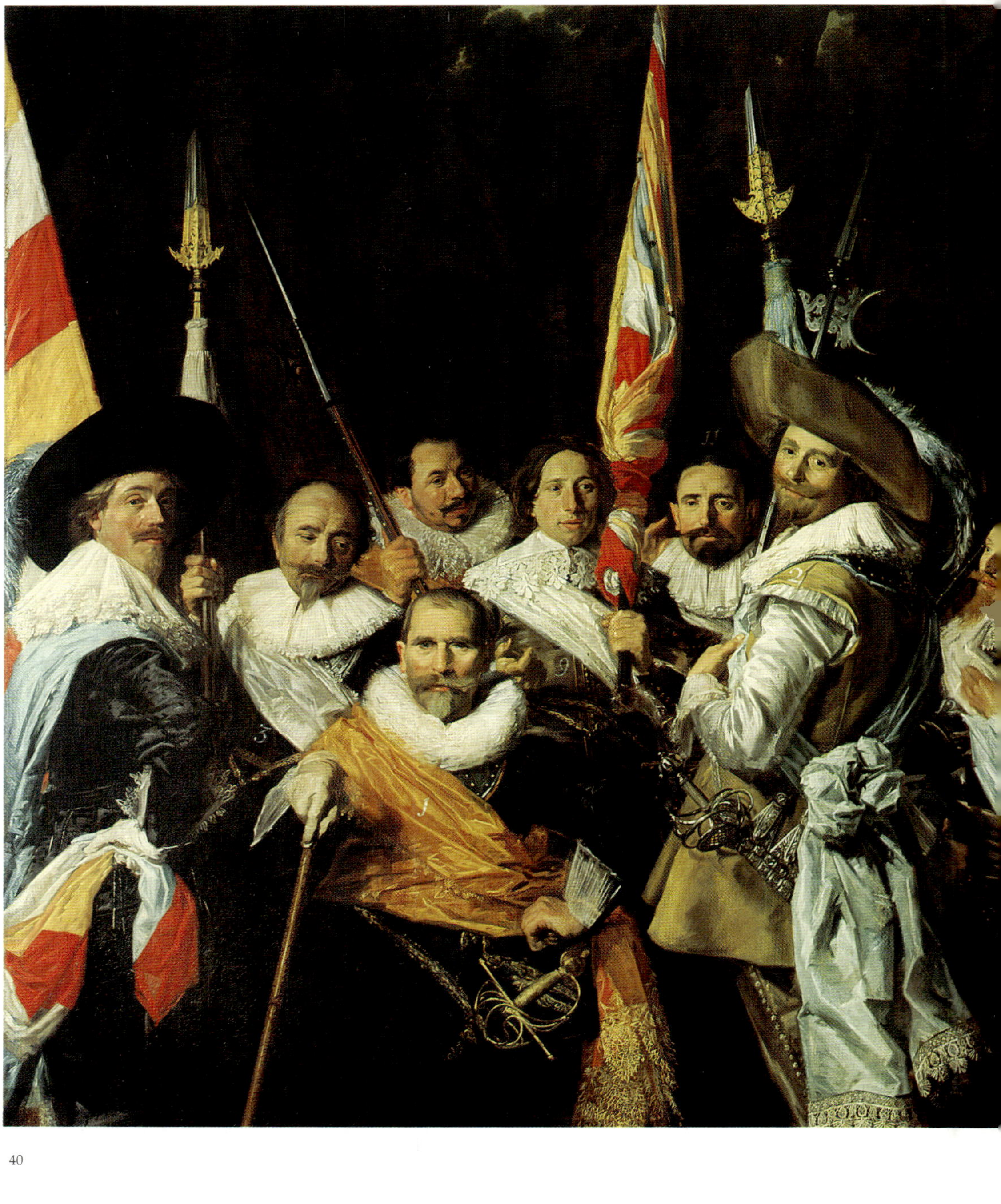

40

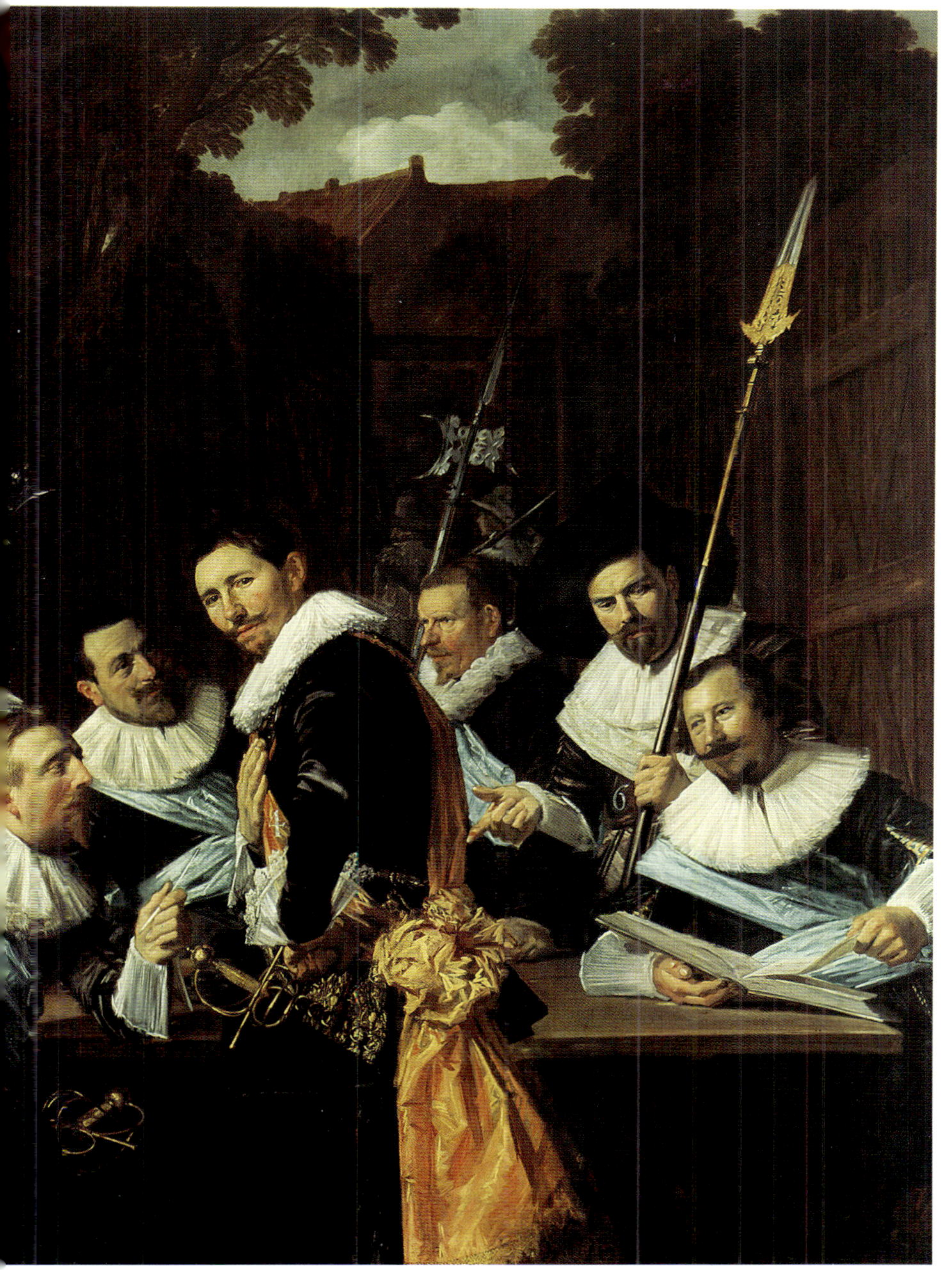

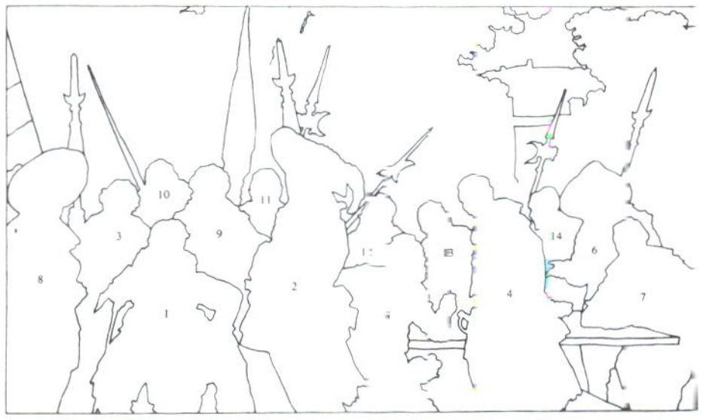

1. Johan (van) Loo, colonel (see also plate 21); 2. Johan Schatter, captain (see also plate 8); 3. Cornelis Backer, captain; 4. Andries van der Horn, captain; 5. Jacob Buttinga, lieutenant; 6. Nicolaes Olycan, lieutenant; 7. Hendrick Gerritsz. Pot, lieutenant (see also plate 21); 8. Jacob (?) Hofland, standard-bearer; 9. Jacob Steyn, standard-bearer; 10. Dirck Verschuyl, sergeant; 11. Balthasar Baudaert, sergeant; 12. Cornelis Ham, sergeant; 13. Hendrik van den Boom, sergeant; 14. Barent Mol, sergeant.

Plate 40. *Officers and subalterns of the St. Adrian militia company*, 1633. Canvas, 207 x 337 cm. Haarlem, Frans Halsmuseum. In the eighteenth century the militiamen were given identification numbers. This militia portrait shows the influence of Amsterdam examples, possibly as a result of the commission given to Hals by the Amsterdam militia in 1633 (see plate 20). Not only did Hals picture most of the men standing, but he also departed from the Haarlem tradition of picturing them according to the hierarchy from left to right. He reserved the most prominent places on the canvas for the highest in rank. The background of the picture may originally have been lighter. Wybrand Hendriks made a water-colour painting after this militia portrait (compare ill. on p. 108).

## HISTORY OF THE ASSEMBLY OF OFFICERS AND SUBALTERNS OF THE CIVIC GUARD OF ST. ADRIAN, 1633

*1633* From information about the subjects in the portrait, it is assumed that the painting was made in this year.
*1695* Item of expenditure for cleaning paintings in the Doelen of St. Adrian.
*1721* Idem.
*1740* A 'Painting Commission' occupies itself with identification of the militiamen. Their names are given on a plaque below the portrait. The men are numbered.
Item of expenditure for cutting frames, 50 guilders.
*1810* Mention of damage to paintings caused by soldiers at exercise.
*1819* New mention of damage, after restoration of painting two years earlier.
*1821* The paintings are brought to the town hall.
*1862* The painting is transferred to the Stedelijk Museum in Haarlem.
*1864* Restoration by Mr. Scholten.
*1870* Before this year, the painting is lined with 'paste'.
*1871* Lined again by Vos and Walter (the painting now has a double lining). The varnish is regenerated and the painting is retouched by Mr. Scholten.
*1906* The varnish is regenerated and the painting retouched by F. Vos, the museum's restorer.
*1908* Varnish regenerated and 'rubbed thin'. The hole in the garden fence is overpainted.
*1913* Taken to the Frans Halsmuseum, opened this year.
*1925* Restoration under the supervision of D. de Wild.
*1986* Restoration by Anne van Grevenstein, Michaela Burek, Carol Pottasch and Liesbeth Abraham.

## RESTORATION 1986

March-December

The varnish of this painting had yellowed strongly and the retouches were discoloured. The paint adhered well and there was very little sagging. Replacing the double lining was considered unnecessary.

Upon removal of the extensive overpainting, it could be seen that in an earlier attempt to smooth the fillings the areas around the losses had been partially sanded away. De Wild's intervention involved removing the varnish and reducing the old overpainting. He left the old remaining filler and reworked it with new bolus putty. Reconstruction was carried out at will, without reference to the water-colour by Wybrand Hendriks, using tempera adjusted in tone using oil paint, which had become completely insoluble.

De Wild overpainted the entire fence and the background trees with a dark brown glaze, avoiding foreground details, such as the halberds.

The varnish and the oil glaze were removed with acetone. As with the other militia portraits, a thin layer of old oil-based varnish was retained over the entire surface. An intermediate layer of dammar varnish was applied and the fillings were effected with a mixture of wax, chalk and pigment in the light brown tint of the ground layer. Reconstructions were made using dammar varnish and dry pigment. The reconstruction of the rapier hilt in fig. 1 was based on the copy by Wybrand Hendriks and advice from a weapons' expert. The painting was sprayed sparingly with a final layer of varnish.

Ill. 40a. Reconstruction of the rapier hilt in fig. 1 by De Wild.
Ill. 40b. First version of the 1986 reconstruction. The first reconstruction of the rapier hilt repeated De Wild's treatment. In removing sizable retouches, it is in principle advisable to limit one's own imagination and to follow the lead of the previous restorer, who may have seen the painting before damage. However, here this argument did not apply, since it is known that the damage occurred in the nineteenth century. A knowledge of weaponry also cast doubt on the acceptability of De Wild's reconstruction. Weapons' expert J.P. Puype gave recommendations for a proper reconstruction. The form of the rapier on the water-colour by Wybrand Hendriks appeared highly reliable.
Ill. 40c. Improved version of the 1986 reconstruction.
Ill. 40d. Detail from the water-colour by Wybrand Hendriks.

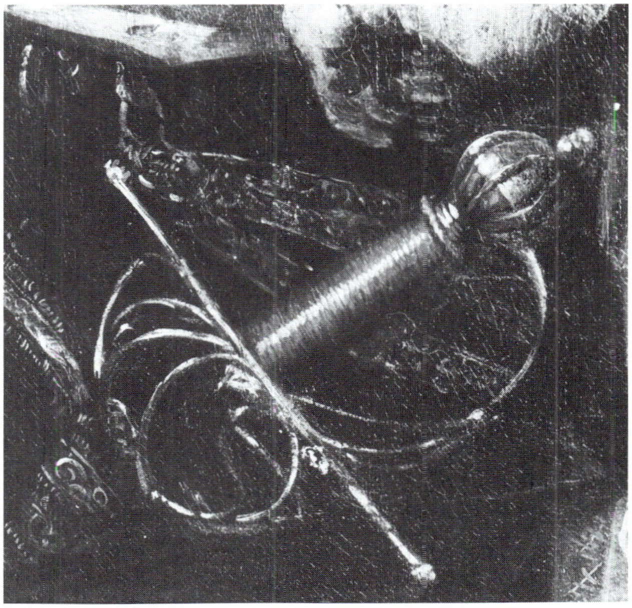

40a

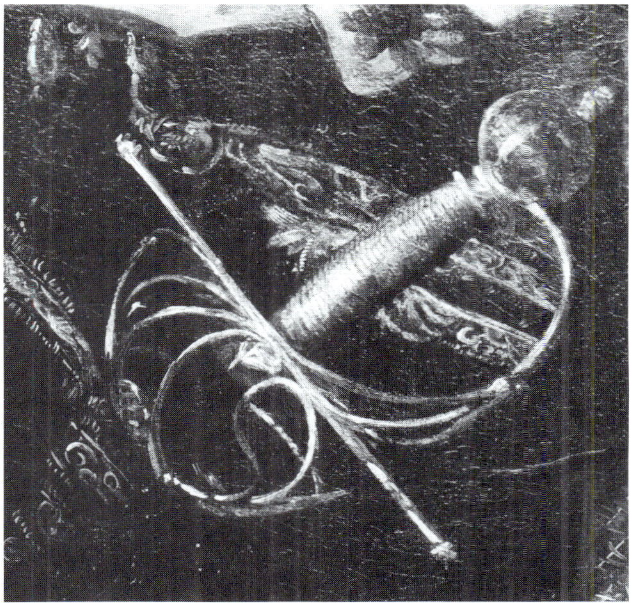

40b

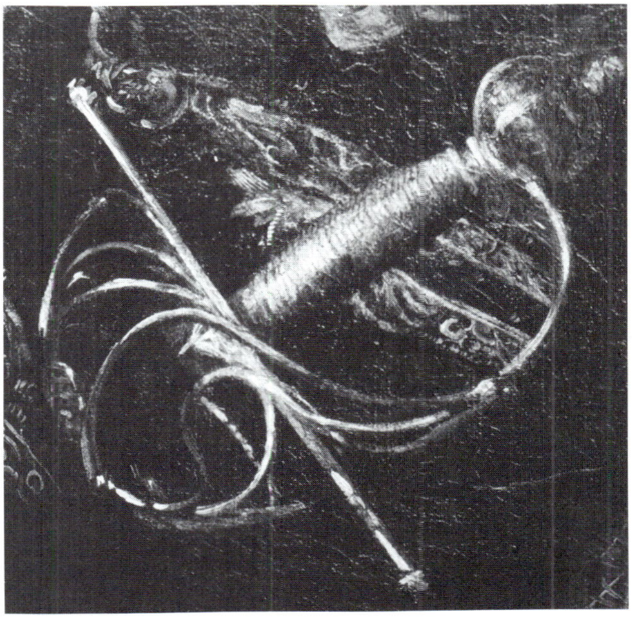

40c

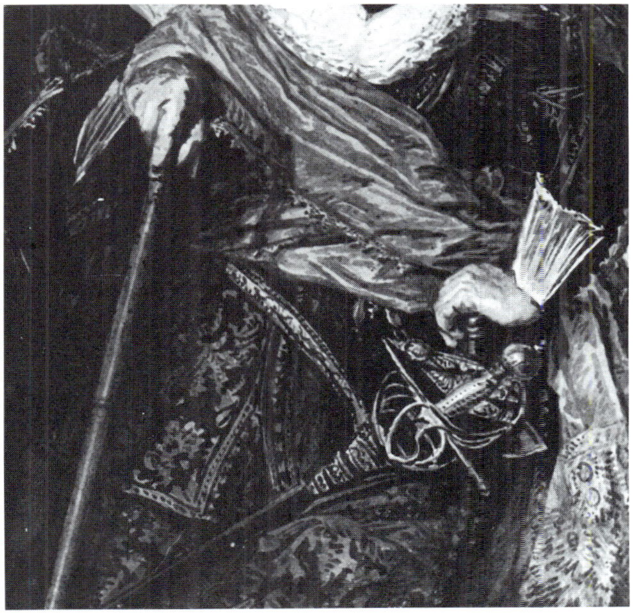

40d

Ill. 40e. Detail of the mouth and chin of fig. 7 during removal of the old varnish and overpainting. The damage - visible in the X-ray - can be predicted: the putty filling was uneven and the reconstruction of the mouth unfortunate. These additions transmitted an unpleasantness which 'contaminated' one's vision of the rest of the portrait. The 'contaminating' effect of retouching has caused many theoreticians of aesthetics to advise against it. But lost, damaged and worn areas also influence our way of looking: the eye is distracted and the three-dimensional illusion, so necessary to painting, is disrupted. In Italy losses are often filled in with a hatched paint structure, invisible from a distance but easily seen from close by. In the case of the militia paintings, signalling the restored areas was felt to be unnecessary given the existence of photographic documentation. The restorer's intervention has been obscured, leaving the illusion intact for the viewer.
Ill. 40f. Loss in the mouth of fig. 7. During a previous restoration, the filling was sanded smooth, some of Frans Hals's paint along with it. An example of the damage restoration can bring. After removal of the old remaining filling material and extensive overpainting, enough of the original paint remained to permit reconstruction of the mouth and moustache. Each tiny indication - a $mm^2$ of paint is sufficient - is treated with the utmost respect in order to arrive at the closest possible reproduction of the original form.

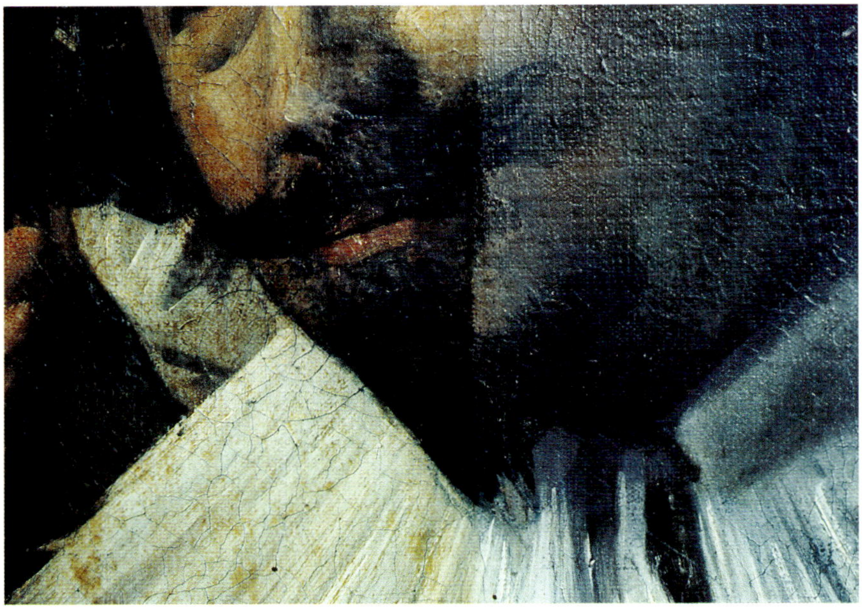

40e

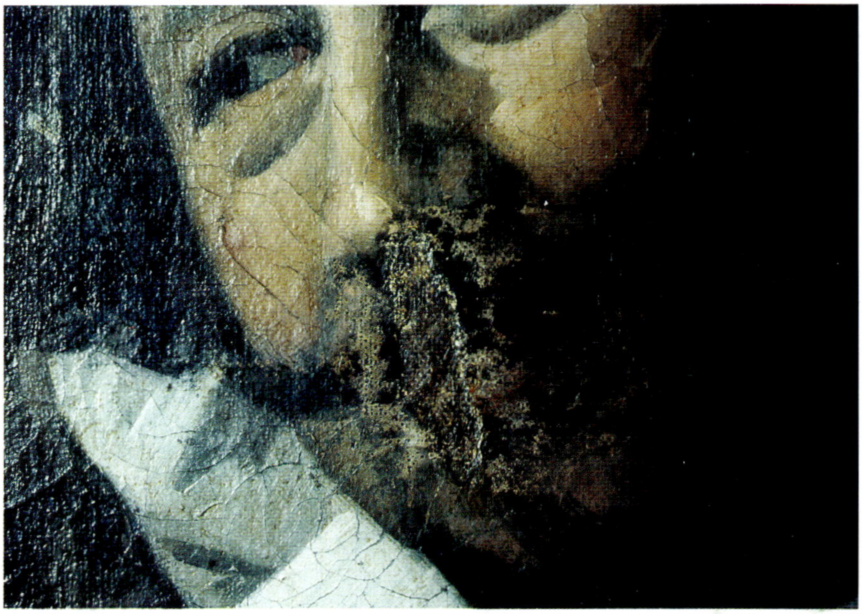

40f

# Restoration

In this chapter restorer Anne van Grevenstein will give an idea of the 'other side' of painting, the more material aspect: what has happned in the course of time and why a painting now looks like it does. The examples, Frans Hals's militia portraits, are used to illustrate a way of looking at and thinking about a work of art. No pretention is made to scientific thoroughness in this respect; nor are the ideas expressed original, they merely form a subject of ongoing discussion.

The restoration team during the cleaning of the *Banquet of the officers of the civic guard of St. Adrian* from 1627: reducing the varnish layer.

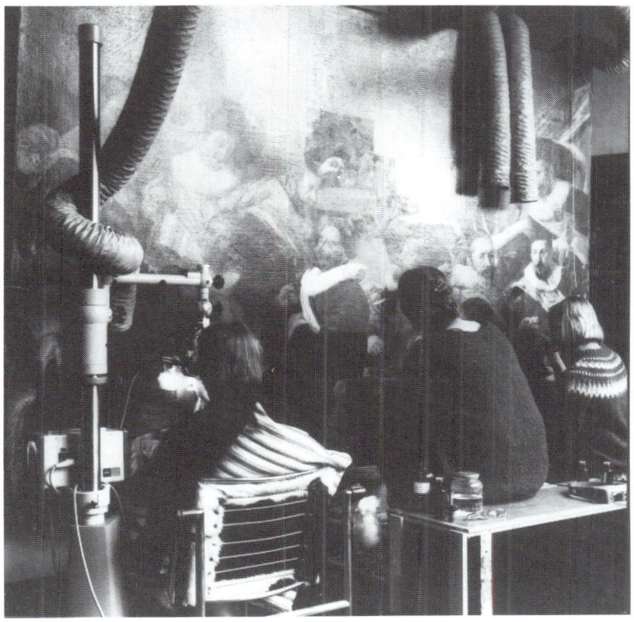

Just as iconography, style and composition are, so to speak, the immaterial building blocks of a painting's 'idea' or underlying invention, so its execution and the technical process are the visible building blocks that give form to the material. The restorer works with this material, this 'receptacle' of the ideas which are the province of the art historian.

The long-standing tradition that an artwork should be attended to by people from two very different disciplines gave rise to many points of opposition in the past. Mutual misunderstanding, lack of respect, secretiveness were the result.

It was a long time before a purposeful dialogue could be established between restorer, art historian, chemist and physicist. Only since the Second World War has there really been extensive interdisciplinary co-operation in this area.

**The history of the work of restoration**

Ever since paintings have been made, they have also been cared for. They have been cleaned: damages have been repaired.

Painters' manuals often contained a chapter giving directions for the cleaning of old paintings in order to make them look new. The most drastic methods were recommended: warm water and soap, scouring powders, caustics, such products as lye, ammonia and even urine. To read these recommendations today is to marvel that so many paintings have managed to survive their 'upkeep'.

Yet it was recognized early on that careless restoration could produce damage. The painter Delacroix (1798-1863) remarked: 'Chaque restauration pretendue est un outrage mille fois plus regrettable que le temps: ce n'est pas un tableau restauré qu'on vous donne mais un autre tableau.' Warnings were given about certain substances and procedures: the painter and restorer De Mayerne, for example, noted in the margin of his treatise (1620-1646) that rubbing with a stiff brush and water was 'mauvais' or bad for the painting. Ironically, the painter - the amateur restorer - had the power to disguise the irreversible damage he did from the eye of the viewer. Abraded areas were simply overpainted. The secretive climate in which this took place is notable. A source from 1622 tells how Hendrick Cornelisz. van Hout instructed the Haarlem artist Jan Marten Jansz. in the 'art of cleaning paintings' and how he must swear to reveal this 'art' to no one else in the world, except his wife and children.

In all likelihood it were not the best painters who undertook this work and fear of competition and losing business is understandable.

A less obvious reason for 'keeping mum' about restoration perhaps lies in the activity itself: the work of art was, as it were, reborn, re-emerging 'new' after its restoration. If such a miracle could be worked with fairly simple means, it was preferable to keep it a secret, allowing the restorer to play the role of magician. Throughout the nineteenth century, these 'magicians' could proceed without interference. Not until the beginning of our century was the painter-restorer confronted with the scientific expertise of the chemist and art historian. For the first time analyses were made of paint and binding mediums and X-rays were taken in order to establish whether or not a painting was 'real'. Natural science was called in if the experts did not agree. Objective data from the laboratory established the 'truth' in such cases as the scandal regarding the false Vermeer in the Museum Boymans-van Beuningen (the Vermeer by Van Meegeren) and opposition by Hofstede de Groot to the experts concerning a 'false Frans Hals'.

Not surprisingly, resistance to this approach was great. In his 1925 defence against the report by F.E.C. Scheffer, professor of chemistry at Delft, Hofstede de Groot aserted that 'one simply can not dispute about art with a chemist.' He found that the expertise of the eye, connoisseurship, was the only true way and waved aside all of Scheffer's arguments. Scheffer had, for example, discovered zinc white, synthetic ultramarine and cobalt blue in the alleged Frans Hals and had further established that the paint was still soft and water-soluble. Hofstede de Groot countered by advancing the knowledge and experience of his restorer who knew of a secret procedure which made old oil paint so soft it could be 'dipped up with a pen-knife'. For Hofstede de Groot, the portrait of 'The laughing man' remained an authentic Hals and he bought it for the sum of 40,000 Dutch guilders.

Science was also called upon when discussions arose about the abrasion of paintings. Cleaning the paintings in London's National Gallery in the 1930s unleashed a 'cleaning controversy' which went on for years. The restorers were obliged to offer proof that their treatment had not removed any of the original paint.

At the time of the restoration of the militia portraits by restorer De Wild in the 1920s, he was also compelled by the directorial committee to give a similar accounting. He secured from the 'Keuringsdienst van Waren' in Haarlem a laboratory analysis showing that there were no traces of the original paint to be found on the cotton-wool he had used.

And so - initially as self-defence, later as a token guaranteeing the safety of a work of art by interdisciplinary co-operation - in the course of this century restoration has become a discipline requiring a combination of manual skill, knowledge of art history and scientific investigation.

**Preliminary studies**

More and more, restoration of a painting goes hand and hand with a thorough technological examination. This is necessary in order to formulate a proposed treatment; one needs to know what is to be restored and to be acquainted with the specific characteristics of a work so as to be able to respect them fully during restoration.

From a general scientific point of view, it is desirable that these informations be accessible or published. Technical data obtained during a restoration still too often remain separate and unintegrated. For a long time traditional art history ignored the physical examination of paintings completely, with the result that today new information is continually being discovered which fits into no customary category.

This makes scientific examination extraordinarily interesting and rewarding. Gradually information obtained can be coupled to 'true' art history, which can then use this wealth of new data to review and adapt its criteria of style and quality. However, assimilating technical information is exceptionally difficult.

Photographic or analytical methods are not always applicable to all situations and the results are sometimes equivocal. For example, with the aid of infrared-reflecto-graphy, the underdrawing beneath a painted surface can be seen, but only when the drawing is black on a white background. Brown sketches or drawings in white or red pastel on a dark background can not be made visible.

X-rays are useless if there is too much lead white in the ground layer. Making an analysis of the composition of the paint is difficult if one does not know what one is looking for, and in addition it is no simple matter to reconstruct the preparation procedures once results have been obtained. Written texts, formulas and theoretical writings by artists can often help to clear up matters and lead to a well-directed examination. Such a source study is usually a task for a specialist in art history.

The restorer, having the painting at close hand for a long time, is often the one to note and record specific things, and also the one who provides the scientist and art historian with particular questions. It is precisely the hourly, daily, monthly contact with a work that makes certain observations possible. Therefore, the restoration atelier is the place where the many 'building blocks' can come together in order to permit a synthesis. Conditions for this are the continuity of the investigations, good documentation and intensive contact with other scientific disciplines.

**Method**

Each work of art has several aspects and can be looked at in a variety of ways. For one person, a painting basically tells a story; another will be moved by the play of colour. Every viewer cares for a work of art for a different reason. Restoration can change a painting in such a way as to emphasize one or another of these aspects. This does not do justice to the complexity of the work of art in question. A painting can be cleaned to a lesser or greater degree; a missing piece can be painted in completely, partially or not at all. Many decisions as to how a painting is to look after restoration depend on its function or the purpose of the restoration. This is why each restoration should be preceded by an analysis. Only after this has been done is it time to look critically at which aspects of the work are the most strongly emphasized and how these should be respected during the restoration.

A restoration should not be regarded as wholly 'aesthetic' or 'scientific'. As much must be known about the work as possible before it can be determined which treatment should be applied and what conse-quences the proposed treatment will have on the preservation of the components, the originality and historical significance of the work, and the aesthetic effect. Professional skill and the technique of restoration must adjust to this complexity, and not the other way round.

In analysing information leading to a correct definition of the problem to be faced, the following factors must be taken into consideration:

- *the story*: anything missing can be vitally important to the narrative or intelligibility of the scene. A yellow varnish can obscure small details, inscriptions and the like.
- *the harmony of colour, the composition and the style*: representations for which the suggestion of a three-dimensional illusion is important suffer greatly from lost areas. If the types of paint used have discoloured in various ways, removing the subduing layer of yellow varnish can disturb the harmony between colour and composition.
- *the material construction*: the original unity of the object - the coherence of paint, support and frame - can break down with the passage of time. Sometimes only a few traces remain to point to the original condition: on the back of a panel, on the edges of a canvas, on an old stretcher, or on an old frame. If these traces are not recognized in time, the danger that they will be lost during restoration is great.
- *the work as bearer of its own history*: some instances of damage or destruction have more expressive or historical value than 'ordinary' accidental flaws, for example, destruction that came about during the time of the iconoclasts. Later changes made for ideological, religious or aesthetic reasons can tell us something about developments in culture and manners of observation.

# Techniques

a. X-ray of the *Banquet of the officers of the civic guard of St. George* of 1627. Right of the head of fig. 2 (A) (see ill. 14a and 14b) and to the right above fig. 9 tears in the canvas are visible. The light spots to the left (B) indicate damaged areas repaired with filling material containing lead white. It can be seen indistinctly that the head of fig. 9 was originally turned in the other direction.
b. Cross-section of paint. The paint sample was taken from the blue sash of the figure at the left (fig. 8) in the *Officers and subalterns of the civic guard of St. Adrian* of 1633. The ground layer is double: a lower layer of light beige, an upper layer of light brown. Both are oil-based. Indigo was used for the blue paint layer, a vegetable dye with a tendency to fade under the influence of light.

**X-rays**
In order to get a clear idea of the extent of the damage, all the militia portraits were X-rayed. Mr. G. van Voorde of the Koninklijk Instituut voor het Kunstpatrimonium in Brussels kindly came to Haarlem with special equipment for this purpose. The equipment permitted large-sized Cronaflex film shots to be made.

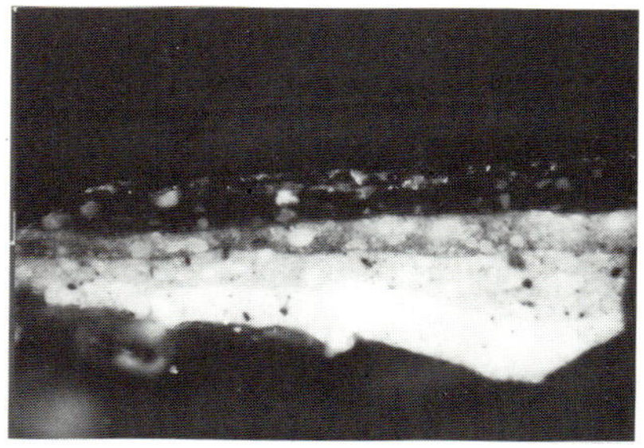

b

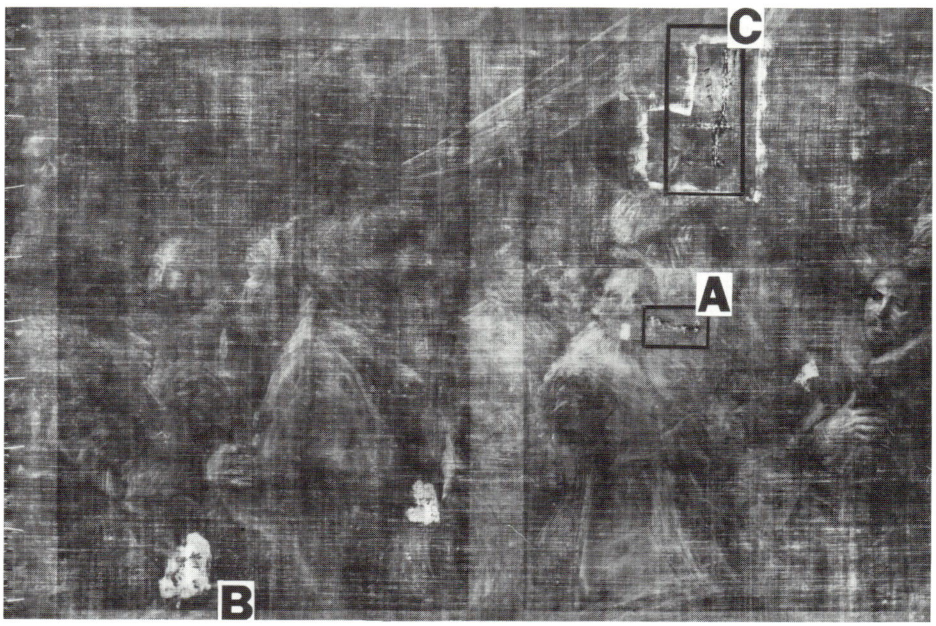


a

The advantage of Cronaflex is that only one or two X-rays on large strips of film need be made. Normal X-rays are 30 x 40 cm., requiring numerous repetitions for a large canvas.

The X-rays were made before the restoration when the militia portraits still held the secret of the damage they had undergone. After closing time, the room in which they hung was completely darkened and the X-rays were made on the spot. The films were developed in Brussels, photographed and printed in manageable dimensions. Without this assistance from the Brussels Instituut, the restoration would have been considerably more difficult.

**What does an X-ray show?**
When an X-ray is made, the painting is situated between the source of the ray and the film. The radioactive rays pass through the painting and come in contact with the sensitive film. The rays do not penetrate metal (lead, iron, etc.) but easily go through organic material like linen, wood or non-metallic paint. The photograph shows different kinds of radiation, ranging from white (all rays are blocked) to black (all rays penetrate the layers), with grey intermediate variations depending on the metal content.

The ground layer containing lead white can be seen as light grey vertical stripes in the fibre of the canvas. Thickly painted areas containing metal also give a white image, for example the lead white in the collars and in the faces and hands.

Details improved or altered by Hals himself (pentimenti) can sometimes be recognized as lighter spots: in this case the X-ray deviates from what can be seen in the painting. Holes and tears in the canvas where there was neither paint nor ground containing lead white show black and are clearly recognizable. Old

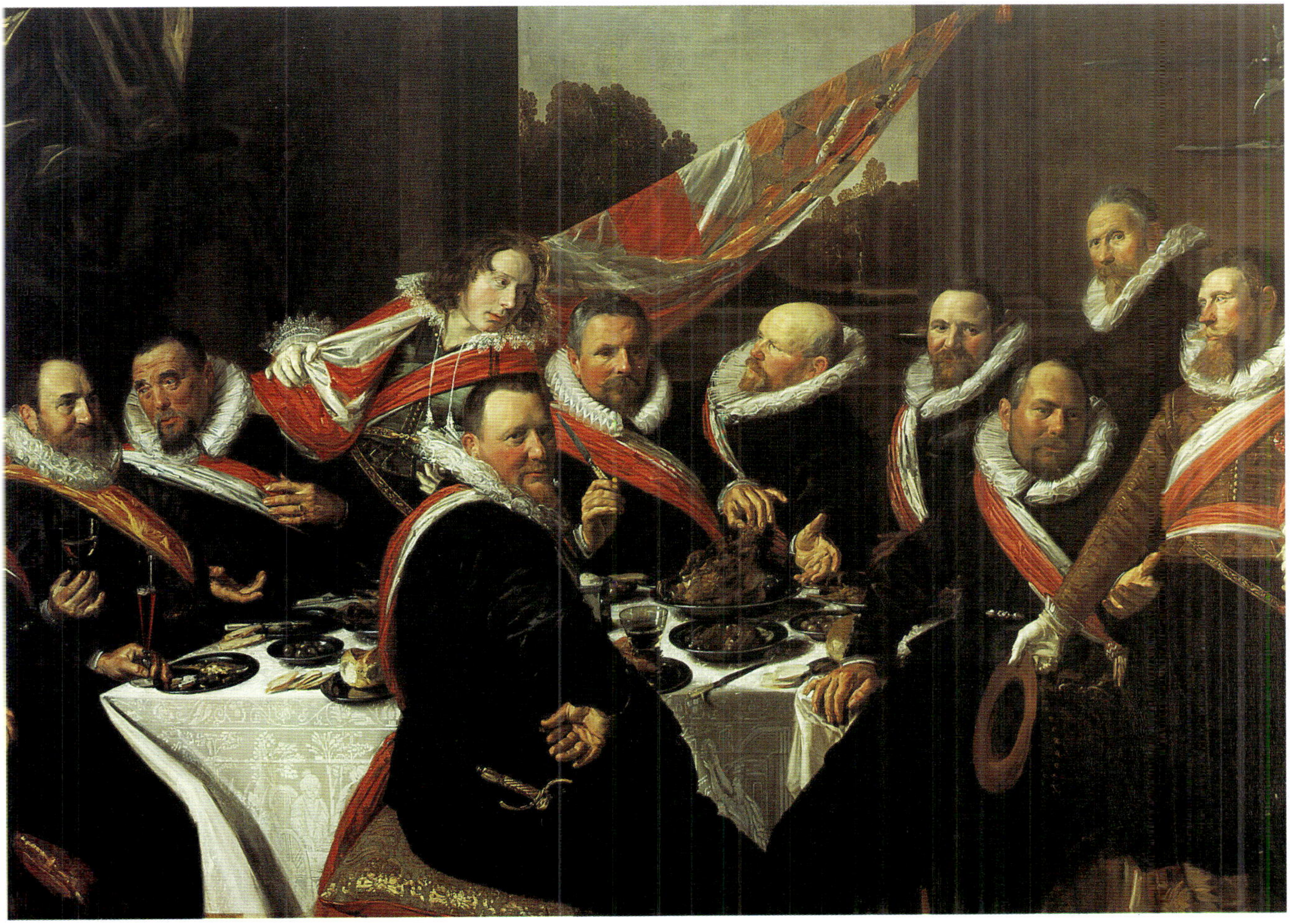

a

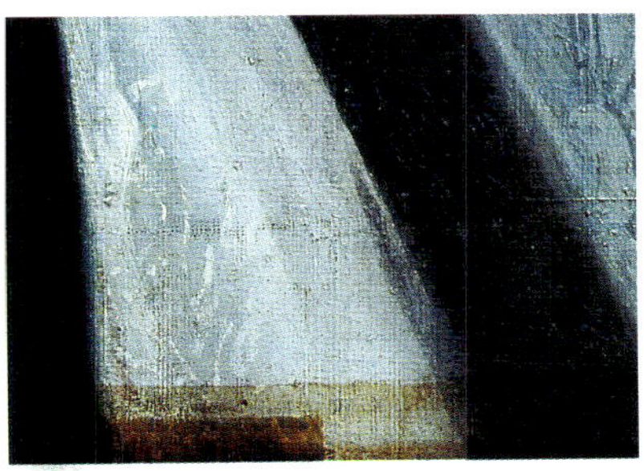

b

a. *Banquet of the officers of the civic guard of St. George*, 1616. Haarlem, Frans Halsmuseum.
b. Detail of the *Banquet of the officers of the civic guard of St. George* of 1616 during removal of the strongly yellowed varnish: the table-cloth.
Bottom left, a strip of old varnish which was not removed during the previous restoration in 1919. This is an early example of candor and objectivity in the profession: traces were deliberately left to show that restoration had been done. Later this method was criticized: it betrayed a lack of professional refinement. Now restoration is documented with photographs.
It was decided to leave the strip of old varnish for the time being, as it is very rare and worth studying in itself.

fillings with lead white show as white spots; old fillings with chalk are black.

**Paint samples and cross-sections**
Paint cross-sections show how a painting is constructed layer by layer. A miniscule paint sample, smaller than the head of a pin, permits very precise analyses to be made. For example, with the aid of a paint sample it can be determined which pigments and binding mediums were used and if an extra paint layer represents a painter's own improvement (pentimento) or a later overpainting. Taking a paint sample calls for the utmost care: each sample is a tiny piece of the painting which is lost to the analysis.

**Ultraviolet rays**
Old varnish shows fluorescent under ultraviolet radiation. In the photograph this can be seen as a light haze. Recent varnish and retouches applied over an old varnish show dark. Making these differences visible aids restoration.

**Choosing various treatments**
There is an obvious difference between two sorts of changes which a work of art can undergo: changes due to normal aging and those due to human intervention (including restorers).

For generations, the dream of restorers was to make the paintings entrusted to them look 'like new'. This dream could well be the origin of the many examples of inadvertent damage done to paintings during restoration. Normal aging produces changes in the material because of light, air, fluctuations in climate and so forth: the natural aging process.

The influence of these factors depends largely on the materials and techniques used by the artist. Or to look at it another way, the choice of the artist has certain inevitable results. The history of the technique of painting tells the story of the development of the choice of materials, their application, how artists break with traditional craftsmanship and wrestle with new ideas to give shape to their 'new art'. The advantage of tradition - history's lesson - is that certain mistakes can be avoided: one can predict what will happen if a formula is not followed to the letter. In innovative times, risks were taken whose consequences were only apparent later. Such risks were adventuresome and inherent to the artist's perpetual quest. Thus certain of his 'mistakes' can have cultural and historical significance.

The viewer, even if he claims to be a layman, looks at such an historical work of art with an educated eye. He possesses taste, judges whether or not something is beautiful and is aware of the norms which dictate how a painting is supposed to look today. It is often said that the reproduction of a painting appears finer than the original. Some art historians work more easily with photographs than with the paintings themselves; the vulnerability of a reproduction is of course infinitely less than that of the original, and this security is reassuring.

People have grown used to an aesthetic ideal which, however 'unhistorical', awakens the illusion of

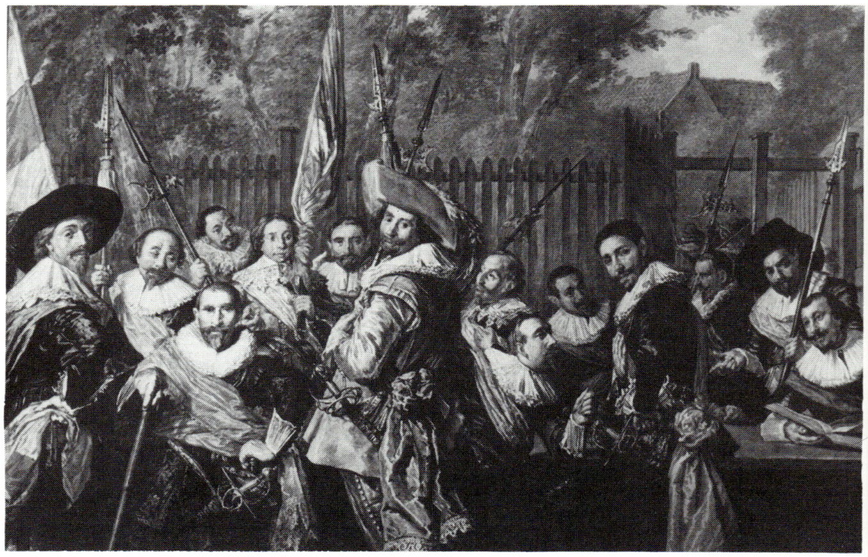

The water-colours which Wybrand Hendriks (1744-1831) made of the militia portraits are a good guideline for the reconstruction of missing pieces and the interpretation of how the paintings have changed through the years. Sometimes, however, the water-colours raise questions, such as this one of the militia portrait of 1633. The brightness of the green is a problem. Were the trees this green when Hendriks saw them and have they since discoloured? Or did Hendriks feel that they must have been green and so painted them this way? Haarlem, Teylers Museum.

having existed in the same form in the painter's studio. From this point of view, a painting seems timeless, eternal, fresh, smooth and gleaming. Unfortunately this is true for only a very short time. For even the paint used during restoration, which helps to sustain this illusion, even the glues and canvas reinforcements , all are subject to aging. After a time, discrepancies arise which can no longer be taken as signs of the normal passage of years but instead point to the fact that a restoration has 'worn out'.

The work of restoration has a cyclical character: every restorer will be followed by a successsor who will have to do the work again.

Another dream of the restorer, one as old as the profession itself, is that his effort will be the last. In 1931 A.M. de Wild said of Frans Hals's militia portraits which his brother had restored in the 1920s: 'The paintings have been in their present condition for a number of years; their appearance has not altered during this time and there is no reason to assume that the perfect condition they are now in will ever change significantly.'

There has always been a feverish search for paint compounds that will not discolour, remain stable and resist solution when varnish is removed. Every restorer had his own formulas, his own secrets.

The illusion of making a painting 'like new' for all eternity has occupied generations of restorers. The incompatibility of the two ideals is clear when one examines what a painting must undergo during a 'complete' restoration: earlier restorations are done away with and everything is begun anew.

Here follows a schematic and somewhat arbitrary picture of what such a complete restoration involves:

- the canvas must be taken off the stretcher. Each time this happens the edges are further weakened by new tack holes. If there are many holes and much fraying, cutting away the edges of the canvas was often chosen as the 'solution'.
- the old lining is removed and the adhesive (wax/varnish or glue) is scraped away. The sturdier the lining, the greater the necessary mechanical force. This work is done after protective paper has been affixed to the front of the painting, often with water-based glue which turns the old varnish layer white and opaque, making it necessary to remove it entirely.
- a new canvas is attached to the back of the painting. Warmth and pressure must be applied in order to achieve the smoothest possible surface. But warmth and pressure have a negative effect on the original paint structure. Even when professional expertise is at its best, there are always risks involved, such as the increase of hairline cracks in the paint, to mention only the least of them.
- the old yellowed layer of varnish on the front must be removed. The solvents used for this must be carefully selected so as to ensure that the original paint will not be affected. More and more experts warn against the fact that solvents which act upon old varnish also influence oil paint. The binding medium (linseed oil) is particularly sensitive to this. This is definitely the case when the solvent can penetrate deep into the structure of the paint. The combination of slow-drying solvents and penetration through hairline cracks and craquelure can have a softening effect. This makes the painting even more delicate to handle when it is again cleaned. Needless to say, the more intensive the removal of the varnish and the longer the solvents remain in contact with the original paint surface, the greater the danger.
- removing old retouches is probably even more problematic. In the past it was thought that an oil painting could only be retouched with actual oil paint. This material was chosen for aesthetic reasons to be sure. The restorer attempted to identify as closely as possible with the artist in order to eliminate signs of damage and age in a kind of symbiosis with him. Sometimes identification was so great that retouches were done only to 'improve' the look of a painting. The restorer's denial of the passage of time was two-fold: he considered the moment of the work's creation to be still going on and he refused to respect the signs of aging.

With the passage of time, retouches with oils acquire the same solubility as the original paint, making the use of solvents extremely dangerous. Occasionally paint was used for retouching that will not dissolve at all, a mixture of egg tempera and oil for example. Doubtless such retouches were meant to last forever.

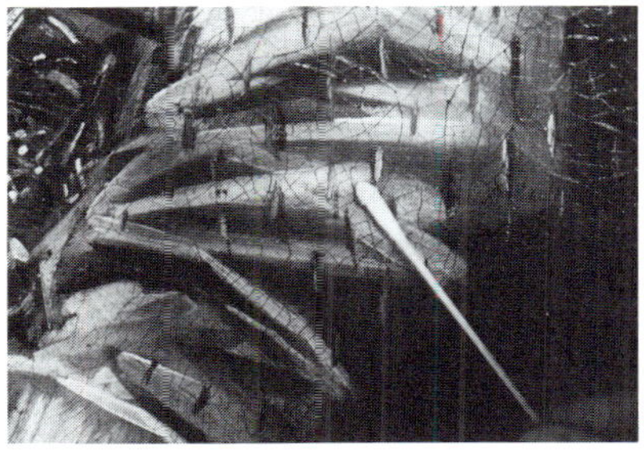

Detail of the sleeve of fig. 2 of the *Officers and subalterns of the civic guard of St. George* of 1639. With cotton swabs soaked in solvent, the old discoloured layer of varnish is removed centimetre by centimetre. All together 30m² of canvas were cleaned in this way.

But if such a retouch discolours, covers the original paint or represents a faulty reconstruction of a missing segment, it signals a lack of humility and self-criticism on the part of the restorer.

About ten years ago what had always been the customary routine of restoration came up for re-examination. It was put forward that every treatment no longer need automatically be a 'thorough' one and that exercising restraint in the matter could only be beneficial for the lifetime of a painting. The often overly keen expectations (smooth, spotless, gleaming) were disclaimed and traces of oldness were accepted. However, as always not everyone is convinced of the rightness of this approach. In each case a dialogue between the restorer and the commissioner of the restoration is necessary to establish the proper procedure.

More often than in the past this will be a meaningful compromise between aesthetic expectations and the need to reduce as much as possible the amount of 'stress' suffered by the work in question.

The restoration of Frans Hals's militia portraits is an example of this type of compromise.

After an extensive preliminary study as described above, a supervisory committee formulated three alternative proposals for treatment:

- leave the paintings alone and adapt the surroundings in which they are shown (dark walls, appropriate lighting)
- remove the yellowed varnish and distracting retouches without further structural alteration
- carry out a so-called total restoration including removal of the old linings and an attempt to smooth the paint surface.

The second proposal was chosen, on the condition that each decision would be taken only after discussion with the supervisory committee. The yellowed varnish, the extensive overpainting and the rough, broadly overlapping fillings were removed. An old, not easily soluble varnish was retained in order to soften the light-dark contrast and for reasons of safety. The old lining, which still gave adequate support, was also retained and no attempt was made to achieve a 'smooth' surface. New retouches were done on fillings with a structured surface for better integration with the surrounding craquelure. Reconstruction of the losses was based on the water-colours made by Wybrand Hendriks (1744-1831) before the paintings were badly damaged in the nineteenth century. Old restoration notes, records from archives and newspaper accounts of what the paintings looked like after cleaning tell a fascinating story about how they have been variously regarded throughout the years, indirectly shedding light on changing attitudes towards works of art in general. Each century treats its art in its own particular way; restoration often mirrors this. This is certainly true as regards the relatively recent problem of easily damaged works of art travelling from place to place.

**The paradox: conservation or exhibition**

Large travelling exhibitions have set new requirements not only for techniques of conservation but also for restoration procedures. Paintings must be able to withstand transport and changes of climate, and the aesthetic criteria of presentation have grown more exacting. When art began to 'move around', warnings about long-term effects were soon heard from the restoration world; accidents which could occur during transport were an immediate and obvious concern. In the most fortunate cases a productive dialogue was carried on between restorers and curators or museum directors. Pioneering steps were taken to improve the technical means of transport, insurance premiums were raised and attempts were made, despite outside pressure, to ensure that certain objects never travelled at all.

The loan of Frans Hals's militia portraits has been prohibited by municipal decree. The restraint shown in their recent restoration reflects this. New linings were not yet necessary for their preservation or to increase their 'life expectancy', providing they were never subjected to the hazards of transport.

*Anne van Grevenstein-Kruse*

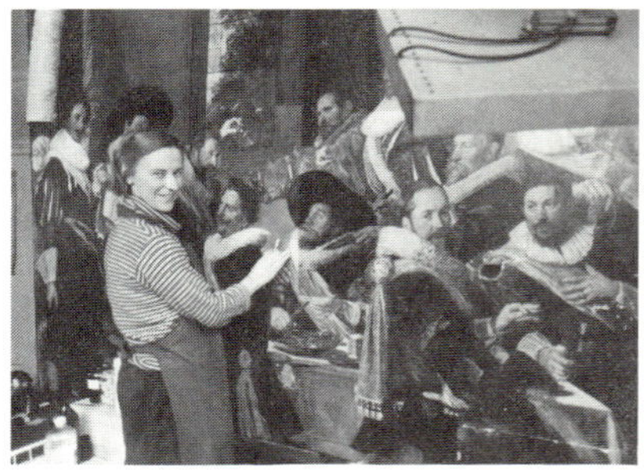

Restorer Anne van Grevenstein with the *Banquet of the officers of the civic guard of St. Adrian* of 1627.

# Glossary



*Lining*

reinforcing the back of an original canvas with a second canvas. Depending on the adhesive used it is called a 'paste lining' (a paste of glue and flour) or a wax-resin lining.

*Binding medium*

substance holding the particles of colour component together in the paint. This can, for example, be an oil or glue.

*Craquelure*

cracks which develop in the paint as a result of aging.

*Dammar resin*

natural resin from a tree growing on Sumatra. Dammar resin is used in making varnish.

*Glaze*

a semitransparent paint layer rich in binding medium.

*Ground layer*

a layer of paint or primer covering the pores of wood or threads of canvas, giving a smooth surface on which to paint.

*Hairline crack*

a tiny crack in the paint, invisible to the naked eye.

*Mastic*

natural resin from a tree growing in southern Europe (*Pistacia lentiscus*). Used in making varnish.

*Underdrawing*

preliminary drawing or sketch done on the ground layer before painting.

*Overpainting*

a layer of paint covering the original paint.

*Pentimento*

a change in the composition made by the painter himself. A correction or overpainting from the artist's own hand.

*Pigment*

the colour component in the paint.

*Regeneration*

Literally: breathing in new life. For example, lightly dissolving varnish that has become opaque because of hairline cracks, making it clear again.

*Retouching*

filling in a missing area in the original paint.

*Cusping*

undulating movement at the edge of the canvas weave, arising when it is put on the stretcher.

*Varnish*

transparant protective layer on top of the paint, which at the same time gives more depth and gloss. Made from resin.

*Abrasion*

damage due to improper use of solvents or sanding procedures during the cleaning of a painting. It results in the loss of part of the original paint.

# Selected reading


***Sources***

Carel van Mander, *Het Schilder-boeck (...).* Haarlem 1604, second impression 1618.

Arnold Houbraken, *De Groote Schouburgh der Nederlantsche Konstschilders en Schilderessen (...).* Three volumes. Amsterdam 1718-21.

Hessel Miedema ed., *De archiefbescheiden van het St. Lukasgilde te Haarlem, 1497-1798.* Two volumes. Alphen a/d Rijn 1980.

***Painting in the northern Netherlands***

Bob Haak, *The Golden Age. Dutch Painters of the 17th Century.* Amsterdam 1984 (with an extensive bibliography).

Jan Briels, *Vlaamse schilders in de noordelijke Nederlanden.* Antwerp/Haarlem 1987.

***Haarlem***

J.J. Temminck, *Haarlem vroeger en nu.* Bussum 1971.

Jan Briels, *De Zuidnederlandse immigratie in Amsterdam en Haarlem omstreeks 1575-1630.* Utrecht 1976.

Pieter Biesboer, *Schilderijen voor het stadhuis Haarlem.* Haarlem 1983.

Frima Fox Hofrichter ed., *Haarlem: The Seventeenth Century.* Exh. cat., The Jane Voorhees Zimmerli Art Museum, 1983.

Alexander de Bruin, *De schilderijen van het Sint Elisabeth's Gasthuis* (in preparation).

***Frans Hals***

Seymour Slive, *Frans Hals.* Three volumes. New York/London 1970-74 (with an extensive bibliography).

Claus Grimm, *Frans Hals. Entwicklung - Werkanalyse - Gesamtkatalog.* Berlin 1972.

Marjan Boot, 'Über Willem van Heythuysen, seinen Nachlaß und die symbolische Bedeutung des Porträts von Frans Hals in München', *Pantheon* 31 (1973), 420-424.

Frances Suzman Jowell, 'Thoré-Bürger and the revival of Frans Hals', *Art Bulletin* 56 (1974), 110-117.

M. Thierry de Bye Dólleman, 'Vier verschillende families "Hals" te Haarlem', *Jaarboek Centraal Bureau voor Genealogie* 28 (1974), 182-212.

H.P. Baard, *Frans Hals.* New York/London 1981.

E. de Jongh, *Portretten van echt en trouw.* Exhibition catalogue Haarlem, Frans Halsmuseum, 1986.

David R. Smith, 'Courtesy and its discontents: Frans Hals's *Portrait of Isaac Massa and Beatrix van der Laen'* , *Oud Holland* 100 (1986), 2-34.

M. Carasso-Kok, J. Levy-van Halm ed., *Schutters in Holland. Kracht en zenuwen van de stad.* Exhibition catalogue Haarlem, Frans Halsmuseum, 1988.

**Restoration**

Knut Nicolaus, *DuMont's Handbuch der Gemäldekunde. Material - Technik - Pflege.* Köln, 1979.

R.H. Marijnissen, *Schilderijen, echt - fraude - vals.* Brussels/Amsterdam 1985.

Helmut Ruhemann, *The Cleaning of Paintings. Problems and Potentialities.* New York 1982 (reprinting).

G.L. Stout, *The Care of Pictures.* Dover Publications Inc. New York 1975 (reprinting).

F. Maringer, *Untersuchungen von Kunstwerken.* Vienna 1977.

Tineke Idema and Marysa Otte, 'Kunsthistorici en restauratoren', *Kunstlicht* Vol. 9 (1988), 2-6.

Seya Dalderup, 'Kunsthistorisch onderzoek en restauratie', *Kunstlicht* Vol. 9 (1988), 7-13.